The Faith Dynamic

*A Treatise on Creationism
and Evolutionary Theory*

E. Basil Jackson, MD, JD, DLitt, PhD

AN IMPRINT OF
GLOBALEDADVANCEPRESS

The Faith Dynamic: A Treatise on Creationism and Evolutionary Theory

Copyright © 2013 by E. Basil Jackson

Library of Congress Control Number: 2013949808

Jackson, E. Basil 1932 —

The Faith Dynamic: A Treatise on Creationism and Evolutionary Theory

ISBN 978-1-935434-20-7

Subject Codes and Description: 1: REL012000: Religion: Christian
Life - General 2: REL106000: Religion: Religion & Science; 3:
REL004000: Religion: Religion: Atheism.

Cover design by Brian Lane Green

Printed in Australia, Brazil, France, Germany, Italy, Spain, UK, and USA

The Press does not have ownership of the contents of a book; this is the author's work and the author owns the copyright. All theory, concepts,
constructs, and perspectives are those of the author and not necessarily the Press. They are presented for open and free discussion
of the issues involved. All comments and feedback should be
directed to the Email: [comments4author@aol.com] and the comments will be forwarded to the author for response.

Order books from www.gea-books.com/bookstore/ or boldbog@aol.com.or
any place good books are sold.

Published by

Post-Gutenberg Books

An Imprint of

GlobalEdAdvancePRESS

DEDICATED TO MY WIFE,
LEILA,
WHO HAS DEDICATED HER LIFE
TO MY WELL-BEING
AND WHO HAS STOOD BEHIND ME
WHEN THE WIND WAS HIGH.

TABLE OF CONTENTS

PREFACE

The twenty-first century is witnessing an unprecedented attack on Christian faith. Richard Dawkins in his book The God Delusion makes it apparent, in his opinion, science and faith are totally incompatible. The argument of Dawkins and others is that in the face of the enormous strides in science, faith is irrelevant and unnecessary.

Basil Jackson, the author of The Faith Dynamic, on the other hand, argues that science and in particular, the theory of evolution is as dependent on a faith commitment and investigates the role of faith as it relates to both science and religion. The value of the present research is that it addresses the presuppositions and assumptions of the evolutionary theory and analyzes the implications for Christian theology, without engaging in apology or criticism of either subject.

An initial problem is the lack of satisfactory definitions of both science and religion. For this study, faith is defined as a strong belief in a supernatural power that controls human destiny and trustworthiness in that belief.

There is no single agreed definition of science. Certain elements are involved – observations, hypotheses, experiments, data collection, evidence, and modification of hypotheses. Scientists work with a set of ideas, assumptions and presuppositions to inform and develop their research until they reach a point where it is impossible to continue with a particular hypothesis. Theories are never absolute, always subject to modification as over time, additional knowledge becomes available.

Science (methodological naturalism or materialism) holds that there cannot be reference to any divine or supernatural activity and thus science is said to be religiously neutral. However, Richard Lewontin, an evolutionary biologist and a geneticist, holds that in science materialism is

absolute, "for we cannot allow a Divine foot in the door."
Michael Ruse, a philosopher of biology, stated that science
and religion cannot be reconciled. Religion has failed and
thus science should be acknowledged as King. On the other
hand, John Lennox, a mathematician and a Christian apologist, wrote that the beauty of the scientific laws only rein-
forced his faith in an intelligent, divine creative force.

In spite of science presenting the appearance of
certainty, it is an ongoing process of enquiry; it is not a
final conclusion. What is accepted as scientific certainty
tomorrow may well be considered outdated. As an example,
the proportion of the human genome that codes for protein
is small and 98% of it has been considered to be useless,
so-called "junk DNA." Scientists, both atheistic evolutionists
and theistic evolutionists have often invoked this redun-
dancy of "junk DNA" as evidence for the random process
of Darwinian evolution. Only a few years ago, Francis
Collins (Director of the Human Genome Project) set this
forth firmly as clear evidence for Darwinian evolution. Jerry
Coyne, Professor of Ecology and Evolution, considered that
the "junk DNA" was a graveyard of dead genes, evidence
for a common ancestor. Denis Alexander, Director of the
Faraday Institute for Science and Religion, also holds that
"junk DNA" is the record of our evolutionary past indel-
ibly inscribed within every cell of our bodies and that we
are all walking genetic fossil museums. However, it is not
"junk DNA." Hundreds of scientific publications now reveal
that this DNA has new levels of functionality and should no
longer be considered "junk DNA."

The author of The Faith Dynamic, considers
Creationism, Naturalism, the Evolutionary Theory, Intelligent
Design, and Theistic Evolution and in each focuses on the
role of the commitment of faith. The conclusion is that while
science, particularly the evolutionary theory, and religion
share many features and characteristics in common, it is
clear that a faith plays an important role in both science and
religion. The evolutionary theory is built on a foundation

of presuppositions and assumptions that are in essence expressions of faith. However, unlike Michael Ruse, an atheist and ex-Christian, who believes that evolution is a religion, the research is unable to reach the point of affirming that evolution is a secular religion.

In the area of research of science and religion, John Stek, Biblical scholar and translator, advised, "Theology must take account of all that humanity comes to know about the world, and science must equally take account of all that we come to know about God." The Faith Dynamic has followed such advice. It is an important work and an invaluable contribution to the on-going debate on science and religion.

— **Prof. Norman C. Nevin**
OBE, BSc, MD, FFPH, FRCPath, FRCP
Professor Emeritus of Medical Genetics
Queen's University, Belfast

INTRODUCTION

AN OBJECTIVE EXAMINATION

This text examines evolutionary theory and creationism objectively without engaging in an apology for or a criticism of either subject. It compares the presuppositions and assumptions of both systems, and examines the role of faith in religion and in the scientific theory of evolution. After discussing the nature of the scientific method and the development of the theory of evolution, the study explores the dichotomy of faith and reason, the ways in which these operate in theories of intelligent design and theistic evolution, and the question of whether scientific evolutionary theory could be considered a secular religion.

This treatise is a formal and systematic exposition that acceptance of the scientific theory of evolution is as dependent upon a faith commitment as is adherence to religion, though the type and quality of the two respective faith systems are different and; consequently, worthy of comparison and contrast. The research concludes that, while science and evolutionary theory share many of the same features and characteristics of faith and presumption, it is presently not appropriate to claim that evolutionary theory is a secular religion, and that when this attitude is asserted it is worthwhile to analyze the predisposition, motivation, conscious and unconscious, involved in the process.

Charles Darwin admitted in his writings that it was extremely difficult to conceive that this immense and wonderful universe, including human beings with capacity to both look backwards and far into the future, was the result of blind chance. A creedal mysterious element seems to be ignored by a significant number of committed Darwinians, many of whom are staunchly anti-theistic and irreligious (cf. Dennett, 1995; Harris, 2006; Stenger, 2007). Most of the Darwinians appear to be oblivious to the system, they and the creationists vociferously espouse and vehemently oppose, are both built on similar psychological dynamic principles. It must be conceded, that an increasing number of courageous evolutionary scientists are willing to confront this serious issue (see Carlson, ed., 2000; McGrath, 2004).

The central theoretical argument was that belief in the scientific theory of evolution is as dependent upon a faith commitment as is religion, though the type and quality of the two respective faith systems are different and, there-fore, worthy of comparison and contrast. The perplexity addressed in this work was: **How may one determine the extent to which both religion and the scientific theory of evolution are dependent upon a faith commitment on the part of their respective adherents?**

The author critically examined appropriate literature available on the subject, as it impinged on the Christian religion. Subjecting available literature to the process of reasoned determination, an examination of the literary evidence produced data by those who both support and oppose the view that presupposition was a *sine qua non* of all scientific thinking. A comparative analysis of the common features and dissimilarities of the foundational faith dynamic for both religion and the scientific theory of evolu-tion, were carefully examined and evaluated to determine whether science could be described as a secular religion. The questions that naturally arise are:

- What role does faith fulfill in the context of religion?

- Is it possible to determine whether the essence of the scientific theory of evolution is also based on faith?

- Is the argument that presupposition is a *sine qua non* of all scientific thinking a valid one?

- What are the principal common features and dissimilarities of the faith dynamic as the foundation for both religion and the scientific theory of evolution?
- On the basis of the above findings, is it possible to describe science as a secular religion?

I must acknowledge, at the outset, that my personal background is such that any conclusions reached may be shaped by my affinity with the Reformed Baptist tradition. Appropriate recognition and respect was given to sources of information that may run counter to any potential personal bias that might otherwise be the case.

— E. Basil Jackson

Publisher's Note: The research included in this volume was originally presented in partial fulfillment of a Doctor of Philosophy in Dogmatics (www. swu.ac.za). The study of dogmatics is the systematic theology division dealing with the theoretical truths of faith. The qualitative research used a paradigm focusing on non-quantifiable measurements. The qualitative findings presented in textbook format provide for a wider discussion of the theoretical concepts and constructs among students. All comments and feedback should be directed to [comments4author@aol.com] and the comments will be forwarded to the author for response.

Topics Discussed in Chapter One

Nature of Science

Evolution as a Term

Methodology of Science

Limitations of Science

The Bias in Science

Subjectivity in Science

The Importance of Adequate Scientific Standards

Study and Review Questions

THE NATURE OF THE SCIENTIFIC METHOD

Nature of Science

Since evolutionary theory is part of the domain of science, it is necessary to define the field with a high degree of specificity and examine the methodology of the scientific enterprise and the relationship of evolutionary theory to this process. Einstein, in an address at the Conference on Science, Philosophy and Religion in 1940, stated:

> It would not be difficult to come to an agreement as to what we understand by science. Science is the century-old endeavor to bring together by means of systematic thought the perceptible phenomena of this world into as thoroughgoing an association as possible. To put it boldly, it is an attempt at the posterior reconstruction of existence by the process of conceptualization (Einstein, 1940).

Judge Overton, in an Arkansas case before his court, spelled out what he considered to be five essential characteristics of science. These were:

1. It is guided by natural law;

2. It has to be explanatory by reference to natural law;

3. It is testable against the empirical world;

4. Conclusions are tentative – that is, not necessarily the final word;

5. It is falsifiable (Overton, 1982).

To most non-scientists these characteristics are an accurate definition of science and a summary of the scientific enterprise. Gower quoted Barber, who points out that even with such a list of essentials in mind, to formulate an adequate definition of science is not as simple and straight forward as it might appear on the surface.

> Although we construct and justify scientific knowledge on the basis of experimental evidence, the way that we do this is much more interesting, and much more problematic, than science textbooks suggest. The suggestion of these textbooks that to adopt a scientific method is to adopt a simple routine fails to do justice to the sophisticated skills which scientists use when they experiment and when they reason from evidence (Gower, 1997: 11).

Whatley stated that science was the term used to describe the knowledge that has accumulated in man's quest to understand the world. He points out that science is a "method of knowing" based on observation and experimentation of the natural world.

> Science is a "way of knowing" based on experimentation and observation of the natural world. We depend on science for unbiased and verifiable information to make important decisions about our lives. Although there are many ways of knowing that may be important in our personal and cultural lives, they rely on opinion, belief, and other factors rather than on evidence and testing (Whatley, 2011).

Warburton opined that the difference between the various views of science by varying scientists usually depends on the different assumptions made about the nature of observation and the inductive method. He stated:

> [the generally accepted view of] the scientific method is surprisingly widespread, even among practicing scientists. Yet it is unsatisfactory in a number of ways. The most important of these are its assumptions about the nature of observation and about inductive argument (Warburton, 2004: 113-114).

Academia depends on science for unbiased and verifiable information on which decisions can be made. There are other ways of knowing that at times may be appropriate and may rely on opinion and belief or other factors rather than on evidence and testing (Carlson, 2000: 22). However, science is also the name given collectively to the methods used for gaining objective knowledge and insight about the universe. The methods of obtaining this knowledge were refined and made more objective and reliable in each generation.

The branches of science are divided into two categories: exact sciences such as physics, chemistry and biology, and non-exact sciences such as history, sociology and disciplines related to the humanities. The exact or hard sciences generally permit more accuracy than the non-exact sciences that tend to be more descriptive. Some fields of science are more easily influenced by personal subjectivity (bias), while others are influenced by an academic frame of reference or methodology. Consequently, it is possible to recognize bias in some subjects while in others it is more difficult (Creationwiki, 2009). Both of these influences on research are of importance in any creation-evolution dialog. Since evolutionary theory falls within the domain of the inexact sciences, personal and academic bias would not be surprising in some of the scientists involved (Mahoney, 1988: 1-2, 6-7, 10).

In the pursuit of the scientific enterprise, the methods available for formal and systematic analysis differ from discipline to discipline, and often the methods of investigation or analysis valid in one field are not applicable or reliable in another discipline. For example, measurement of mass plays a great role in physics while it is relatively insignificant in historical analysis. Only the element of logic is common to the multitudes of methods of investigation. Merriam-Webster defines logic as "a science that deals with the principles and criteria of validity of inference and demonstration or the science of the formal principles of reasoning." It is a discipline of study which supplies the norms and standards to evaluate truth and separate valid conclusions from those not adequately supported. Logic is considered a universal, generalizable academic process; namely, the science of rational thought.

In any discussion of science, is it essential to clarify the meaning of the terms; namely, whether one is referring to accumulated results or to methodology. In a generation that tends to worship science, it must be clear that historical studies are different from the material sciences. Material sciences, such as physics and chemistry study those properties of matter that may be investigated with the aid of repeatable experiments. Historical science deals with things that have taken place in the past and repeatable experiments are not possible. The origin of the universe and the origin of life are examples of historical investigation. Subjects such as origins may be considered by cosmology and biology, but that is only for the sake of convenience. These investigations are actually non-repeatable and historical in nature. Those who have no understanding of the difference between historical and material sciences may require material proof for historical subjects. No meaningful dialog is possible before this essential difference is clarified and all concerned in such a dialog must realize that historical and physical sciences should not be inappropriately mixed (Mahoney, 1988: 1-2, 6-7, 10; Popper, 1985:134).

For these reasons, it is mandatory to define the use of the term "scientific" in any dialog. Sometimes the term is used to mean an attempt to explain how things actually are, while at other times the word "science" is used to mean an explanation without any recourse to *anything* supernatural. This second definition would be acceptable only with confirmation that there *never* was any supernatural intervention in the history of the universe. To assume or claim that these two definitions of science are interchangeable is to beg the question and perhaps to conceal an already established cryptic worldview. (Mahoney,1988: 1-2, 6-7, 10).

McCarthy, a Roman Catholic cleric, attempted to construct an accurate definition of science:

> Science is composed of insight on the part of the knowing subject, meaning on the part of the real objects that he knows, and understanding on the part of the intellect which provides his medium of thought. It is not a mere collection of unrelated facts verified by experience. It is structured knowledge, and the structure arises from the natural development of the mind itself. Material science is the collection of facts; formal science is the understanding of the facts in the intellect of the knower ... The recognition of what the intellect knows and how it knows what it knows divides the field of science into material and formal knowledge of reality. It also divides the field into the lower level of knowledge of the facts (scientia) and the higher level of understanding of the facts (intellectus). It is understanding that advances science towards even greater intelligibility and protects its conclusions from those forms of unscientific understanding called pseudo-science (McCarthy, 1991: 48-49).

A common idea is that science is limited in its objectives to the five senses and that by definition it excludes metaphysics, the fundamental nature of being. It should be remembered that energy, information and ideas, and even moral standards are not physical in nature. They are rather factual and considered legitimate objects of science. The function of science is not only the discovery of data about things, rather how to establish certainty about known data. Science discovers data/facts, and these change with each new discovery; truth is a certainty that does not change. Absolute truth is disclosure that comes only through faith.

Based on the forces and processes controlling evolution, when it focuses on origins, evolution must be placed among the historical sciences and cannot be considered an operational science. Since these events can never be observed or repeated, all theories dealing with the origin of life and the universe fall into the category of historical science. Historical sciences use scientific methodology built on the foundation of assumptions or presuppositions. When the initial assumptions are wrong, the conclusions will be wrong. Theories are never absolute and always subject to change as additional knowledge becomes available over time.

An additional characteristic of theories is that the basic ideas do not tend to be cumulative. This means that previously acquired data/facts tend to be discarded as new information is accepted. Theories are generally not accepted because they have been confirmed empirically, or rejected because they have anomalies. The acceptance of changes in established theories is often because of conceptual changes rather than empirical findings. The principles of rationality used by scientists in theory evaluation tend to be similar to theories themselves in that they are not fixed but tend to modify over the course of time (Popper, 1985:134; Niewoehner, 1997:52; Whitehead, 12926:13);

An assumption is a basic building block of theory development and an attempt will be made to demonstrate that an assumption is akin to faith. For example, a creationist assumes (has faith-trust) that God created the earth and an evolutionist may assume (has faith-trust) that random chance created the earth. Neither assumption can be confirmed empirically, but both assumptions may be useful in interpreting facts that are unclear. Creationists and evolutionists take the same facts and interpret them according to their a priori assumptions and presuppositions. It is clear that if an initial assumption is wrong then it is likely that the final conclusion will also be wrong. (Perlas, 1982: 29). Assumptions and presuppositions are fundamental in the historical sciences. In this work, an attempt was made to demonstrate that the creation/evolution issue was riddled with unproven assumptions and presuppositions on both sides of the divide. Understanding the difference between historical and operational science may reduce the confusion in the evolution/creation debate. The origin of life on earth and the beginning of the universe cannot be observed.

The fundamental assumption of creationism is that there is a God, while the essential assumption of evolution is that there is no God. These are metaphysical issues that lie outside the province of science (Wald, 1963:26).

In the practice of the scientific enterprise, clear recognition of the existence of personal assumptions is necessary. An example of this thinking is summarized by McGrath in an analysis of statements and ideas by Richard Dawkins. McGrath questioned why the logic of Dawkins leads to the notion that there is no God. He points out a host of unstated and unchallenged assumptions underlying Dawkins' argument (McGrath, 2005:142-153; Dawkins, 2006:157-158). McGrath outlined these assumptions and presuppositions. It is assumed that:

1. The scientific method is incapable of adjudicating the god hypothesis, either positively or negatively;

2. God need not be invoked as an explanatory agent within the evolutionary process;

3. The concept of God as a "watch-maker" was of significance in earlier thinking and it is assumed that it remains typical of Christian thinking today (McGrath, 2005:142-153).

William Paley proffered the existence of a Creator, using the now famous metaphor of finding a watch in the woods and distilling from that the existence of an intelligent, unseen watchmaker. In his book *Natural Theology or Evidences of the Existence and Attributes of the Deity, Collected from the Appearances of Nature*, first published in 1802, Paley laid out a full exposition of natural theology, the belief that the nature of God could be understood by reference to His creation, the natural world. Paley introduced one of the most famous metaphors in the philosophy of science, the image of the watchmaker:

When we come to inspect the watch ... the inference we think is inevitable, that the watch must have had a maker

... who comprehended its construction and designed its use (Paley, 1802:119, 129).

McGrath noted that these incorrect assumptions were inadequately grounded presuppositions; consequently, he concluded that Dawkins' atheism was firmly implanted in the biological evidence and that these propositions were faith-based (McGrath, 2005:52-53). Scientists, consciously or unconsciously, have a basic *faith* or assumption: that eventually all life will be explainable by science (Wald, 1974:9; Eigen, 1971:59; Cech, 1995:95).

Many scientists and philosophers appear to share an expectation and faith that when the scientific world picture is complete, it will be possible, within the parameters of biology, physics and chemistry to explain all aspects of human existence. Presently science cannot provide such a comprehensive explanation of human existence and it is not at all clear that the future development of science must lead in this direction (Hasker, 1983:99; Watson, 1982:44; Rifkin, 1983:298).

Nevertheless, it is reasonable to consider the possibility that science has its own faith-based belief system. After a careful review of this issue, Rolson stated:

> Making this survey, can we insist that the probabilities must always have been there, or at least the possibilities, since what did actually manage to happen must always have been either probably probable or, minimally, improbably possible all along? Push this to extremes, as one must do, if one claims that all the possibilities are always there, latent in the dust, latent in the quarks. Such a claim becomes pretty much an act of speculative faith, not in actualities, since one knows that these events took place, but in probabilities or possibilities being omnipresent. Is the claim some kind of induction or deduction or the most plausible case conclusion from present actualities? (Rolston, 1998:425-426).

All science proceeds from the assumption that nature is ordered in a rational and intelligible way. When physicists discover findings that confirm their initial faith-based assumptions, this tends to justify their confidence. Formerly, the practice of science accepted the laws of nature to be unchanging and absolute. Accordingly, to be a scientist it required faith that the universe was governed by dependable, immutable, absolute, universal, mathematical laws of unspecified origin and that these laws would never fail. This need for faith is echoed by Collins who stated that the natural sciences have a positive presumption of faith of one type or another (Collins, 2003:142-153). This view was echoed by Davies, who has pointed out:

> ... science has its own faith based belief system and that all science proceeds on the assumption that nature is ordered in a rational and intelligible way. When physicists probe to a deeper level of subatomic structure, or astronomers extend the reach of their instruments, they expect to encounter additional elegant mathematical order. And so far their faith has been justified. In the not too distant past the laws of physics were regarded as completely off limits. The job of the scientists was to discover the laws and apply them, not inquire into their provenance. The laws were treated as "given" – imprinted on the universe like a maker's mark at the moment of cosmic birth – and fixed for evermore. Therefore, to be a scientist, you had to have faith that the universe is governed by dependable, immutable, absolute, universal, mathematical laws of an unspecified origin. You've got to believe that these laws won't fail, that we won't wake up tomorrow to find heat flowing from cold to hot, or the speed of light changing by the hour (Davies, 1983:1-8).

Evolution as a Term

Evolution, as the term is generally used, is an attempt to explain the derivation of one organism from another by the study of natural causes operating to produce change over time. As Rush summarized, in the field of biology modern evolutionary theory includes the following propositions:

1. Variation is a ubiquitous feature of all living things. It is continuously (and normally) produced spontaneously.

2. Selection is the result of interaction of specific sets of environmental conditions with variations in specific plants and animals. Selection is the force that gives rise to and alters the categories of living things.

3. The interaction between varieties and selection results in adaptation or extinction. Adaptation is always relative to particular organisms and specific environments. Adaptation is never permanent.

4. All forms of life are ultimately related to each other by genealogical connections.

5. There are no non-material forces at work in the evolutionary process, nor are there any "pull" factors in evolution.

6. There is no radical dichotomy between humans and other animals (between "culture" and "nature"), just as there are no radical dichotomies between any things in nature at all. Species are ranges of variation that integrate into each other at the margins (Rush, 1962:284).

At times confusion has resulted from a failure to appreciate that the term "Darwinism" is used in a number of different ways each meaning something slightly different.

1. It is used, for example, as an explanatory concept to indicate a specific theory regarding the mechanism of evolution (Mayr, 1991: 575)._

2. It is also used as a communication device of Darwinian evolutionary naturalism to describe a philosophical worldview, which is based on faith in its tenets (Hösle & Illies, 2005:6).

3. In addition, the term evolution is sometimes used in association with a theory of preceding purpose and in such a case, may not be inimical to the idea of creation (Warfield, 1915:190).

Since the concept of evolution was first introduced, many distinguished scientists have expressed acceptance of the evolutionary theory. (Ayala, 1978:64; Waddington, 1962:28; Dobzhansky, 1958:109; Dimitrov, 2008). On the other side of the evolution-creation dialog, however, a number of distinguished scientists, while rejecting preceding purpose, have accepted the concept of a Supreme Being and/or have refused to accept the idea that the genesis of life on earth occurred by chance and/or natural cause. (Schwartz, 2006:34; Crick,1981:51; Erbrich,1985:34). Hanegraaff gives a graphic depiction of scientists with some doubts about aspects of evolution. He wrote:

> The field of paleoanthropology is fraught with ape-men fiction, frauds, and fantasies. In the category of fiction is Pithecanthropus erectus (Java man). Nineteen doctrinaire evolutionists who participated in the Selenka expedition – a trek bent on demonstrating that the evolutionary conjectures concerning Java Man were true – produced a 342-page scientific report demonstrating beyond the peradventure of a doubt that Pithecanthropus erectus played no part whatsoever in evolution (Hanegraaff, 2009: 306).

It is clear that there is a certain measure of reluctance in the minds of many scientists to accept creation in *any* form. Carlson labeled this negative view as scientific imperialism or scientism, as many distinguished scientists rigidly insist on a purely materialistic philosophy when considering the question of origins. (Carlson, 2000:12).

Methodology of Science

The scientific method is the process by which scientists, collectively and over time, attempt to construct an accurate, reliable, consistent and non-arbitrary representation of the world. This method uses a series of facts, hypotheses, laws and theories to explain observations in the natural world. However, personal and cultural beliefs influence both perceptions and interpretations of natural phenomenon. The aim of science is to reduce these as much as possible when developing a theory. The scientific method constantly attempts to minimize the influences of bias and prejudice in the experimenter when testing a theory or a hypothesis (Wilson, 1952:32).

Science, as an empirical discipline, is involved in observation, using one or more of our five senses (hearing, sight, smell, taste, or touch) to gain knowledge about the world that others will be able to repeat the observations. One can observe only in the present. No scientist was present over the millions of years to witness the postulated evolutionary progression of life from the simple to the complex. Observation of the actual event is impossible and the events are not repeatable today. All evidence the scientist has exists in the present. Consequently, evolution is a belief system about the past, based on the judgment of scientists who were not present. These faith-based presuppositional assumptions are an attempt to explain the origination of all the present data. This most certainly is a system of beliefs often held with ardor, faith and at times with evangelical zeal. In this text, it is suggested that evolution has as many characteristics of a belief system as does religion.

The only way one could always be certain about conclusion about anything, including origins, depends upon knowing everything there is to know about the subject. Unless one knew all evidence were available, one could never be sure that correct conclusions were reached. One would not know further evidence that may be discovered that could change the conclusions previously held. In addition, a person could never reach the point where all the evidence had been discovered. No one can ever be absolutely certain about such matters. In the Christian religion, this incompleteness gives rise to the need for faith and revelation (Barbour, 1990:1).

The prerequisite for the scientific enterprise is conscious or unconscious acceptance of the faith-based-presuppositional-assumption that there is rational order in nature. If the natural world is random and lacks order, scientific study would be impossible. However, the reason the world might be law-governed is ultimately a question not for science but for philosophy. Science at this stage engages ab initio (from the beginning) in the faith-based- presuppositional-assumption that the world is law-governed. Science cannot progress without basic philosophical commitments about the nature of the world and of humanity. Science depends on a consistent order and uniformity in nature (Ratzsch, 2000:18-19).

As previously noted, Davis also emphasized this view. He stated that science is based on the assumption that the universe is thoroughly rational and logical at every level. He claimed that atheists accept that the laws of nature exist without reason or sense and that the universe is ultimately absurd. He stated that as a scientist, this was hard to accept. There must be an unchanging rational ground in which the logical, orderly nature of the universe is rooted (Davies, 1983:179). Carlson (2000:129-131, referring to Meyer's Science & Christianity: Four Views) noted that it is claimed by creationists that the existence of this order inherent in nature is not only the *sine qua non* (outcome) of the scientific enterprise but that the actual presence may reveal the hand of a designer. This is a scientific question, not merely a question of personal faith or religious experience. To answer this question fairly, science must not be restricted by naturalism. It is to some degree a matter of faith to believe that there is a Creator or Designer, but it is also a matter of faith to disbelieve in that possibility. Here again evolution and religion appear to be on the same "faith" track!

Lisle emphasized that the basic assumption in science and religion is that the universe is governed by a set of laws. He wrote that everything in the universe, every plant and animal, every rock, every particle of matter or light wave, is bound by laws that it has no choice but to obey.

As a devout Bible-believing creationist, he points out that the universe obeys certain rules – laws to which all things must adhere. These laws are precise, and many of them are mathematical in nature. Natural laws are hierarchical in nature; secondary laws of nature are based on the primary laws of nature, which have to be exact in order for the universe to exist. He questioned from where did these laws come and why do they exist. If the universe were merely the accidental by-product of a big bang, then why should it obey orderly principles – or any principles for that matter? He concluded that such laws are consistent with biblical creation. Natural laws exist because the universe has a Creator God who is logical; and has imposed order on His universe (Lisle, 2006:75).

The goal of science is to study nature, but the world is so complex that in such an enterprise one has to pass through rigorous stages of information-collection and analyses. This means that at any given time the available scientific information will consist of different categories of information – some fully certain and some less than certain. These categories may be expressed as follows:

- Presuppositions
- Hypothesis
- Assumptions
- Theories
- Facts
- Laws
- Interpretations
- Schools of opinion
- Models
- Deductions
- Inferences

An assumption is not as reliable as an observation and a theory is not as reliable as a fact. These are the two types of information found in science and this differentiation is important. There are theories of science and facts of science. Theories of science represent all the information about which certainty does not as yet exist. This category is a necessary pre-requisite for the development of science, but issues within this category are never considered as the final reality about any question or subject. Theories of science are transient and only a few such theories survive intact for more than a generation, they are modified or completely abandoned. Facts of science represent all the information that is known with a high degree of certainty but not absolute certainty (Mitchell, 2012). Unlike theories, which are expected to change as new "facts" are discovered or new "interpretations" of facts are required, facts tend to be stable and without any expectation that change will be mandated by further discoveries. As Herman Sissons wrote:

> The scientific method is in many ways a highly disciplined application of the kind of reasoning processes humans use all the time. First, we experience something – we see the sun come up in the morning, for instance, and set every evening. In a scientific study, this is what is called "data." Then we ask what it means, we try to explain it. How it is, for instance, that the sun comes up every morning and sets every evening? In science the explanation is the "theory." But science adds several qualifications to these steps. The first is replication of the data. Scientists agree that data must be subject to being checked by other scientists. So scientists study only objects and events that other scientists can also observe if they choose. Whatever a scientist studies, from the stars to how people behave, the basic requirement is that other scientists can also observe and analyze it. (Sissons, 2010).

Limitations of Science

The basis of a purely secular science, not in any way influenced by theism, is to question everything and to take nothing for granted. This is in marked contrast to classical Reformation theology in which God controls, orders, and determines, for nothing can be done except the will of God (Barth, 1958: 148). Science relies on assumptions to advance its cause, but these assumptions are not to be taken as fact. Assumptions are only postulations, to indicate that science acknowledges that these assumptions are not the actual way the universe may work, but rather constitute a model that scientists can use to better their understanding of the universe. Science constantly changes its basic assumptions. There are important questions science will never be able to answer. These questions do exist and it is the task of science to answer them as much as possible. (Godel (1906-1978), as reported by Krista Tipett, who shocked the world when she revealed that some mathematical models cannot be proved in the realm of mathematics – which does not necessarily mean that they are not accurate), but mathematics itself cannot demonstrate their certainty (Tipett, 2010:202; Triggs, 1993: 1).

Accordingly, science has a number of limitations that must be recognized. There are inherent limitations of science, exemplified by a variety of questions that can never be definitely answered given the limits of human science (Horgan, 1996:7). Some of the limitations of science are undoubtedly due to the motivation for its existence in the first place. Review of the tenets of Darwin's theory, raises the possibility that the theory itself was developed, not from a desire for truth per se, but, in all probability and unconsciously, from a compulsion to control the environment in order to increase the likelihood that the human genes will propagate. This is a reasonable interpretation from a psychoanalytic perspective and is consistent with the theory as it developed.

There is a variety of questions that can never be definitely answered, given the limitations of human science. One website gives a few examples:

1. How exactly was the universe created?

2. Could our universe be just one of an infinite number of universes?

3. Could quarks and electrons be composed of still smaller particles, ad infinitum?

4. What does quantum mechanics really mean?

5. How exactly did life begin on the earth?

6. Just how inevitable was life's origin and its subsequent history?

7. How does a single fertilized cell develop into multi-cellular organisms?

8. How does the central nervous system process information?

The recognition of the religious limits of the scientific method was understood around the time of Darwin. As none other than "Darwin's Bulldog" T. H. Huxley wrote in 1880:

> Some twenty years ago, or thereabouts, I invented the word "Agnostic" to denote people who, like myself, dogmatize with utmost confidence... (McGrath, 2005:53).

McGrath further recalled that Huxley was so tired of hearing pontifications of both dogmatic atheists and dogmatic theists that he was forced to conclude that God questions could not be settled on the basis of empirical science and that even the arch-evolutionists, Stephen Gould, was forced to admit that science because of its limitations can only work with naturalistic explanations. Consequently, science can neither affirm nor deny the existence of God (McGrath, 2005:55).

Heft has enunciated clearly how both science and theology have limitations and blind spots. He stated that theology has its blind spots when it refuses to accept the findings of careful science and when it over-interprets some of its own sources (Heft, 2005:10). Collins expressed the limitation of science in that science can work only with naturalistic explanations and that it can neither affirm nor deny the existence of God, but that the natural sciences do create a positive presumption of faith (Collins, 2003:142-153).

The Bias in Science

It appears that science, at least on occasion, does not live up to the expectation which it generally purports to give, namely to be "the god of this age." Science is an amazing and useful tool in the search for reality. God, according to theists, has provided a wonderful universe for us to examine and study with the assistance of a rational mind and those who fail to do so suffer an overwhelming loss. It is important to be sensitive to the fact that science *qua* science does have serious limitations, as previously noted, even though it is often presented to the public as an all embracing and accurate *kerygma (preaching)* of "truth." This is just not the case. The accepted model for the scientific enterprise generally has been that science is built on four basic premises (Warburton, 2004:111):

1. Scientists are completely objective in their interpretation of scientific facts.

2. Scientific methodology is totally rational.

3. Scientific truths are superior to religious or philosophic truths.

4. Science has already disproved the existence of God.

Notwithstanding, this model has generally been accepted by those who have accepted science as the only way to find reliable truth, a close analysis of these criteria will demonstrate how a fallacious notion. Science is always a process, not a conclusion. What is accepted as scientific certainty today, may well be considered out of date tomorrow. Consequently, any attempt to find an absolute reconciliation between religion and science is a dead end and will not happen since scientific views are always changing. Theories are always tentative and are modified as new discoveries occur. As a result, any theology that attaches itself to one scientific conclusion today may possibly be an orphan tomorrow.

Science does not develop by the accumulation of individual discoveries and inventions, but rather science periodically changes the way it looks at and interprets facts. Science grows by such changes and revolutions but not in the traditionally accepted linear fashion of fact upon newly discovered fact. In a period without such developmental steps, scientists tend to interpret facts in the same way.

Schroeder recounted a rather sad example that illustrates the need for this concern regarding bias in the scientific enterprise. He reported what happened to Charles D. Walcott, the Director of the Smithsonian Museum.

> Yet old ideas cling even in the face of contradictory evidence. It's a biological fact that the song the sparrow learns in its youth is its song for life. We humans are not so very different. When data mount, ever more convincing arguments against a favored paradigm, all sorts of mental mechanisms allow us to retain our preconceived notions of reality. If we have spent much of a life time attempting to prove the validity of a premise in question, the emotional stakes are high. Cognitive dissonance, humanity's inherent ability to ignore unpleasant facts, helps us in our struggle to retain the error of our ways. Walcott had discovered an imprint of a crustacean in shale that was, in his opinion, too old to contain such a complex fossil as this specimen, so Walcott buried the specimens in the files of his laboratory, where they lay undisturbed until re-discovered some eighty years later (Schroeder, 1997:35).

These different scientific perspectives and inherent limitations are defensible within the broader fields of human behavior and cognition. They are acceptable as tertiary commitments that are logically unrelated to the evolutionary theory program but none the less characteristic of a field characterized by anti-theistic biases and other strong reductionisms. Just as in each theological schism, i.e. theological and faith-based system, there is much in evolutionary theory worthy of scientific consideration by both sides of the philosophic divide. Science is powered by the primary motivation of a desire to understand the minutiae in the physical world and this desire trumps a desire to change the world. Theology, however, has a natural role in this age of science because it shares with science this search for intelligibility. As Hastings noted:

> ... it is only appropriate for Christians to develop a curiosity for knowledge about creation and science that will evoke a sense of wonder and worship. Any attempt to integrate science and theology must be vigorous, though always tentative and guided by the essentials of Christian faith, or historic Christian orthodoxy as this has been revealed in Scripture properly interpreted, and expressed in the Creeds. Christian theology and science in fact share a common commitment to the fearless pursuit of truth no matter its source, in a hands-on or empirical fashion. Both acknowledge that knowledge is gained by more than mere abstract reasoning. This not only validates science, but also theology. Theological discoveries are made in a fashion similar to how scientific discoveries are made. Scientists tend to privilege fact to what is scientifically verifiable, to the neglect of historical fact. In fact, both have merit (Hastings, 2011).

Subjectivity in Science

It must be a rigid rule in the practice of the scientific enterprise that all personal commitments, whether theistic or atheistic, must never be permitted to interfere with epistemic values. In the scientific endeavor, it must ever be kept in mind that if such an influence is tolerated then the ability to formulate theories will be skewed and the search for authentic knowledge will be impaired. Religious commitments, whether theistic or non-theistic, ought not to interfere with the normal functioning of the epistemic value system of the scientific community. Great mischief occurs when extra-scientific dogma becomes a substitute for epistemic values as cognitive relevance, predictive accuracy, coherence, explanatory scope, unifying power and/or fertility. Progress toward the goal of authentic knowledge will be impeded when religious commitment is permitted to skew the theory-evaluation process with the result that one epistemic value takes inordinate precedence over all others (Van Till, 1988:41). Thomas Kuhn was also sensitive to the presence of subjectivity in science. He noted that science was a social enterprise and as such is subjective. He argued that "every individual choice between competing theories depends on a mixture of objective and subjective factors" (Kuhn, 1977: 325).

The great danger exists that personal values may result in the temptation to prove a priori convictions and a cryptic worldview whether religious or philosophical. When this occurs, the result is not the acquisition of authentic knowledge of the world and the result is likely to be a creedal confirmation or an attempt to demonstrate the validity of a cryptic a priori, which is a frequent dynamic of evangelical theology. In the opinion of this author, it would be more useful and accurate to label it "Para-scientific distortion."

It is clear that the epistemic goal of the scientific enterprise is to obtain fact- based knowledge. This is accomplished by empirical investigation leading to the development of theories of structure, function, history and functioning of the physical universe. There is no common handbook, which spells out exactly what the rules are for the scientific endeavor. In the absence of such a definitive rule- book, Van Till and his associates suggested four categories of functioning criteria for judging the quality of scientific research or the adequacy of scientific theory and the acquisition of authentic knowledge (Van Till, 1988:33-39). These are as follows:

1. **Competence** --In order to engage in a scientific endeavor one must first have acquired a degree

of knowledge and the prerequisite skills which are required to perform the empirical and analytical activities with a sufficient degree competence.

2. **Integrity** --The highest level of personal integrity is necessary and this is all the more so because of the conceptual bias and affective contaminants which are often involved in the scientific pursuit. This is probably more so in the case of evolutionary research than in any other branch of science. The best available check for this level of personal honesty and absence of bias is that the activity must be exposed in the public forum so that other investigators have the opportunity to examine the results and repeat the research. Contradictory evidence must be openly reported for this purpose.

3. **Sound judgment** --This psychological process involves:

   a. The act or process of forming of an opinion after consideration or deliberation of all the known facts;

   b. The mental ability to perceive and distinguish relationships, both physical and psychological;

   c. The capacity to form an opinion by distinguishing and evaluating;

   d. The capacity to assess situations or circumstances and draw sound conclusions.

4. **Collegial Sensitivity** --This is collegiality, not contrived but authentic, characterized by respect for others, interdependent professional behaviors and collaborative decision making (Hertzog, 2000:17).

When the criteria for competency and honest analysis are met, the next step is to consider the criteria that the scientific community may use in evaluating the value of competing scientific theories (Van Till, 1988:33-39). "Private interpretation" may be acceptable in the theological enterprise, but is both dangerous in the practice of science. The current insistence of many scientists involved in the study of evolution is to give assurance that the scientific endeavor is confined exclusively to the intelligibility of the *physical* world (Wald, 1963: 101). All will agree that the stated method of science is to be objective. In order to achieve this goal, scientists look for maximum agreement that must be found in what is publicly accessible. The danger in this endeavor is that any non-empirical claims to certainty, which might raise their ugly heads, may be diagnosed as irrelevant and mere attitudes.

The Importance of Adequate Scientific Standards

It is clear from an examination of the work of numerous scientists, irrespective of their philosophic orientation, that there is no such thing as a unique method in science. It is also clear that scientists use many methods of investigation, most of which are also used in a variety of other fields of human endeavor. There is no unique standard method which is applicable in all endeavors and which is essential to all scientific progress. Whether "science" even as rigorously defined can "prove" anything, depends of the definition of the word "prove." However, for practical purposes some observations can be considered to be "proved" when, as far as is known at that particular time, such a result has always happened in the past. It is then anticipated, but not proved, that it will be likely to happen again in the future.

Kerkut, having reviewed what in his opinion constitute seven non-provable assumptions upon which evolution is based, concluded that "these seven assumptions by their nature are not capable of experimental verification" (Kerkut, 1960: vii, viii). Milliken is even more critical of the deficiencies of the scientific enterprise. He declared "the pathetic thing is that we have scientists who are trying to prove evolution, which no scientist can ever prove" (Milliken, 1925, quoted in *The Nashville Banner*, August, 7th). Ayala also takes the position that "a hypothesis is empirical or scientific only if it can be tested by experience ... A hypothesis or theory which cannot be, at least in principle, falsified by empirical observations and experiments does not belong to the realm of science (Ayala, 1974: 700.) Johnson also speaks of the inherent limitations of science and notes, for example, that "a vast historical scenario like 'evolution' necessarily involves a degree of speculation that is absent from, say, the typical chemistry experiment" (Johnson, 2000: 72).

On occasion, it appears that some scientists find it is difficult to accept that "Scientific Truth" is not absolute. From the point of view of science, there is *never* absolute truth in the sense that no observations can ever be made in the future which would necessitate further modification of the theory in question. Those scientists who have an emotional need to hold adamantly that scientific theory has been miraculously transmuted into fact, manifest a terrier-like determination to believe what they need to believe irrespective of whatever facts may confront them. Some scientists have demonstrated this evidence of the mechanism of denial in the public statements and writings. Howells, for example, has pontificated: "Evolution is a fact, like digestion" (Howells, 1944:5). Watson takes the same position. "Today the theory of evolution is an accepted fact for everyone but a fundamentalist minority" (Watson, 1982:44).

Eric Lyons (2007) summarized the cognitive rigidity of some leading evolutionists:

> For several decades, leading evolutionists have attempted to sell their beloved theory as "fact." In 1944, W.W. Howells wrote: "Evolution is a **fact** like digestion" (*Mankind So Far,* New York: Doubleday, p.5, emphasis added). Eight years later, Richard Goldschmidt arrogantly asserted: "Evolution of the animal and plant world is considered by all those entitled to a judgment to be a **fact** for which no further proof is needed" (*American Scientist* 49:84 [1952], emphasis added). J. Savage penned a book in the mid-1960s, titled Evolution, in which he alleged "the **fact** of evolution is amply clear" (1965, preface, emphasis added). In a 1980 Newsweek

article, Stephen J. Gould gave us one of the more memorable quotes on evolution, saying, "Evolution is a **fact**, like apples falling out of trees" (as quoted by Jerry Adler, 3 Nov. 1980, 96[18]:95, emphasis added). More recently, Thomas Hayden, writing for U.S. News & World Report, exclaimed: "By now, scientists say, evolution is no longer 'just a theory.' It's an everyday phenomenon, **a fundamental fact** of biology as real as hunger and as unavoidable as death" (2002, 133[4]:43, emphasis added). (Lyons, 2007).

An example of the danger of confusing theory with fact is well demonstrated in the discoveries of Newton regarding gravitation. This particular "truth", the discovery of which was perhaps the greatest feat of the human mind, had to be modified by the subsequent discoveries made by Einstein. For everyday use, however, Newton's theory of gravitation remains "truth" in that it is an adequate explanation for most purposes. However, because of the nature of the scientific enterprise we must anticipate that in the future there will be further modifications of Einstein's "truth" as new facts are discovered.

Study and Review Questions for Chapter One

1. What was Einstein's definition of science?

2. Explain Whatley's view of science

3. What are the two divisions of science and examples?

4. How do historical sciences differ from the material sciences?

5. How are the five senses related to science?

6. Describe an assumption.

7. How does God as the "watch-maker" related to creation?

8. Explain the term "evolution."

9. How does bias relate to science?

Topics Discussed in Chapter Two

Creationism

Evolution

Study and Review Questions

CREATIONISM
AND EVOLUTION THEORY

Creationism

The fundamental assumption of creationism is that there is a God, while the essential assumption of evolution is that there is no God. These are metaphysical issues that lie outside the province of science (Wald, 1963:26). It is a fact that evolutionary theory is not based on known scientific laws or scientific evidence. Creationism, as described in Genesis, is consistent with known laws and evidence.

It is self-evident that creationism is built on the foundation of faith. Many scientists tend to focus exclusively on the material dimension and reject the metaphysical. It is the assumption of this author that since religion is based on faith, the scientific enterprise is also based on a pre-suppositional hypothesis, which is another dimension of faith.

To determine the extent to which both creationism and the scientific theory of evolution are dependent upon a faith commitment by their adherents, this treaties had five objectives.

1. To establish the role of faith in the context of religion;

2. To determine whether the scientific theory of evolution is also essentially a faith-based system;

3. To examine the validity or otherwise of the argument that presupposition is a *sine qua non* of all scientific thinking;

4.   To compare and contrast the principal features and dissimilarities of the faith dynamic as the foundation for both religion and the scientific theory of evolution;

5.   To clarify on the basis of observed data whether science may, in fact, be described as a secular religion.

Evolution

This author affirms that evolutionary theory was constructed on false assumptions and weak science. Although scarcely a few decades old, the scientific theory of evolution has developed a high profile within the cognitive sciences (cf. Eccles, 1991; Barkow *et al*, 1995; Plotkin, 1998). Evolutionary theory has also been characterized by a number of tertiary commitments that are not logically related to the evolutionary program, such as anti-theistic biases and other strong reductionisms (Dawkins, 1986). In the ongoing conflict between the Christian and the naturalist worldviews - as exemplified in the creationist position and that of the evolutionary theorist - it appears that little attention has been paid to the fact that both are built upon a foundation of 'faith', irrespective of what terminology is actually employed to describe their respective phenomena. This text deals essentially with the similarities of the psychological dynamics found in each system.

The scientific theory of evolution demands a faith-based cognitive response in a first coincidence that led to further similar and sequential coincidences. In its basest form, this makes it as much a belief system as any religion. Evolutionists have yet to posit a mechanistic first coincidence. Thus far, their best efforts have yielded only the faith-based assumption that each step must have a necessary survival advantage, the means by which evolution from simple to complex has occurred (cf. McIntyre, 1999; Rose & Rose, eds. 2000).

Evolutionary theory remains a controversial field. This

is so not only where it impinges upon matters relating to
science and theology, but it also draws criticism from its
own ranks, from the social sciences and from within evolutionary biology itself. That notwithstanding, however,
evolutionary theory has become a prominent force in the
landscape of the human sciences. As seekers of objective truth, therefore, it behooves us to search beyond the
rhetoric and examine its fundamental claims and logic. As
scholars committed to the pursuit of truth in the cognitive
and behavioral sciences, this may provide us with a knowledge base required for an informed dialogue on the issue.
For Christian believers who are committed to the doctrine
of a personal, intelligent Creator who sustains and governs
his creation, such an approach also provides them with
a fresh opportunity to clarify their thinking regarding the
origins of life and to consider how the dynamic of faith may
be foundational to both positions.

Evolution Questioned

Scott Atran documented evidence that the theory of
evolution was no longer unchallenged or unchallengeable.
In a careful and detailed way, a number of professional scientists* have opined that the theory of evolution is in serious
trouble. In recent thinking, a significant change has occurred
and the role of science and empirical evidence is no longer
accepted without question by the general public and sometimes even by scientists themselves. It is not enough to rely
exclusively on the bare fact of acceptance within the public
sphere or in the isolated towers of academe. So much has
been consigned to the realm of the private and the objective
that doubts have even arisen regarding the worth of science
itself. Like the medieval church, a cadre of scientists and
scholars feel that science must rest its claims to authority in
something beyond itself and in fact must appeal to a metaphysical basis. It is insufficient to say that scientific rationality *is* rationality. One must be told why this is so. Science
remains in need of rational justification (Atran, 1998: 347).

Today there are numerous organizations of scientists who support creation theory. **

_____

*For a list of these, see the website: creation.com/scientists-alive-today-who-accept-the-biblical-account-of-creation.

**Answers in Genesis; Creation Research; Science Education Foundation; Institute for Creation Research; The Creation Super-Library and others. Some publish peer-reviewed journals, such as the Creation Research Society's *CRS Journal* and the *Journal of Creation* by Creation Ministries International.

John Baumgardner, an eminent geophysicist, stated in a public interview:

> Evolutionists do not have a viable mechanism for macroevolution at any stage, whether we're talking about the origin of a first living cell or the origin of new structures in existing organisms. Natural selection and mutation alone are pitifully inadequate to account for what we see, especially with our current understanding of molecular biology. (Baumgardner, 1998). (Interview reported by James Bell)

History has repeatedly demonstrated that theories are made to be broken and abandoned as new facts are identified. Changes have already occurred in evolutionary theory. As Simmons cogently asserted:

> Few scientific theories have stood the test of time. With each new generation of scientists come the "correct" answers, yet, repeatedly, many of these well-conceived ideas are disproved; what was widely accepted as fact often turns out to be wrong. Sometimes, very wrong! Knowing whom to believe or what information is reliable has continued to be a challenge. It may remain so for a long time to come (Simmons, 2004: 299).

Horgan poetically opined, the empirical basis of objective science has thus nothing "absolute" about it. Science does not rest upon rock bottom. The bold structures of its theories rise, as it were, above a swamp. It is like a building erected on piles driven from above into the swamp, but not down to any natural or "given" base; and when we cease our attempts to drive our piles into a deeper layer, it is not because we have reached firm ground. We simply stop at least for the time being (Horgan, 1996:36). Behe makes the same point and notes that the need for modification and change of evolutionary theory is clearly demonstrated in that eminent biologists have been led astray in following Darwin's theory and concepts (Behe, 2007:188-189).

Study and Review Questions for Chapter Two

1. What is the fundamental assumption of creationism?

2. What are the foundational assumptions of evolution?

3. On what basis do scholars question evolution?

Topics Discussed in Chapter Three

The Ephemeral Nature of Theory

Metamorphosis of Theory to Fact

Subjective Experience

The Enigma of Consciousness

Evolution Questioned

Worldview

Similar Tracks: Faith-Trust

Study and Review Questions

THE NATURE OF THEORY

The Ephemeral Nature of Theory

In this text, *theory* is used as a generic term for a tentative explanation of phenomenology or of observed phenomena. However, theory and hypothesis are considered synonyms. Academically, the concept of theory, is a contemplative and rational type of abstract or generalizing thinking. Scientific theories must be predictive and testable, and it must be possible to use the theory to predict the results of observations to be made, and then the theory is tested by seeing whether the actual results agree with predicted outcomes. A satisfactory theory, in the final analysis, must be one that satisfies the desire to understand. In addition, a theory is not understood as necessarily standing in contrast to fact. A theory may be either mistaken or factual. Also, it is assumed that a theory is an attempt to describe reality rather than merely a technique for reproducing observations. Theories evaporate as the mist on a bright summer morning, how then can one ever be sure that a theory is true? Theocharis and Psimopoulos both excoriated this skeptical question in an essay, *Where has Science gone Wrong,* in which they blamed the "deep and wide spread malaise" in science on philosophers who had attacked the notion that science could achieve objective knowledge, citing Popper, Lakatos, Kuhn and Feyerabend as examples (Theocharis & Psimopoulos,1987:595-598).

Ratzch wrote that the history of science illustrated the fox-terrier-like rigidity with which some scientists adhere to a particular theory and the reluctance to accept new evidence that conflicts with present views. That this phenomenon afflicts even the most prominent minds is demonstrated in the case of Albert Einstein. When he first proposed the theory of relativity, Einstein discovered that it predicted that the universe was, from the beginning, expanding from an infinitesimal volume. This was in complete disagreement with the current accepted cosmological model, that proposed an infinitely old universe, which was held in a static state for infinite time. Einstein was manifesting his faith in "the common wisdom of the day." He came to realize that his findings indicated that the universe had a beginning and this contradicted his worldview. However, in the face such convincing evidence Einstein grudgingly abandoned his hypothesized self-stretching space property and acknowledged "the necessity for a beginning" and "the presence of a superior reasoning power." This "reasoning power" was not recognized as the God of the Bible, but Einstein's decision reflects academic integrity (Ratzch, 2000:99, 104).

Science in general has been preoccupied with the physical world and this reflects its inadequacies for examination of the metaphysical realm. As Dolphin observed, speaking of the limitations of science, moral issues and even aesthetics such as the experience of beauty have generally not been accepted as within its purview. Likewise, the model that is useful for a purely physical world is inadequate to examine such issues, the existence of such a dimension cannot be denied because current methods of science are not competent to explore it.

> Science does well when many measurements of phenomena can be made and independently confirmed by others (hopefully objective) observers. And science does poorly when attempting to deal with the spiritual world. (Dolphin, 2006).

Horgan, writing in *Scientific American*, reflected on the question of beauty and how others have struggled with this issue:

> My friend David Rothenberg, a philosopher at the New Jersey Institute of Technology, is, I think it's fair to say, obsessed with the problem of beauty. He has been pok-

ing, prodding and pondering the problem for many years. He has trekked around the world to interview scientists who, in one way or another, study beauty (even if they shun that term) and attempt to explain it, if not explain it away ... His new book considers not just music—in which Rothenberg, as a musician, has a special interest—but beauty in all its manifestations, and especially visual art, whether Paleolithic cave paintings or the ethereal, sculptures of bowerbirds. Rothenberg does all the things that conventional science writers do. He interviews experts in their labs and in the field, weighs the evidence for their theories, offer his assessments and so on. But he also engages with his material in utterly original ways. In an attempt to understand the music of other species, he has played his clarinet with a lyrebird in Australia and with a humpback whale in Hawaii (Horgan, 2011:13).

He further wrote:

Rothenberg argues passionately that we are not the only species with an eye and ear for beauty and a compulsion to create. He is dissatisfied with theories that attempt to explain beauty in strictly functional, evolutionary terms, as a mere side effect of mating or communication. These theories, he asserts, do not do justice to the richness and complexity of art, whether human or inhuman. He proposes that a laughing thrush lets fly a new aria and a satin bowerbird adorns his sculpture with blue flowers not just to attract mates but for the sake of beauty itself, for the sheer joy of creation, just as human artists do (Horgan, 2011:13).

Creation by a Supreme Being, or even by a Designer, cannot be denied by science *qua* science. Whether such is a possibility must at least be given the status of a theory or hypothesis and then it can be scrutinized and examined critically. The onus is, therefore, not just on the supporters of evolution or atheists, but Bible believing Christians must also be sensitive that they cannot operate on the premise that if something cannot be true, because it must not be true, because it runs counter to one's religious or scientific beliefs, this would eventuate in intellectual suicide.

Because the process of evolution has never been observed, to accept the theory of evolution requires some degree of faith-trust as does creationism. Evolution in this context means the theory of common descent proposed by evolutionists. The main tenet of the theory of common descent is that all living creatures have descended from one or a few common ancestors, these ancestors being made up of one or of a small number of cells, namely uni-cellular or multi-cellular life forms. These life forms then pass through a plethora of gradations and eventually change into humans. The main mechanisms given by evolutionists for this great change are random mutations and natural selection. Faith, or acceptance of what cannot be demonstrated empirically, is an essential ingredient in the theory because none of these assumptions have been observed by any human, which is understandable because, according to the evolutionary view of history, humans did not appear on the scene until the last stages of a multibillion year process (Gould, 1977: 45).

Metamorphosis of Theory to Fact

Failure to remember the nature of science and what are its objects and parameters have both on occasion resulted in a deliberate, often subtle and perhaps unconscious metamorphosis of the theory of evolution into evolution as a fact. This could possibly represent naiveté on the part of those involved, but it is more likely the result of the gross and malignant denial of those who refuse to recognize the limitations of the theory they espouse and cling to with religious and fundamentalist devotion. This is an example of the denominational and sectarian involved in the theory of evolution. Burgess, who heads the Department of Mechanical Engineering at Bristol University, spook to this issue:

> The media and educational system often present the theory of evolution as a scientific fact. However, there is no scientific evidence for the evolution of man or any other class of animal. Evolution is simply an atheistic

philosophy which states that everything can be explained by natural phenomenon and that life arose without any input from a Creator. The atheistic bias of modern science is reflected in the fact that even if all the data point to an intelligent designer, such a hypothesis is excluded from science because it is not naturalistic. Scientists like Newton and Pascal would be astonished at the atheistic bias of modern science. They would also be dismayed that the general public is being misled with the claim that evolution is a fact (Burgess, 2004:7-8).

Consider some of the following examples of this denial-based phenomenon:

1. Mayr has opined that "no educated person any longer questions validity of the so-called theory of evolution, which we now know to be a simple fact" (Mayr, 1977:78). In other words, those who fail to accept the unproved theory of evolution as a fact are uneducated ignoramuses.

2. Ayala, who uses legal language, argues that scientists agree that the evolutionary origin of animals and plants is a scientific conclusion "beyond reasonable doubt" and that in any case there can be no doubt that the staggering amount of genetic variation in the natural population provides ample opportunity for evolution to occur (Ayala, 1978: 64).

The use of denial in the consideration of the "myth" (so considered by many scientists) of "the survival of the fittest" has been noted even by ardent evolutionists (Schmidt, 1993:90). In his description of evolution, Darwin proposed a mechanism which was to be summarized in this tautological phrase coined by Herbert Spencer, the philosopher of *laissez-faire*. He stated that in the process of evolution, some types are *fitter* than others and in the struggle for existence and survival only the *fitter* variants would survive to propagate their kind (Bethell, 2005: 206, quoting Spencer, 1864:444). As a result, animals and plants would eventually adapt to their surroundings and those that failed to adapt would die out. Nature has this "evolving mechanism" built into it. Thus the mechanism of evolution as an idea and as a theory was born. By the time of the centennial celebrations at the University of Chicago in 1959, the total ascendency of evolutionary thinking was affirmed. Sir Julian Huxley (grandson of Thomas Henry) pontificated that "the evolution of life is no longer a theory, *it is a fact.*" To corroborate his dogmatism he added, "We do not intend to get bogged down in semantics and definitions" (Huxley, 1960:41).

In spite of the development of the theory and the accolades bestowed upon it by those who worship at its altar, the basic question of "the survival of the fittest" has never been satisfactorily answered. No specific criterion of fitness has ever been identified other than the fact of survival. The essence of Darwin's theory of natural selection is simply that some organisms leave more offspring than others. This was acknowledged by British geneticist C. H. Waddington who spoke at the same Darwin centennial. He reminded the audience that natural selection, which was at first considered a hypothesis, was in need of experimental or observational confirmation, turns out on closer inspection to be a tautology, a statement of an inevitable although previously unrecognized relation. It stated that the finest individuals in a population (defined as those which leave the most offspring) will leave most offspring (Waddington, 1962:385). Koestler was in agreement:

> In the meantime, the educated public continues to believe that Darwin has provided all the relevant answers by the random formula of random mutation plus natural selection – quite unaware of the fact that random mutations turned out to be irrelevant and natural selection a tautology (Koestler, 1978: 354).

Subjective Experience

Another major difficulty for classical Darwinians relates to *qualia,* the distinctive characteristics of human consciousness and subjective experience. Such *qualia* include the experience of color, the affective response to musical sounds and even the experience of pain. Many Darwinian psychologists simply refuse to look at the problem. Daniel Dennett stated that the challenge is to construct a theory of mental events using the data that the scientific method permits (Dennett, 1987:18). He made the claim that there was no distinction between what is conscious and what is not, that simply means that consciousness should no longer be understood as being some inaccessible, private experience. He opined that there was no reality of conscious experience independent of the effects of various vehicles of content on subsequent action. Since Dennett believed that reality must be scientifically accessible, he added that postulating special inner qualities that are not only private but also un-confirmable and un-investigable is obscurantism. In addition, the whole issue of unconscious experiences, which are the grist of the psychoanalytic enterprise, has not yet been examined from the perspective of evolutionary theory (Dennett, 1987:18).

For science to conclude that there is no such state as the experience of pain, which is exceedingly dubious, since we are all only conscious of pain. What science cannot do is explain away the distinctive features of consciousness while pretending that it has not done so. Consciousness and the ability to be self-consciousness together with and capability to reflect about one's own state, would be eliminated by a scientific program at the cost of bringing into question the status of science. It seems ludicrous to reject the idea of there being a self, which is the subject of experience. However, in the absence of a self there is no real subject capable of making rational decisions. The representatives of science, in a personal vendetta against the subjective have not only undermined the reality of personal experience but has apparently destroyed the subject of that experience. Any empirical approach will find it difficult to discover an experience of the self because by definition it is always the self, that is having the experience.

The Enigma of Consciousness

It appears that the origin and significance of consciousness remains one of the great dilemmas for evolutionists because a purely physiological theory or empirical methodology was not formulated to explain the phenomenon. Just because biologists complete their empirical investigations does not mean that they have answered all relevant questions. No purely physiological theory has yet been able to explain consciousness, as Wolf argued "human consciousness is too remarkable to have evolved our moral sense" (Wolf, 2006:182-193). Since the process responsible for this wholly private experience will be seen to degenerate into seemingly quite ordinary, workaday reactions, no more or less fascinating than those that occur in any other physiological process.

In spite of its claim as a "theory of everything," evolutionary theory still has made no dent in this area. Each individual has the ability to recognize his/her consciousness but since it is located in a private, non-physical universe of thoughts and sensations, it is not possible for others to observe it. Indeed, we can only infer the consciousness of another through their behavior and through communication with them via the physical universe. Many superb thinkers are convinced that human consciousness is too remarkable to have evolved and our moral sense defies the narcissistic imperatives of nature (Wolf, 2006:184).

Worldview

The dictionary definition of worldview is a comprehensible philosophy or conception of the universe and of human life. In other words, worldview is the fundamental cognitive orientation of an individual encompassing the entirety of their perspective on life. It is the view or interpretation that everyone has of reality as a whole. It is the comprehensive philosophy of god, nature, life, death, and history. It is the over- all perspective, the fundamental point of view, the basic outlook on life. In every scientific endeavor, the worldview of the researcher is controlling. It is impossible to separate a person from his or her faith-trust. Few would question the view that faith has a pervasive influence on the life of an individual. Faith will also influence the culture that fabricates the understanding about reality and the ideas of history. A faith commitment affects much more than the view of history. As Kenneth Woodward wrote:

> By any secular standard, Jesus is also the dominant figure of western culture. Like the millennium itself, much of what we now think of as western ideas, inventions and values finds its source of inspiration in the religion that worships God in his name. Art and science, the self and society, politics and economics, marriage and the family, right and wrong, body and soul – all have been touched and often radically transformed by Christian influence (Woodward, 1999).

Burgess echoed the same viewpoint, though in more Evangelical language. He points out that human origin cannot be proven scientifically and therefore a person must have faith in either creation or evolution. One of the reasons why "origins" is so important is that belief in creation or evolution leads to different worldviews and values. Belief in creation leads to the view that humans are accountable to a Creator and that life should be governed by biblical principles. In contrast, evolution encourages the view that humanity can ignore the moral law (Burgess, 2004: 146). Noebel has observed:

> Darwin, Huxley, Russell and the pro-evolution activists inform us that mankind is the product of evolution and chance. Wundt, Watson and Skinner with their disciples have formulated a psychological system based on the assumption that there is no spiritual dimension to man. Nietzsche and his followers claim that belief in God is a mark of weakness and that every person has the ability to define his own morality. Marx and Lenin assert that there is no God while Dewey and his followers state that life is a mere accident of nature (Noebel, 2001: viii).

Anti-evolutionists are convinced that the secular humanist worldview is in direct conflict with Christianity and is battling for the hearts and minds of people the world over. The essential conflict is not between science and religion. That is a red herring. The battle is drawn between humanism as a front for evolution without God and theism and supernaturalism. Humanistic values have become a way of life for many, having taken the predominant position in universities, the news media, the judiciary and the behavioral sciences. In particular, the humanist *kerygma* is enunciated by the narcissistically-oriented and pervasive entertainment industry. The atheistic-based theory of evolution has become the prevalent mode of thinking in much of society and although the overwhelming majority of Americans believe in the existence of a personal god, ninety percent of the leadership of the National Academy of Sciences declare themselves to be atheistic (Johnson, 2000: 86). Secular humanists continue in their evangelistic fervor to promote their religious worldview, as admitted by Dewey (Dewey, 1962: 87).

Every worldview, whether Christian, Humanist or Marxist, has its own foundation of faith-based presuppositional-assumptions. Each view demands basic assumptions about the nature of reality in order to grant meaning to specific approaches to it. Theological and philosophical assumptions permeate each aspect of one's worldview and these must be recognized and admitted in any attempt to understand the implications of the worldview in question.

Christians believe that the Christian belief system, based on biblical revelation, is authenticated true and is significant for every aspect of human endeavor. As Henry stated, "The Christian belief system, which the Christian knows to be grounded in divine revelation, is relevant to all of life" (Henry, 1990:47). However, it is important to point out that no reputable Christian scientist espouses the idea that the Bible is an actual scientific textbook. As David Bailey noted:

The Bible is not a scientific textbook, nor was it ever intended to be read in this way. The Bible describes humankind's grand and sublime search for God, the meaning of
life, morality and salvation. Technical questions such as the
age of the earth and the history of biological species are
much better studied with the tools of modern science, tools
which many believe to have been granted to mankind for the
express purpose of better understanding the physical world
around us. (Bailey, 2011).

Giler, an outstanding sociologist and economist,
echoed the same sentiment, as quoted by Neff: "Christianity
is true and its truth will be discovered anywhere you look"
(Neff, 1987:35). Professor C. E. M. Joad, an eminent
former atheist philosopher, enunciated the same conviction and wrote, "I now believe that the balance of reasoned
considerations tells heavily in favor of the religious, even of
the Christian view of the world" (Joad, 1955: 22). His search
was for absolute truth rather than truth that evolves with
each new discovery. "A religion which is in constant process
of revision to square with science's ever-changing picture
of the world might well be easier to believe, but it is hard to
believe it would be worth believing" (Joad, 1955: 241).

The Christian worldview and its sources was summarized by Noebel:

1. Source is the Bible.

2. Theology is Theism.

3. Philosophy is Supernaturalism.

4. Ethics are Absolutes.

5. Biology is Creationism.

6. Psychology is Mind/Body.

7. Sociology is Traditional Home, Church and State.

8. Law is Biblical and Natural Law.

9. Politics are Justice, Freedom and Order.

10. Economics are Stewardship of Property.

11. History is Historical Resurrection.

(Noebel, 2001: 330):

On the other hand, the secular humanist worldview and its sources, as summarized by Noebel, included:

1. Theology is atheism.

2. Philosophy is naturalism.

3. Ethics are relativism.

4. Biology is Darwinian evolution.

5. Psychology is self-actualization.

6. Sociology is non-traditional family.

7. Law is positive law.

8. Politics are globalism/world government.

9. Economics are socialism

10. History is historical evolution

(Noebel, 2001: 330).

Everyone, whether Christian or secular humanist, has a worldview. The importance of understanding the ramifications of one's worldview has been clearly enunciated by Noebel:

> If Secular Humanism is a religious worldview it has, by present interpretation of the "separation of church and state" doctrine, no place in the public school system. We do not, of course, expect Biblical Christianity to be the only worldview taught in America's schools. But we do expect fair representation. At the very least, this study should "level the playing field" so that Christian students and their parents will recognize worldview bias and understand how to take effective countermeasures to preserve their point of view (Noebel, 2001: 33).

The religion of secular humanism has its evangelists and peddlers of devotional literature in wide positions of influence in society. Skinner, Maslow, Carl Rogers, and Eric Fromm, all former Humanists of the Year, have all had a tremendous influence on psychology. Carl Sagan, another Humanist of the Year, has preached his humanistic homilies on a widely heralded television series somewhat reminiscent of a typical American televangelist (Terzian, 1997:xiii). Norman Lear has produced and otherwise influenced a number of shows on television. Ethical decisions are made by the Humanist of the Year-1986, Faye Wattleton, former director of Planned Parenthood. Humanist Isaac Asimov wrote tirelessly for his evangel (Asimov, 1982: ix-x). It is clear that the religion of Humanism, with its primary doctrine of evolution and its worldwide missionaries, are as active, and, perhaps, even more active, than any Christian evangelical outreach.

Similar Tracks: Faith-Trust

The evidence appears to be accumulating that religion, especially the Christian religion, is not alone in being built on a foundation of faith – or on a faith-based-presuppositional-assumption. Hasker has emphasized that philosophically, naturalism, insists that the natural world is complete in itself, self-contained and self-sufficient. According to naturalism, everything that exists or occurs lies entirely within the domain of natural processes. Nothing comes into nature or influences it from outside. There is no "outside." Nature is all there is (Hasker, 1983:108). However, both the worldview of the biblically-based theist and that of the secular humanist, of whatever hue, owe their existence to a rather similar foundation built on faith. The belief system known as Secular Humanism relies heavily on the evolution theory for credibility. All that exists is held by faith to be self-perpetuating by a never-ending evolutionary process. Scarcely a page of any of the publications written by proponents of secular humanism fails to cite evolution as an established fact central to all existence.

(See, for example, the website http://www.allaboutphilosophy.org/secular-humanism.html).

A rather typical pro-humanist and pro-evolution publication of the Council for Secular Humanism reads as follows:

> Although the theory of evolution cannot be said to have reached its final formulation or to be an infallible principle of science, it is nonetheless supported impressively by the findings of many sciences. There may be some significant differences among scientists concerning the mechanics of evolution; yet the evolution of the species is supported so strongly by the weight of evidence that it is difficult to reject it. Accordingly, we deplore the efforts by Fundamentalists (especially in the United States) to invade the science classrooms, requiring the creationist theory to be taught to students and requiring that it be included in biology textbooks. This is a serious threat both to academic freedom and to the integrity of the educational process. We believe that creationists surely should have the freedom to express their viewpoint in society. Moreover, we do not deny the value of examining theories of creation in educational courses on religion and the theory of ideas; but it is a sham to mask an article of religious faith as a scientific truth and to inflict that doctrine on the scientific curriculum. If successful, creationists may seriously undermine the credibility of science itself. (Council for Secular Humanism, 1980). .

A common charge frequently brought against creationists is that their approach to natural history is influenced by their faith. However, the approach of evolutionists is also influenced by their faith. The theory of evolution is an attempt to account for the natural world without God. It is an expression of Naturalism, the predetermined belief that the only form of reality is the physical one. Anything that is not physical, and cannot therefore be investigated and measured by the scientific method, is not real and does not count. The theory of evolution sets out to demonstrate that the world is self-explanatory; everything can be explained without God by the operation of natural laws and of change, the random collision of atoms, and molecules and the random mutation of genes. But atheism is a faith. It is as much an act of faith to believe that God does not exist as it is to believe that He does. The reality of a spiritual being,

Who is not by definition susceptible to scientific investigation, must be a matter of faith one way or the other.
Scientist, because of their understanding of the nature of
the scientific enterprise, will put aside the idea of supernatural causality when they enter the laboratory; their job
is to find natural causes. But the fundamental question is
precisely: is there more to life than science can explain? To
rule out the possibility of a supernatural causation from the
start, as naturalism does, is to make a dogmatic statement
of faith, and begs the question this research is attempting to
answer: is the natural world self-explanatory? (Down, 2007:
24).

While it is true that lack of belief in a Creator is not
necessarily dishonest in a scientific sense, Darwinians
commit a logical error in their assumption and presupposition that science as such is the ground of their metaphysical
dismissal of God. Evolutionists, however, at times, in their
assigning of significance to the mechanism of natural selection, have almost reified the concept and given it the status
of a distinctive foundation of "faith" credited with evicting
the Creator. Sir Julian Huxley has heralded evolution as an
inescapable fact:

> Charles Darwin has rightly been praised as the "Newton of
> biology"; he did more than any single individual before or
> since to change man's attitude to the phenomenon of life
> and to provide a coherent scientific framework for ideas of
> biology, in place of an approach in large part compounded of
> hearsay, myth and superstition. He rendered evolution ines-
> capable as a fact, comprehensible as a process, all embrac-
> ing as a concept (Huxley: 1960: 13).

It appears that religion is an essential part of human
psychological makeup and if it is not fulfilled in one way,
it will search for another, whether in theistic or atheistic
science. Davies points out that, in spite of all appearances,
mankind lives in a world that is still fundamentally religious.
He stated:

... ranging from countries like Iran and Saudi Arabia, where Islam remains the dominant social force, to the industrialized west, where religion has fragmented and diversified, occasionally into vague pseudo-scientific superstition, the search for a deeper meaning to life continues.

However, he continues:

... scientists also search for meaning by finding out more about the way the universe is put together and how it works, about the nature of life and consciousness; they can supply the raw material from which religious beliefs may be fashioned (Davies, 1983:3).

The scientist and the theologian approach the deep and ultimate questions of life and the universe from different starting points. Science is an empirical enterprise and based on observation and experimentation from which theories are formulated. Regularities in nature are discovered that indicate laws in nature based on which predications may be made and further experimentation planned. Competent scientists, with integrity, are always willing to abandon a theory and formulate a better one when the empirical findings indicate the need.

The Christian religion, on the other hand, is based on revelation, and since it claims to be unalterable truth communicated to the believer, rather than through the rigid process of collective investigation, it is difficult to modify to fit changing ideas and concepts. This is when true believers are confirmed by their faith. Many scientists deride such a notion and are not impressed by the convictions of those who have had religious experiences and who invariably put more weight on their personal experience than on scientific experiments (Davies, 1983:6).

Early in its conflict with theism, both science and evolutionary theory learned that the most effective way to demolish or at least attenuate a religious system is to produce a more acceptable substitute. In this connection, Horgan reports the convictions of Stent:

Stent was still convinced ... that a purely physiological explanation of consciousness would not be comprehensible or as meaningful as most people would like, nor would it help us to solve moral and ethical questions." Stent thought the progress of science might give religion a clearer role in the future rather than eliminate it entirely, as many scientists had hoped. Although it could not compete with science's far more compelling stories about the physical realm, religion retained some value in offering moral guidance. Humans are animals, but we're also moral subjects. The task of religion is more and more in the moral realm (Horgan, 1996:14-15).

Davies agreed:

Any scientist will verify that, if religion has been displaced from peoples' consciousness, it has certainly not been replaced by rational scientific thought. For science, despite its great impact on all our lives, is as elusive and inaccessible to the general public as any exclusive religion (Davies, 1983:2).

It is a psychological truism that every Christian believer, from Saint Thomas and ever afterwards, has had the experience of doubt at some time. This is an extremely common phenomenon and reflects the fact that at times for most people faith comes somewhat short of certainty. It is fascinating to note that even Darwin himself, the high priest of the new secular faith, that he had recognized as tentative, at times walked in the valley of "horrid doubt." In 1881, in a personal letter to William Graham, he confessed, as follows:

Nevertheless, you have expressed my inward conviction, though far more vividly and clearly than I could have done, that the Universe is not the result of chance. But then with me the horrid doubt always arises whether the convictions of man's mind, which has been developed from the minds of lower animals, are of any value or at all trustworthy. (Darwin, 1881).

Darwin realized that if living organisms survived only on the basis of mindless natural selection, then it inescapably followed that human reason was also the product of natural selection. The conclusions of human reason could, therefore, never be known to be true, but only valuable in accord with their contribution to the survival of the human species. Such an implication for any meaningful human enquiry can cause "horrid doubt" as depicted in Darwin's autobiography. He wrote:

> But then arises the doubt, can fill the mind of man, which has, as I fully believe, been developed from a mind as that possessed by the lowest animal, be trusted when it draws such grand conclusions. (The grand conclusion in this context is the evolutionary hypothesis itself). Man will never be able to discover purpose to existence, for he cannot determine if his conclusions are true. All scientific enquiry is undermined (Clark, 1976: 39; Darwin, 1887:108).

Thomson believed that Darwin's doubts may have evolved from the catastrophe of the loss of his daughter. "God the Creator of pain and suffering is never quite explainable by Malthus's arithmetic, however, and Charles Darwin himself turned away from religion as much or more because of the "senseless" death of his 10-year-old daughter Annie than any logic" (Thomson, 1997:XXII). However, no clear evidence for this opinion has yet surfaced. Numbers has commented on this rather frightening atavistic perspective as follows:

> The metamorphosis of idea into concept, to observation, to theory and to established fact has been developed with denominational fervor previously rarely seen outside the political and theological arenas, and it demands adherence and cognitive submission to the altar of some Darwinian principle. A startling example of intolerance is well illustrated in the suggestion that children of Christian believers who would teach their children some theory other than evolution should be caged in zoos or quarantined because they pose a serious public health threat to the social order. If Dawkins played the role of point man for late-twentieth-century naturalistic evolutionists, Tufts University philosopher Daniel C. Dennett gladly served as their hatchet man. Displaying a degree of intolerance

more characteristic of a fundamentalist fanatic than an academic philosopher, he called for "caging" those who would deliberately misinform children about the natural world, just as one would cage a threatening animal. "The message is clear," he wrote: "those who will not accommodate, who will not temper, who insist on keeping only the purest and wildest strain of their heritage alive, we will be obliged, reluctantly, to cage or disarm, and we will do our best to disable the memes [traditions, ideas, behavior, or style that spreads within a culture] they fight for" (Dennett 1995, 519-20). With the bravado of a man unmindful that only 11 per cent of the public shared his enthusiasm for naturalistic evolution, he warned parents that if they insisted on teaching their children "falsehoods — that the earth is flat that "Man" is not a product of evolution by natural selection — then you must expect, at the very least, that those of us who have freedom of speech will feel free to describe your teachings as the spreading of falsehoods, and will attempt to demonstrate this to your children at our earliest opportunity" (Dennett 1997). Those who resisted conversion to Dennett's scientific fundamentalism would be subject to "quarantine" (Numbers 1988:13).

Publication of this type of rhetoric by a respected scientist and academician raises the question: Has a scientific Inquisition returned? It used to be that in society, theology reigned supreme, but times have changed. Bickel and Jantz have given an excellent description of the change that has occurred.

Theology was once called the "Queen of the Sciences" because it addresses the whole person – emotional, intellectual and spiritual – and seeks to bring the natural and the spiritual together. Not anymore. For the past 150 years, science has successfully challenged the notion that there is a God who created the universe. Today, science leads our culture and stands in the forefront of intellectual integrity, while theology has been relegated to the realm of philosophy and personal preference. Science gives us the technology and cure for diseases. The findings and benefits of science are universally applicable to peoples of all countries, ethnicities, and faiths. Science seems to be the only universal constant in our lives upon which we can rely. Science is king. Even more, for many people, science is God (Bickel & Jantz, 2008:93).

Again science and religion appear to be on the same track, exhibiting many similarities and using similar mechanisms.

Study and Review Questions for Chapter Four

1. Describe the basic nature of a theory.

2. What is the essence of Darwin's theory natural selection?

3. Why is the origin of consciousness significant?

4. What is the meaning of "worldview?"

5. Why is Henry's statement on the Christian belief system important?

6. How does the secular humanist's worldview relate to the following:

   a. Theology; b. Biology; c. Sociology; d. Economics?

7. How did the death of Darwin's young daughter influence his thinking?

8. Why was theology once called the "Queen of the Sciences?"

Topics Discussed in Chapter Four

The Theory of Evolution

Pre-scientific Concepts

Forerunners of Darwin

The Search Continues

Examination of the Fossil Record

The Contribution of Chevalier de Lamarck.

Chambers and Organic Evolution

Uniformitarianism

Darwin's Giants

The Influence of the Enlightenment

The Evolution of Darwin

Modern Developments

The Current Landscape

Non-polemical and Non-Apologetic

Evolution a Potential Threat to Naturalism

Study and Review Questions

CHAPTER FOUR

THE DEVELOPMENT OF A THEORY

The Theory of Evolution

The theory of evolution is an attempt to explain origins and, to the best of current knowledge, by what mechanisms the process has occurred. It is an attempt to describe a process (some would say an unplanned and undirected process) that combines elements of random genetic change or mutation that are accumulated through natural selection. The term evolution, however, can mean many different things, which is why a precise definition is crucial. Rolston appreciated the bi-polar nature of evolution as the development of the theory has continued along two divergent tracks. He wrote:

> Biology has developed two scales. Molecular biology, discovering genes and DNA, has decoded the "secret of life" (once ascribed to the Spirit of God). Evolutionary history has located the secreted in natural selection operating across enormous time spans with the finest selected to survive. The two levels are theoretically interrelated (Rolston, 1998:415).

Some meanings are uncontroversial, such as things change over time or that organisms adapt to their changing environments. Common examples include bacteria developing resistance to antibiotics or finch beaks varying in size over weather cycles. This is small-scale evolution, known as microevolution, and no one disputes that this process does occur. In microevolution, no new species crop up, bacteria remain bacteria and finches remain finches. Macroevolution, on the other hand, is the metamorphosis of one species into another and is, and remains a central feature of Darwinism.

Gould described Classical Darwinism:

> Classical Darwinism makes two major claims: first, all organisms (life forms) are related back through time to a common ancestor. This is commonly called common descent or universal common ancestry. Second, the process that brought all organisms into existence from a common ancestor is natural selection acting on random variations. It is claimed that this process operates by chance and necessity, apart from any evident intention of direct design. According to contemporary Neo-Darwinism, one organism becomes more fit than another through random mutation of genes, or, in layman's terms, sheer luck or trial and error (Gould, 1980: 66).

In essence, the theory of organic evolution involves three basic ideas:

1. Living things change from generation to generation, producing descendants with new characteristics.

2. This process has been going on so long that it has produced all the groups and kinds of things now living, as well as others that lived long ago and have died out, or become extinct.

3. These different living things are related to each other.

Pre-scientific Concepts

Since humans first appeared on the earth, there have been perennial questions about the universe and how it originated and especially concerning humanity itself. The earliest records of human history, for example, the Akkadian, Sumerian and Babylonian, focus on how gods created the world, the origin of human beings, animals, plants and the complexity of the heavens (Leeming, 2010: 84; Barbour, 1997: 58, 65; Kuyper, 1903: 37, 38, 117 f). The account recorded in the first chapters of Genesis is especially significant to Jews, Moslems and Christians because it is accepted as a revelation from the Creator. Each type of animal and plant, according to the Genesis account, is said to reproduce "after its kind" (Genesis 1:21) and this had traditionally been interpreted as "after the same species," an exegesis frequently aimed at precluding the possibility of macroevolution. Collins has stated regarding *min*, the Hebrew word translated "kind" as follows:

> Some suggest that the word "kind" is roughly equivalent to "species" and that the text is opposed to any notion of a new species developing from old ones. There are two problems with such statements. First, the meaning of "min" does not support it; and second, it is not what Genesis actually says. As to the semantics of "min", the term here is not as technical as "species;" it rather means something like "category" or "variety" and its basis for classification is the appearance.

Collins adds a footnote:

> Some creationists hold this view, but the claim more commonly comes from opponents of all forms of creationism (Collins, 2006:58).

The philosopher Munitz has described some of the mythological conceptions of the creation event, some of which may have influenced the Genesis account.

> The type of thinking was initiated by the Milesian school of pre-Socratic thinkers – Thales, Anaximander, and Anaximenes – in the sixth century B.C. and was carried forward in many directions. One of the most remarkable outcomes of such speculations, representing a culmination of their materialist thought, was to be found in the atomist school. Originally worked out in its main features by Leucippus and Democritus in the fifth century B.C., the teachings of atomism were later adopted as a basis for the primarily ethical philosophy of Epicureanism ... It elaborates the conception of a universe whose order arises out of a blind interplay of atoms rather than as a product of deliberate design; of a universe boundless in spatial extent, infinite in its duration and containing innumerable worlds in various stages of development or decay (Munitz, 1965: 438).

These ideas are remarkably reminiscent of the Darwinian theory of evolution. The early Greeks were extremely interested in the origin of the universe and its contents and favored theories based on mythic revelation and religion. However, even at that relatively early stage of human history, some of these early Greek thinkers leaned toward purely materialistic explanations founded on reason and they proposed rather crude prototypes of the theory of evolution. Aristotle (384-322 BC), after having spent years studying animals, concluded that the species are fixed. He went on to propose that the species are, in fact, eternal and that both creation and evolution are erroneous and unnecessary notions (Lennox, 2000:128). It is difficult to be certain, however, of just what Aristotle meant because he wrote in a deliberately obscurantist style. The pre-Socratic Greek Milesian philosophers evidently received their concepts of evolutionary cosmogony from the even more ancient religious leaders of Egypt, Babylonia and Sumerian. The basic unity of all ancient religions is a pantheistic, poly-theistic, astrological, Spiritist, evolutionary cosmology that is a remarkable feature of the ancient world. This indicates that in all probability evolution is not in any way a modern "scientific" discovery, but rather a revival of a primeval mythic world religion. Osborn is even more specific. He wrote:

> Aristotle believed in a complete gradation in Nature, a pro-gressive development corresponding with the progressive life of the soul... He put his facts together into an evolu-tion system which had the teaching of Plato and Socrates for its primary philosophical basis ... Like his master Plato, Aristotle insists there is but one world, that is a central body like the earth surrounded by a finite number of planets. This one world, of course, which makes up the entire universe, contains all existent matter ... Aristotle argues that the one world or universe we know is eternal, without beginning and without end (Osborn, 1929:48).

Abel emphasized that the notion of evolution is certain-ly as old as written history:

> Although it is customary to credit the inception of this theory to Charles Darwin and his immediate predecessors, a rudi-

mentary form of this notion can be traced back to the beginnings of written history itself. In fact, the belief that life had its origin in a single basic substance is so wide-spread among the various peoples of the world, primitive or civilized, that it can be considered one of the few universal themes in the history of ideas (Abel, 1973:15).

Cornford echoed the same theme:

The Milesian system pushed back to the very beginning of things the operation of processes as familiar and ordinary as a shower of rain. It made the formation of the world no longer a supernatural, but a natural event. Thanks to the Ionians, and to no one else, this has become the universal premise of all modern science ... They believed that the order arose by differentiation out of a simple state of things, at first conceived as a single living substance, later by pluralists, as a primitive confusion in which "all things", now separate, were together (Cornford, 1965: 21-22).

In Hesiod's great poem, *Theogony,* the same materialistic assumptions are depicted in Miss Hamilton's paraphrase:

Long before the gods appeared, in the dim past, uncounted ages ago, there was only a formless confusion of Chaos brooded over by unbroken darkness. At last, but no one ever tried to explain, two children were born to this shape of nothingness ... What took place next was the creation of the earth, but this too, no one ever tried hard to explain. It just happened. The poet Hesiod, the first Greek who tried to explain how things began, wrote:

Earth the beautiful, rose up,

Broad-bosomed,

She that is the steadfast base of all things.

And the fair Earth first bore the starry heaven,

Equal to herself,

To cover her on all sides and to be

A home forever for the blessed gods.

(Hamilton, 1942: 77-78)

A comparison of the Babylonian "creation tablets" with the revelation regarding origins in Genesis shows marked differences. Often the mythological notions of the early Akkadians, Sumerians and Babylonians and the developing concepts of the early Greeks are placed in juxtaposition with the creation account given in the Hebrew scriptures. These are often compared and contrasted with the biblical account, often, it would seem, with the implication that they are all of the same mythological nature and possibly from the same source. However, it is clear, for example, that the Genesis cosmogony is antithetical to that of the creation tablets such as those which have been preserved in an epic poem composed to honor Merodach, the patron god of Babylon.

a. The tablets begin with chaos.

   The biblical account begins with perfection (Genesis 1:1)

b. The tablets consider the heavenly bodies to be gods.

   Genesis depicts them as matter created by God.

c. The tablets are infused with polytheistic mythology.

   Genesis is a revelation of monotheism.

d. The tablets are characterized by atavistic superstition.

   The biblical account of creation is characterized by righteousness and holiness. (Foster, 1995:438; Bottero, 2004: 246; Jacobsen, 1976: 273)

The theory of evolution was not original with Darwin. It is clear that it was an ancient concept, which may possibly have been revived as a methodological weapon in the developing conflict between religion and science as stimulated by the Enlightenment. From the point of view of biblical inspiration, there is perhaps something to be said for the idea that the ancient mythological fantasies are not equal with the Hebrew account, but degradation from it.

Forerunners of Darwin

Beginning in the 18th century, the French naturalist, Comte de Buffon (1707-1788) and British physician Erasmus Darwin (1731-1802) – the grandfather of
Charles Darwin – began to speculate about the possibility
of a species gradually changing or evolving into another
species. At the same time G. W. F. Hegel (1770-1831) in
Germany and Herbert Spencer (1820-1903) in England
were preaching a *kerygma* of progressive social development or evolution over time (Elliott, 2003: 1-2).

Topoff has stressed the role played by Erasmus
Darwin, who was one of the most celebrated personalities in
England during the last decade of the 18th century. A physician, philosopher and poet, his writings on evolution utilized
evidence from embryology, comparative anatomy, biological
systematics and zoogeography. His influence is reflected in
the fact that two years after his death, the word "Darwinian"
was in common use and his book, *Zoonomia* had been
translated into French, German and Italian. Four years after
its publication, Thomas Malthus (1776-1834) elaborated
Erasmus's ideas in his *Essays on Population*. Nine years
later, Lamarck expounded a theory of evolution, based on
Erasmus Darwin's notion of the effects of use and disuse.
Another 63 years would elapse before his grandson Charles
Darwin would publish *On the Origin of Species* (Malthus,
1798:10; Topoff, 1997:104-107).

The Search Continues

In the early nineteenth century, the notion that species
might have developed from pre-existing species was slowly
but gradually gaining acceptance. There were a variety of
factors operative at that time in Western science that con-
tributed to this development, namely:

1. Examination of the fossil record

2. The work of Chevalier de Lamarck

3. Robert Chambers and organic evolution

4. Uniformitarianism

Examination of the Fossil Record

Early in 1800, a British civil engineer, William Smith (1797-1875) began to record the differences in the fossils found in various layers of rock strata. He noted that each era of rock formation appeared to have its own unique population of living things. It was left to Cuvier (1769-1832) to reconstruct these earlier life forms from their fossil remains. He concluded that there was evidence of systemic development over time, from invertebrates to fish, to reptiles and finally to mammals. During the 1820s and the 1830s British geologist William Buckland (1784-1856) and anatomist Richard Owen (1804-1892) fired up public imagination with their descriptions of dinosaurs from the age of reptiles. At the same time Adam Sedgwick (1785-1873) identified trilobites from the earliest eras. As Ulett noted, with reference to these developments, by the mid 1880s the concept of progressive development over time was the generally accepted idea among the public, with humans being the last to appear. It was also generally accepted that the earth was very old – a *sine qua non* of evolutionary theory (Ulett, 2010).

The Contribution of Chevalier de Lamarck

It was left to the French naturalist Chevalier de Lamarck (1744-1892), to present in 1820 the outlines of the first comprehensive theory of evolution. He believed in the spontaneous generation of simple living organisms which were acted upon in some mysterious and unknown way, perhaps by electrical stimulation. This energizing force then continued to act on the organisms and this was responsible for the development of organisms into more complex forms. The focus of the energizing force was on those organs which are currently useful and necessary. Those organs which were not being used were deprived of stimulation and consequently atrophied (Gould, 1980: 65-71).

The doctrine of acquired characteristics was widely accepted in Lamarck's time. No reputable scholar or scientist would have thought of doubting it till the close of the nineteenth century. The number of individuals before the nineteenth century who rejected the inheritance of acquired characters was very small. The atmosphere was to change radically, as a 1966 textbook of biology stated:

> Acquired characteristics are not inherited because environmental factors (which do not affect the genes in the sex cells) cannot influence the next generation (Hall and Lesser, 1966: 304-305).

Nobel Prize winning geneticist Muller emphasized the demise of the Lamarckian notion. He pointed out:

> despite the strong influence of the environment in modifying the body as a whole, and even the protoplasm of its cells, the genes within the germ-cells of that body retain their original structure without specific alternations caused by the modification of the body, so that when the modified individual reproduces it transmits to its offspring genes unaffected by its own acquired characters (Muller, 1959: 988).

Unfortunately for Lamarck neither his scientific views nor his poetry were accepted by Cuvier who was his superior in the French Natural History Museum, and few scholars paid attention to his views. Curvier was convinced that the secret lay in the sharp breaks in the fossil records and not in the idea of species changing over time (Rudwick,1997:229).

Chambers and Organic Evolution

Robert Chambers (1802-1871) revived the idea of spontaneous generation of elementary life forms. He believed that organisms progressed in a linear fashion that was somehow preordained. He had no explanation for the lack of intermediate fossils or any explanation of how change in a species could occur. For these reasons his opponents ridiculed him and this rejection was to have a profound effect on Charles Darwin who determined that his ideas would be scrutinized, proven and scientifically acceptable before he made them public (Wyhe, 2007:178) ; Chambers, 1994: xi).

Uniformitarianism

Neptunism was an idea that dominated geological thought during the early 1800s. The notion was first proposed by German geologist Abraham Werner (1750-1817) in the late 1700s. The thesis was that rock strata, fossils and the earth's geological features were results of a gradual retreat of a vast primeval ocean that had once covered the earth. Cuvier added the concept of repeated catastrophic floods which terminated each geologic era and which in the process deposited characteristic fossils. These ideas were somewhat acceptable to Christian apologists because geologic history still had a beginning and an end. (Ospovat, 2008)

In 1795 Scottish naturalist and deist, James Hutton (1726-1797) formulated his alternate theory of steady-state volcanism. As a deist he could not accept God's active intervention in geologic history and as an empiricist he objected to hypotheses of past catastrophes to account for current geologic characteristics. Hutton posited a cyclical process of igneous rock mountains and volcanoes rising from the earth's molten core, and then eroding to create inhabitable land. As the lands built up, bottom layers would push down into the core. The resulting pressure would push up new earth (Rance, 1999).

Hutton stated that in creation there was no beginning and no end and that, therefore, there was ample time for organic evolution. His theories received little or no scientific support in Britain. Breaks in the fossil record and the supposed sedimentary origin of most rocks discredited his theory of volcanic gradualism.

In 1830 the naturalist Charles Lyell (1797-1875) began to emphasize the theory of modern uniformitarianism. He insisted that scientists should only use observable processes in their attempts to explain nature. He believed that the inner heat of the earth was sufficient to shape geologic features and that the most common rock forms, granite and basalt, are not sedimentary but igneous. The abrupt appearance and disappearance of species in the fossil record convinced him that each species was created separately by God in a local milieu. Gradual geological change suggested that organisms would need to adapt to a changing environment and uniformitarianism gave ample time for these changes to accumulate (Lyell, 1881:168).

Darwin's Giants

It appears, therefore, that in spite of the prominence given to his name and work Charles Darwin was not the originator of the theory of evolution, even though he referred to the theory as "my" theory of natural selection (Thompson, 2001:212). This in no way is a depreciation of his great and significant pioneering work. There were many, however, who came before him and on whose shoulders he stood. In this connection Barzun stated:

> Darwin was not a thinker and he did not originate the ideas that he used. He vacillated, and retracted, and confused his own traces. As soon as he crossed the dividing line between the realm of events and the realm of theory he became "metaphysical" in the bad sense. His power of drawing out the implications of his own theories was at no time very remarkable, but when it came to the moral order it disappeared altogether, as the penetrating evolutionist Nietzsche observed with some disdain (Barzun, 1959:84).

Topoff notes:

> Darwin's first use of the word "evolution" was in his second major book, The Descent of Man, published in 1871. The following year, it was added to the sixth edition of the Origin. In an important sense the Origin also did not address the question suggested by its very title, namely speciation. Instead, it focused on changes within a single lineage over long periods of time. The issue of how a single group of organisms with a shared gene pool could split into two or more genetically distinct populations remained unexplained until well into the 20th century (Topoff, 1997:106).

Darlington was even more scathing in his observations. He also noted that Darwin in *The Origin* of Species did not address the question suggested by the title of his work, namely speciation. Instead, it spoke of the evolution of animals from "one living filament". Darlington noted:

> Erasmus Darwin (who died before Charles was born) had assembled the evidence of embryology, comparative anatomy, geographical distribution and, so far as man is concerned, the facts of history and medicine. These arguments about the fact of transformation were all of them already familiar. As to the means of transformation, however, Erasmus Darwin had originated almost every important idea that has ever appeared in evolutionary theory (Darlington, 1959: 61-62).

Rifkin has stressed:

> Darwin borrowed very heavily from the popular economic thinking of the day. While by Darwin's own admission, Malthus's economic writings were a key influence in the development of his theory, Darwin was equally influenced by one of the other great economic philosophers of the eighteenth century, Adam Smith. An examination of Smith's and Darwin's writings shows how deeply indebted the latter was to the thoughts Smith penned in The Wealth of Nations, published in 1776 (Rifkin, 1983: 86).

The Influence of the Enlightenment

The idea of evolution, or creation by natural law, was to have a recrudescence as a result of the Enlightenment. As religious authorities were becoming less important and powerful during the 1700s natural philosophers struggled to develop explanations for life that were completely materialistic. Denis Diderot (1713-1784) and Baron d'Holbach (1723-1789), both dedicated materialists, proposed that all living forms had developed as a result of chance mutations from organisms which had themselves spontaneously germinated. D'Holbach wrote that there is "no necessity to have recourse to supernatural powers to account for the formation of things" (Thiry, 1797: 25). Pierre Laplace

(1749-1827), in his famous response to Napoleon, stated that he "had no need for God in (his) hypothesis" (O'Connor, 2006). In spite of some significant discoveries in astronomy by William Herschel (1738-1822), eighteenth century scientists found zero evidence to support these types of materialistic speculations (Israel, 2001:710; Hoskins, 2008: 289-291).

As previously indicated, in the early 1800s the French naturalist George Cuvier (1769-1832) laid the foundations of modern biology on the basis of empirical research. He focused on the internal structure of a variety of species rather than on external characteristics and he concluded that there were only a few types of animal organization and that the various species represented variations of these types. His observations convinced him that species bred true to type with minimal variations and that therefore, the origin of new species through evolution was impossible. (Waggoner, 1996).

Cuvier was the chief of the French Museum of Natural History during the Napoleonic era and initiated the first comprehensive collections of fossils and biological specimens. In his research, Cuvier found that there were no demonstrable changes in living organisms over time either in the fossil record or during recorded history. He was also impressed with the evidence of sharp breaks in the fossil strata that corresponded to epochs of geologic history and that each successive layer of rock strata contained a different array of fossil types. This suggested catastrophic changes and extinctions that he felt might possibly be due to floods. Cuvier's followers looked for and could not find any source of repopulating of regions following such catastrophes and they concluded that God or some type of vital force in nature must, therefore, have re-created life similar to the models that had survived. As this theory was fully developed in the mid-1800s, it was postulated that the earth had experienced a series of floods or ice ages which had shaped geologic features and that this was followed by the new creation of life in each age (Waggoner, 1996). Religious concepts remained an essential element in the ongoing search.

The value of Cuvier's notions and ideas was that it permitted Bible-believing Christians to reconcile the fossil record with the Genesis account by equating the days of creation with geologic stages and with God engaging in further creation of species after each catastrophe. It was also apparent to them that there was a design in each species and this was considered proof or at least strong evidence that, since there was design, there must also be a Designer, namely God (Rudwick, 1997:131).

The Evolution of Darwin

Darwin became involved in the creation versus evolution debate when in 1831 he was recommended to serve as a naturalist on H. M. S. Beagle. He had been trained in Cuvier's creationist biology and he took Lyell's *Principles of Geology* with him on the voyage (Secord, 1997: ix-xliii). As a result of his observations, he gradually accepted the ideas of Lyell. His observation of the birds and tortoises on the Galapagos Islands gradually convinced him that his previous ideas of gradualism were incorrect and that a more scientific view was that existing species had evolved from pre-existing ones.

On his return to England from the voyage on the Beagle, Darwin settled into a life of observation and a search for biological understanding, but he was careful not to make his views and opinions public. It was during this period that he developed the idea of "natural selection". In 1858, influenced, perhaps, by the fact that naturalist Alfred Wallace (1823-1913) had developed ideas similar to his own, Darwin announced his theory and the following year he published *On the Origin of Species* (Kutschera, 2003: 343–359).

Darwin gradually gained stature in the British scientific community. He used his time to oversee the identification and classification of the specimens he had brought back on the Beagle and he published a variety of scientific articles and a popular narrative of his experiences on the voyage. He became more and more obsessed with how the mechanism of evolution might work. In 1838 after reading an essay by Anglican cleric Thomas Malthus (1766-1834) on population, Darwin experienced a possible answer to some of his concerns. Malthus was convinced that as the world's population would eventually surpass the available food supply only the fittest could and should survive. Darwin began to apply Malthus's theory to all living organisms (Darwin, 1996: vi).

Using the basic principles and ideas enunciated by Malthus, Darwin proceeded to develop the theory of "natural selection" which he considered to be capable of driving the evolutionary process. Assuming over-population, it was also reasonable to assume that only the fittest could survive to reproduce. With sufficient time and a changing environment, as postulated by uniformitarian geology, it was reasonable to assume that selected varieties would gradually change into different species (Malthus, 1798: 10).

Darwin was well aware that previous concepts of evolution had resulted in fierce scientific opposition, so he kept his ideas private. During the years 1842 to 1857, he published seven books on basic science, but nothing about evolution. His wife, to whom he was devoted, was a pious Christian and he personally saw great value in the social role of religion. He had definite concerns that his theory would have a negative impact on religious faith by demonstrating that humans were a product of nature. Darwin stressed that he was not trying to destroy religion. He stated that, "In my most extreme fluctuations I have never been an atheist in the sense of denying the existence of God" (Jones, 1994:46). He was also concerned that his theory of evolution would cause problems by showing that the process of survival of the fittest, which produced species, was cruel in contrast to the activity of a loving God. In all probability, it was during this period that Darwin lost his own personal faith as he struggled with the problem of evil. It is important, however, to keep in mind that Darwin made statements about religion that appear to be conflicted and that these probably reflect his personal psychological dilemma at different times. An example of such conflict is when he implies that belief in a Creator is a psychological-cultural residue and that the idea of a universal beneficent Creator does not seem to arise in the mind of man until he has been elevated by long-continued culture (Jones, 1994:46).

Darwin was to be shocked out of intellectual exile in 1858 on receipt of a letter from Alfred Russel Wallace (1823-1913), that contained an outline of a somewhat similar theory of natural selection. He too had been impressed with the theories of Malthus. Darwin showed Wallace's letter to Lyell, who was one of the three people who knew of Darwin's work on the same theory. Lyell then arranged for the joint publication of essays on the theory of evolution by both Wallace and Darwin in 1858. Darwin was anxious to present his evidence for natural selection before the scientific community, and proceeded to work assiduously to complete his classic book, *On the Origin of Species*, in 1859. This book was to have a revolutionary impact on biological thought (Larson, 2002: 8).

Charles Darwin, as a serious scientist and observer, was determined to provide an empirically grounded basis for belief in evolution. He also desperately wanted to persuade his readers of a particular mechanism of evolution, namely, the natural selection of whatever was involved in the ongoing struggle for existence. In his first aim Darwin was successful. Within a decade of the publication of *Origin of Species*, many readers became convinced of evolution. However, with respect to his second aim and desire to convince people regarding the significance of natural selection, he had less success. Most people favored some form of evolution by saltationism, a sudden change from one generation to the next, being unaware of the warning of the Swedish botanist, Carl Von Linné (1707-1778), *Natura in operationibus suis non facit saltum.* (In its activities nature does not make a sudden leap). Lamarckian inheritance of acquired characteristics, or some other mode of change, was also regarded as being of possible significance in this regard (Gliedman, 1982: 92).

In spite of his enthusiasm and Herculean efforts, Darwin failed in his desire to place the study of evolution on a solid scientific foundation as an academically accepted professional scientific enterprise. A kind of bastardized Germanic evolution did make its way into academia, but it was more concerned with hypothesizing about histories than with mechanisms. It focused more on Ernest Haeckel's law of "ontogeny recapitulating phylogeny" than with what Darwin had suggested in *The Origin of Species*. Darwin's desire to have evolution accepted as a mature professional research discipline was a complete failure (Richards, 2008: 136-142).

One of the principal reasons for this failure is that from age thirty Darwin was an invalid and the spreading of the *kerygma* of the new biological *euangelion* (gospel) had to be done by his supporters, the most notable and notorious of whom was "bulldog" Thomas Henry Huxley (1825-1895). Britain was desperately in need of reform in widespread areas and Huxley, as an expression for change, was eventually able to sell physiology to the medical profession. As a result of his missionary endeavors, Huxley was also able to sell structure and morphology to the education establishment on the grounds that hands-on empirical study was more effective training for modern life than the outmoded classical education so much favored in Britain. Huxley too had his share of ambivalence regarding religion. "I find no difficulty in imagining that, at some former period, this universe was not in existence, and that it made its appearance in consequence of the volition of some pre-existing Being" (Huxley, 1903: 429). Huxley then continued to use his missionary experience in spreading the gospel of evolution.

The philosopher Herbert Spencer (1820-1903) proved to be of great assistance to Huxley in his proselytizing efforts. Spencer was willing to encourage his fellow Victorians that the way to true virtue lay through evolution, which by this time had also formulated a series of commandments no less than the Christian religion. Huxley was already preaching evolution as the most acceptable and scientific worldview at working men's clubs, from the podia during presidential addresses, and in debates with members of the clergy – notably Samuel Wilberforce (1805-1873), Bishop of Oxford. He even assisted in the founding of new "cathedrals" of evolution, officially labeled as natural history museums, which were stuffed with relics of dinosaurs recently discovered in the American West (Lucas, 1979: 313-330). The Para-religious ideology was already in motion!

Modern Developments

An important phase in the evolution of evolution began around 1930 (Larson, 2006:222). This was the era during which a number of mathematically trained scholars, such as J. B. S. Haldane, fused Darwinian selection with Mendelian genetics, and thus provided the conceptual foundations of what became known as the synthetic theory of evolution or Neo-Darwinism. An attempt was beginning at this point to reduce the probabilistic reputation of evolutionary theory and to produce a product that was more definitive and scientific. At this stage, however, no scientist had a clear understanding of the actual mechanism of evolution. Initially the increased knowledge of genetics was of little help in finding a satisfactory explanation. However, eventually, advances in genetics continued and "the unit of evolution became the gene, and evolutionary change was to be measured in terms of changes in gene frequencies (Hull, 1973:34).

Rapidly the experimentalists and naturalists, notably Theodosius Dobzhansky in America and E. B. Ford in England, started to put empirical flesh on the mathematical skeleton, and finally the dream of a professional evolution with selection as its core was realized (Provine, 1988: 857-887; Dobzhansky, 1973: 125-129).

The new style evolutionists, the mathematicians and empiricists, desired to professionalize evolution because, as their progenitor Darwin, they wanted evolution to be accepted as a professional discipline in universities. There is a possibility, however, that like many of their colleagues they had been initially attracted, consciously or unconsciously, to the developing doctrines of evolution precisely because of its quasi-religious or suspected metaphysical aspects. Such psychological dynamics could well have been operative, regardless of whether these formed the basis of an agnostic/atheistic humanism or merely represented a cryptic attempt to revitalize an old orthodox religion that had lost its spirit and vigour. Unfortunately, there are no records extant that indicate that any type of psychoanalytic analysis was attempted on such new converts, so the possibility remains speculative. There is support for the notion that a number of supporters of evolutionary theory did desire to maintain a value-impregnated evolutionism that delivered moral messages with a social emphasis, even as it strived for greater progressive scientific advances (Ruse, 2003: 1524).

The concept of the importance of unconscious dynamic factors influencing both negatively and positively is still seen in clinical analysis today. It therefore appears reasonable to conclude that such dynamic psychological factors may have been operative throughout the history of evolutionary theory.

From the conservative end of the political spectrum, the enormously influential social philosopher Herbert Spencer, already an evolutionist, freely worked Darwinian concepts into his progressivist philosophy of social development... As social theorists, Spencer and Darwin became inexorably linked in the public mind during the nineteenth century... For men like [Andrew] Carnegie, Darwinism became a religion, or an alternative source of human moral or ethical values (Larson, 2009:136-7).

The result of these developments was that by the 1940s and 1950s, the study of evolution consisted of two parts. There was, on the one hand, serious empirical work being done that contained few if any exhortations to moral or social action. In addition, almost all of the leading evolutionists were turning out a new quasi-religious quasi-scientific genre of works of a more popular nature focusing on social change and the methods by which it could be achieved. By the 1950s, evolutionary works, such as those by the Darwinian palaeontologist G. G. Simpson, discussed democracy and education and a new missionary Endeavour, namely, conservation. In 1944, Simpson published *Tempo and Mode in Evolution,* which was straight science dealing with natural selection and the fossil record. Then in 1949, he published *The Meaning of Evolution,* which began his return to pure science (Simpson, 1967:345).

Little has changed since the introduction of Neo-Darwinism. There is today, for example, professional evolutionary biology that includes mathematical, experimental divisions, which are not suffused with an axiological dimension. In addition however, coexisting at the same time with a scientific approach and often from the same individual, evolution as a secular religion does exist. Much of the confusion stemming from the question of whether evolution is a "religion" arises from a failure to recognize these two direct dimensions of evolution theory. As a general rule this secular "religion" of evolution is built on a background of explicit materialism and it attempts to solve all the major world problems, from racism to education to conservation.

Edward Wilson, for example, is considered one of the most outstanding current professional biologists and is the respected author of numerous major works of straight science. In his *Toward a Humanistic Biology*, he assures us that evolution is a myth that is now ready to take over Christianity. Without any apparent hesitation he describes evolutionary doctrine as essentially religious in nature and as a rival for traditional religion: The final decisive edge enjoyed by scientific naturalism will come from its capacity to explain traditional religion, its chief competition, as a wholly material phenomenon. Theology is not likely to survive as an independent intellectual discipline (Wilson, 1982:56-58).

As an ardent progressionist, Wilson saw moral norms from the need to keep the evolutionary process moving forward. In his view, this translated into a need to promote biodiversity, for he believed that humans evolved in a symbiotic relationship with nature. There is no doubt, therefore, that this popular type of evolutionism does exist and that it is often an alternative to religion (Lipson, 1980:138). It is supremely gratuitous for Wilson or any other scholar to assume *a priori* that a supernatural dimension is impossible and unwarranted or that reported descriptions of it are mythic and fallacious, because in so stating this opinion he or she is demonstrating a faith-based-presuppositional-assumption which will be demonstrated to be the kernel of both evolutionary and religious thinking (Wilson, 1982:56-58).

Theory of evolution still causes argument, not only related to science and theology, but also from its own ranks in the social sciences and within evolutionary biology (Provine, 1988:10). In spite of such tensions, evolutionary theory has become a prominent force in the human sciences. As seeker of objective truth, it behooves scholars to search beyond the rhetoric and examine its fundamental claims and logic. Scholars committed to the pursuit of truth, in the cognitive and behavioral sciences, this may provide a knowledge-base required for an informed dialog. For Christian believers who are committed to the doctrine of a personal, intelligent Creator who sustains and governs His creation, such an approach also provides them with a fresh opportunity to clarify their thinking regarding the origins of life and to consider how the dynamic of faith and faith-based-presuppositional-assumptions may be foundational to both positions.

As evolutionary theory continued to develop it was characterized by a number of tertiary commitments that are not logically related to the evolutionary programme *per se*, such as anti-theistic biases and other strong reductionisms (Dawkins, 1986:48). There is an ongoing conflict between a Christian naturalist worldview. This is exemplified in both the creationist and the evolutionary theorist positions. Little attention is paid to the facts that both are built upon a foundation of "faith", irrespective of what terminology is actually employed to describe the respective phenomena. This work deals essentially with the similarities of the psychological dynamics found in each system and the meaning of "faith" as an essential element in both positions.

In addition, even though scarcely a few decades old, current evolutionary theory has already developed a high profile within the cognitive sciences, as illustrated with the growing number of textbooks on the subject, (Eccles, 1991; Cosmides & Tooby, 1995; Plotkin, 1998) and has been involved in a variety of theories such as "computational theories," that is, functional descriptions of what information processing devices, including brains, are designed to do. Such theories constrain and inform the search for cognitive and neural processes. Evolutionary theory, is characterized by primary commitments to modularity of mind, the use of evolutionary biology's adaptationist program to generate hypotheses regarding mental modules, and the use of cognitive science methods for testing such hypotheses (Marr, 1982: 42). As has been indicated, it is characterized by a number of secondary commitments and positions on

important issues that are not necessitated by the evolutionary approach.

The Current Landscape

Charles Darwin admitted in his writings that it was
extremely difficult to conceive that this immense and wonderful universe, including human beings with capacity to
both look backwards and far into the future, was the result
of blind chance. A creedal mysterious element seems to
have been conveniently ignored by a significant number
of committed Darwinians, many of whom are staunchly
anti-theistic and irreligious (cf. Dennett, 1995; Harris, 2006;
Stenger, 2007). Most of the Darwinians appear to be oblivious to the system, they and the creationists vociferously
espouse and vehemently oppose, are both built on similar
psychological dynamic principles. It must be conceded,
that an increasing number of courageous evolutionary
scientists are willing to confront this serious issue (see
Carlson, ed., 2000; McGrath, 2004).

Non-Polemical and Non-Apologetic

This work does not represent a polemic against or an
apology for either a creationist or an evolutionary hermeneutic of observed phenomenology. It is perhaps rather
naively assumed and accepted, that all those involved,
whether journalists, theologians or scientists of whatever
hue, are honest, have integrity, a reasonable degree of psychological health and maturity, and will not make any claim
or statement that they know to be mendacious. In this work
there will be a sincere attempt not to depreciate or disparage anyone for their personal views, sincerity, integrity,
knowledge of science or intellectual endowment. The bad-
mannered accusatory invective and antagonism that has
been demonstrated between various viewpoints can only
remind one of the evil, malignant and mendacious antagonism that frequently exists between a variety of religious
and denominational viewpoints, and the psychopathologi-
cal dynamics often reflect the similarity of the psychological

processes involved. In a similar manner, the belligerent commitment to evolutionary philosophy on the part of so many intellectuals today may reflect the fact that they need to believe and have faith in evolutionary theory rather than in the fact that they can see no other satisfying solution to the complexities of the biological world. Strident evolutionists may have learned well from religious provocateurs.

Notwithstanding, it is clear that there are honest and objective scientists and thinkers in both communities. There are, for example, a number of organizations that have published lists of scientists of accepted credentials, more, it would seem, as propaganda than for the dissemination of scientific information. Such lists are used on both sides of the creation-evolution divide and are relatively worthless (Morris, 1997: 351-371)

Should it come as a surprise to many that scientists, like theologians, often disagree and that some may even do it in an amicable and affable fashion in spite of what the history of denominationalism would suggest? It is important to take note of what particular evidence is being offered to defend or defeat what particular conclusion. Proof of necessity is more difficult than proof of sufficiency. God certainly would be a sufficient condition for the existence of the universe, but the universe cannot be cited as a necessary condition for the existence (or non-existence) of God. In the same way, the mere sufficiency of evolutionary theory to explain many natural phenomena says nothing about the necessity of the theory. Thus, much of the current literature is not compelling enough to change anyone's mind one way or another. Discussions about the relationship between contemporary knowledge and religious faith will likely broaden to include serious consideration of non-western religions. Polkinghorne goes farthest in this direction though hardly enough in considering the potential for relativizing the traditional Christian theism he so ably and strongly defends. Polkinghorne, a superb scientist and a gentleman, speaks gently but cogently to the issue of the relationship of science and theology. In *Faith, Science and Understanding,* he discussed a number of key issues that arise in the interaction between science and theology.

> The underlying basis is the conviction that both disciplines have things of value to say to each other because both, in their differing domains of experience, are concerned with the search for truth attained by the formulation and evaluation of motivated beliefs. In the desire for an open search for understanding, the personal and subjective elements of human experience must be accorded equal weight with the impersonal and subjective aspects which constitute science's self-limited domain of enquiry. Theology's appeal to revelation is seen as being a recourse to illuminating experience, analogous to science's recourse to observation and experimentation, and not an appeal to some ineffable and unquestionable authority (Polkinghorne, 1986:121).

For a different perspective by a fellow scientist, readers would do well to consult *Dreams of a Final Theory* by Stephen Weinberg, who shared the dais with Polkinghorne at a summit on "The Interface of Science and Religion", sponsored by the American Association for the Advancement of Science. Weinberg informed the summit that he is in favour of dialogue between religion and science, but was careful to add that he does not anticipate a constructive dialogue. Religion, Weinberg added, is "an insult to human dignity" (Weinberg, 1999, Avise, 1998: 85).

Evolution a Potential Threat to Naturalism

Evidence from the medical field may well demonstrate that the proclamation of the atheistic *euangelion* of materialism may be shooting itself in the foot. In the 1990s scientific studies of religious communities began to deliver solid evidence that religious belief has significant benefits for believers in terms of health and longevity, as well as reproductivity. John D. Martin (2010) notes:

> Perhaps the best known researcher into the religion/health connection is that of Dr. Harold Koenig of Duke University, who has demonstrated a statistical increase in health and a decrease in mortality among those of his

patients suffering from chronic or life-threatening illnesses who professed strong religious convictions ... Less startling, perhaps even expected, are the findings that religious persons of all types tend to have larger and more stable families.

Martin reported further on Koenig's work:

1. In nations in which the birth rate has fallen below replacement rates, traditional values tend to be replaced with philosophical materialism.

2. Nations in which this occurs place their future in jeopardy.

3. Decline in religious beliefs tends to be associated with the birth of fewer and weaker individuals.

4. This finding does not support evolutionary theory in which reproductive success is all that matters (Martin, 2010).

Here is an indication of the possible mendacity of the Dawkins gospel that proclaims that all that matters is reproductivity. On the basis of his own tenuous logic and belief in evolution as the only explanation for the origins, nature, and ultimate fate of humanity, Dawkins trumpets his "discovery" of the religious "meme" or how religious ideas spread from mind to mind, like genes in a gene pool. As Martin (2010) notes, "the 'meme' must also be subject to selection pressure, and the meme that best contributes to the survival of its carriers is assured of survival and further reproduction."

One of the major characteristics of religion is that it creates civilizations, and all the great civilizations in history had a religious foundation and infrastructure. Attempts to do the opposite as in China and Russia have proven to be a devastating failure. The continuing presence of religious sentiment, ideas and practices in a community or nation appears to be a prerequisite for the survival of the group. Dawkins claims that religion proves to be a successful and powerful pious religious "meme" and has a powerful influence on the survival of the human race. Religion and the religious impulse, according to the same postulated laws of the "survival of the fittest" have a definite effect on the "survival of the metaphysically fittest" (Dawkins, 1976: 84).

In view of the fact that different scientists of superb academic credentials and personal integrity have varying views while involved in the same scientific enterprise, it should be possible to search for truth without internecine denominational antagonism. The effort is to present a fair and balanced review.

Study and Review Questions for Chapter Four

1. Why are the first chapters of Genesis important to Jews, Christians, and Moslems?

2. What evidence do you have that the concept of evolution was not original with Darwin?

3. Explain Neptunism.

4. In what year did Darwin first mention evolution in which published source?

5. How did Cuvier's notions and ideas permit Christians to reconcile the fossil record with the Genesis account?

6. Did Darwin deny the existence of God?

7. How is modern evolutionary thought often seen as an alternative to religion?

8. How does "Proof of necessity is more difficult than proof of sufficiency" fit into the creation/evolutionary dialog?.

Topics Discussed in Chapter Five

The Naturalistic Bias

The Theological Roots of Naturalism

The Ubiquity of Presuppositions

Faith and Reason

Kuyper's Analysis of Faith

Applicability of Kuyper's Integration

Spirit and Faith

Faith and Cognitive Psychology

The Essentiality of Faith

Study and Review Questions

NATURALISM AND FAITH

The Naturalistic Bias

Naturalism may be considered as the hypothesis that the natural world is a closed system, in the sense, that nothing that is not a part of the natural world affects it. In other words, naturalism is the denial of the existence of supernatural causes. In rejecting the reality of supernatural events, forces, or entities, naturalism is the antithesis of supernaturalism.

As a substantial view about the nature of reality, naturalism is often called metaphysical naturalism, philosophical naturalism, or ontological naturalism to distinguish it from methodological naturalism (Mastin, 2008). The latter is the presupposition that all science and history, in order to promote a successful investigation, must presume that all causes are natural causes. To presume anything else is not considered scientific. The idea behind this principle is that natural causes can be investigated directly through scientific method, whereas supernatural causes cannot, and hence presuming that an event has a supernatural cause for methodological reasons halts further investigation. For instance, if a disease is caused by microbes, one may learn more about how microbes interact with the body and how the immune system can be activated to destroy them, or how the transmission of microbes can be contained. But if a disease is caused by demons, one may learn nothing more about the etiology because demons are said to be supernatural beings unconstrained by the laws of nature. In utilizing methodological naturalism, science and history will never admit that an *a priori* is possible because, super-natural causes do not exist. A typical example of this type of claim is seen in the opinion of Francisco Ayala, a former Dominican priest, who has stated that evolution is a necessity in order to account for biology's flaws in design (Miller, 1999: 102).

The Theological Roots of Naturalism

In view of this anti-metaphysical bias on the part of naturalism, it may come as a surprise to many that the roots of naturalism are essentially theological. Plantinga stressed this:

> ...analysis of the evolution-creationism dilemma indicates just what naturalism is. The adherents of naturalism consider it as a scientific discovery while its detractors think of it as atheism in disguise. The truth, according to Plantiga, is that naturalism is actually a rationalist movement which has been built on a foundation of religious thought and tradition that mandated a world that operates according to natural laws and processes. Theological naturalists today find it impossible to permit science the latitude to incorporate non-material explanations for the world or even to consider such a hypothesis. For them science must be firmly and absolutely restricted to naturalistic explanations and yet the religious conviction that the world operates according to laws is the foundation of their system of naturalism. God must be excluded (Plantinga, 1997:18).

Atheistic naturalism was not the initial response to Darwin's theory of evolution. His arguments for evolution can be traced back to earlier theological naturalists and not surprisingly Darwin concluded his major tome with an appeal to theological naturalism. He wrote in *The Origin of Species*:

> To my mind, it accords better with what we know of the laws impressed on matter by the Creator that the production and extinction of the past and present inhabitants of the world should have been due to secondary causes, like those determining the birth and death of the individual (Darwin, 1872: 477).

This is an argument straight out of theological naturalism (Stone, 2009). God created via laws rather than through
intervention. In addition, to prove his position, Darwin had
support from clerics who agreed that evolution led to a
noble conception of the deity. This argument continues to
the present day as theological naturalists elaborate on how
theism fits into the evolutionary framework. The early naturalists argued that divine action ought to be down-played in
order to satisfy concerns about dysteleology, evil, salvation
and the nature of God (Urpeth, 2009). Today's theological
naturalists have inherited the problem of explaining just
why naturalism works so much better. Not all naturalists are
atheists and there are many theists who advocate materialist explanations. They advocate naturalist explanations
because they believe in a non-intervening God. The sentiment that motivates naturalism still remains essentially and
deeply religious. The 'naturalism equals atheism' model fits
neither the history of naturalism nor the state of naturalism
today (Van Till, 1999:246-247).

It is impossible to understand the practice of the scientific enterprise today without an understanding and appreciation of the cryptic and pervasive tensions of naturalism
which have influenced the development of science over the
past four centuries (Schafersman, 1997

Many of these are the products of the *kerygma* of naturalism. In the scientific enterprise, as in ordinary human
thinking, assumptions and premises of a crucial nature often
go unnoticed and are considered so obvious that no justification is required. Alfred North Whitehead wrote, "Such
assumptions appear so obvious that people do not know
what they are assuming because no other way of putting
things has ever occurred to them" (Whitehead, 1926: 49).

It appears that the intent of the *euangelion* of the
Naturalist dogma has been the virtual reification of science,
that is, concretization of science into a deified state. During
the past four hundred years, science has made amazing

discoveries and improved the lives of many. Science investigates the natural world with great success and now is taken for granted and its findings are considered synonymous with knowledge and truth. Science has its weak points and challenges. Perhaps the biggest challenge that science has faced is from religion, not that religion opposes science but that in some ways religion and science are co-partners.

Naturalism may be thought of as the restriction of science to exclusively naturalistic explanations of nature for reasons that are essentially religious. It may be found surprising that theological naturalism is *not* based on atheistic influences, or on empirically based research. It is rather based on metaphysical reasoning. Theological naturalism demands that science operate only within well defined parameters to which it must conform or it will not be recognized as science or as scientific. Science is not simply empiricism but it approaches an issue with a built-in bias of cryptic answers already in place. This is a move away from empiricism in the direction of rationalism. Theological naturalism also plays an important role in how science is evaluated. Theories with sometimes quite obvious evidential problems tend to be accepted if they conform to the tenets of theological naturalism. The topsy-turvy nature of the world of science is demonstrated that theological naturalism has influenced science but that science independently corroborates theological naturalism. As Niewoehner has noted, few people understand the strict control and limitations that theological naturalism has mandated for the scientific enterprise. For example, these include issues such as the following:

- The theology of a greater God
- Religious rationalism and deism
- The problem of evil
- Theological opposition to miracles
- Anthropomorphizing God

- Danger of the God of the gaps
- Infinite regression
- Intellectual necessity

All of these categories represent some of the theological ground rules placed on science, namely, scientific explanations must be purely naturalistic. Religious thought control permeates the practice of science that demands theological naturalism. It is therefore a myth that science is free of religious influences (Niewoehner, 1997: 23).

Jerome Stone has given a concise definition and explanation of theological or religious naturalism:

> Religious naturalism is a set of beliefs and attitudes that affirm that there are religious aspects of this world which can be understood within a naturalistic framework. There are some happenings or processes in our experience which elicit responses which can appropriately be called religious. These experiences and responses are similar enough to those nurtured by the paradigm cases of religion that they may be called religious without stretching the word beyond recognition. Charles Milligan, life-long student of American religious naturalism, puts it, by religious naturalism "I take to be any naturalistic world view or philosophy in which religious thought, values and commitments hold an important and not merely incidental part. Or perhaps more simply, where religious discourse plays an integral role." (Stone, 2009).

To be fair and balanced in this review of naturalism, it must be noted that there are a number of scientists of repute who have adopted and made the choice of a modernist worldview within the mainstream religious community:

> Among the better known of these theistic evolutionists are Ian Barbour, Nancy Murphy, Howard van Till, Philip Hefner, Robert John Russell, Arthur Peacocke and John Haught. None of these is remotely as prominent as the leading members of evolution's offensive platoon, but as a group – supported by the considerable financial resources of the John M. Templeton Foundation – they dominate the tiny segment of the academic world that is concerned with the relationship between science and religion. All accept methodological

naturalism as the basis of scientific thinking, and therefore they also accept the Neo-Darwinian picture of evolution as governed at all levels by some combination of physical law, chance and natural selection. They concede that evolution so defined has regularly been employed by scientists and philosophers to support atheism and to disparage theism, but they insist that this need not be so and argue that at a deeper level evolutionary science and non-fundamentalist theology are compatible and perhaps even mutually reinforcing (Johnson, 2000: 89).

The Ubiquity of Presuppositions

Naturalists traditionally deny the necessity of biblical revelation as a necessary presupposition for the intelligibility of our lives. It is true that the church has its share of naïve fideists who have never learned the rationality of the Christian faith. Scientists too, however, have their share of naïve fideists who have never learned that for two centuries it has been recognized that empiricism has serious limitations. It is possible that even a scientist may be philosophically duped into believing that it is only science that can provide real and exhaustive knowledge.

As Niewoehner pointed out, naturalists have a series of presuppositions. They believe that nature equals reality and that whatever is not physical is not real. They conclude that as science provides knowledge of nature it provides exhaustive knowledge of all reality. However, by doing so they take the position that love, morality, honesty and evil, which cannot be examined empirically, are therefore not real and must be mere fabrications of the human mind. One is forced to conclude that we can know nothing truly about such abstractions. If the naturalist, on the other hand, takes the position that the scientific method presupposes nothing, he has immediately and explicitly refuted himself, having candidly demonstrated his own cryptic presuppositions (Niewoehner, 1997: 52; Whitehead, 1926: 12-23).

Popper is careful to point out that creationists share the same dilemma. When creationists insist on labeling their position as "scientific creationism" they may be getting in over their head. There are some specific questions they must address if they insist on using the term "scientific."

- Are they sure they want to admit that creationism is falsifiable?

- Are they willing to subject the theory to rigorous scrutiny and   examination, without the bias of possible consequences?

- Are they willing to examine the theory for possible flaws?

- Are they willing to accept that as a theory it may need revision?

- If they understand that theory qua theory has a number of associated implications, then have they thought of what that might do to inerrancy, since by definition a theory is not fixed in granite and must be accepting of change based on subsequent understanding? (Popper, 1959: 76).

In Popper's opinion, both evolution and creationism are *theories* and their future depends on how well they survive rigorous criticism. He insists that antecedent presuppositions are always present because they are the *sine qua non* of the cognitive process. All presuppositions, in both camps, must be recognized, examined and debated and the perennial orientation of seekers after truth must be openness to severe criticism and a non-grudging willingness to examine alternatives or rival theories. The atheist-naturalist believes that the universe came from nature, in some as yet unknown way, and the theist believes that the universe comes from God. Neither can prove their convictions because they are both unproven presuppositions (Popper, 1959: 76; Barnhart, 1996: 35).

Faith and Reason

In any discussion of faith, there must first of all be an attempt to formulate a clear definition of the term if adequate communication is to be achieved. It is, however, an extremely difficult goal to articulate just what faith is and to elucidate its metaphysical, epistemological and ethical implications, because the concept has such a nebulous consistency.

> Faith seeking understanding is an attempt to articulate faith, to elucidate its metaphysical, epistemological and ethical implications ... The approach of faith seeking understanding is not, however, monolithic. Different thinkers in the tradition have different understandings of the powers of human reason, and of the exact role that reason plays in articulating faith, and different philosophical convictions (Helm, 1997: vii-viii).

The words of Sir. William Osler (1849-1919), Canadian research scientist, are as applicable today as when he wrote, "Nothing in life is more wonderful than faith – the one great moving force which can neither weigh in the balance nor test in the crucible" (Jones, 1994: 45). In this discussion, faith will be considered first using the commonly accepted significance of the word:

- As a strong belief and conviction in a supernatural power that controls human destiny, and

- As the conviction of the trustworthiness of such a belief.

However, it must first of all be noted that even the term "faith" has an evolution of its own. The first definition of *pistis* in the Liddell and Scott Greek Lexicon is "trust in others." The Latin *fides* has the same significance. If both *fides* and *pistis* mean "trust" how did "faith" come to be defined in the culture as "firm belief in something for which there is no proof?"

Schoenheit continued this analysis in "Truth or Tradition" as follows:

> To understand this one must remember that a dictionary definition is only a record of how people are currently using the word in their speech and writing ... The linguistic evolutionary process ... may be traced as follows:
>
> (1) People started to use "faith" as "belief in something for which there is no proof", (2) that usage was put in a

dictionary as a definition of "faith", (3) people who did not know what faith is looked it up in a dictionary, and saw that definition, and thereafter used it that way. This process continued over time until now almost everyone thinks "faith" is "belief in something for which there is no proof." In fact that definition was used in the popular television medical series, "House" in April 2006 ... Most people now do not appreciate that the basic meaning of "faith" is "trust ... However, if there is nothing to trust in and nothing "trustworthy" to believe, then to ask people to "take it by faith" is wrong, and contributes to the misunderstanding of God and the Bible." (Schoenheit, 2006).

It is rather surprising that a clear description of faith is found in the pages of the *American Atheist*, written by Allegro, who was a member of the Dead Sea Scrolls editing team. He opined that it may be, despite a highly prized rationality, that religion still offers humanity the best chance of survival, or at least of buying a little more time in which to devise some more reasoned way out of the dilemma. He continues:

1. If so it must be a faith that offers something more than a formal assent to highly speculative dogma about the nature of a god, and his divine purpose in creation;

2. It must promise its adherents a living relationship that answers man's individual needs within a formal structure of communal worship;

3. It has to satisfy the emotions without violating believers' intellectual integrity;

4. It must avoid the tragic divisiveness of ethic or social affiliations by finding a common reference in our biological heritage (Allegro, 1970: 30).

It is difficult to imagine that this perspective of faith could have been penned any better and clearer by the most erudite and devout Evangelical!

The next question, and one that is perennial for both philosophers and theologians, is, How does faith accord with reason? Dallas Willard, in his forward to Johnson's book on naturalism, clearly defined reason as the human ability to determine what is real or not real by *thinking*. He wrote, "Just as, centuries ago, the honest thinker had to be willing to follow the inquiry even if it led to a godless universe, so today the honest thinker has to be willing to follow the inquiry even if it leads to a God-governed universe" (Johnson, 2000: iii). He also points out that rationalism, which he denotes as a common psychological virus in both theological and scientific thinking, is the use of reason to make certain the answers one discovers are those that accord with one's worldview (Johnson, 2000: 9). In this garb, scientific naturalism in the 1920s had identified itself as a philosophical doctrine that was issuing numerous promissory notes that scientific investigation might or might not be able to later redeem. The character of rationalism on occasion reflects unconscious subterfuge hiding behind the cloak of benign authority (Livingstone, 1971: 4,13; McGiffert, 1961: 212).

The perception of Hellenistic philosophers was that reality was rational and therefore was subject to reason. Philosophy has assumed since the time of the early Greek thinkers that in the beginning there were the fundamental particles that compose matter, energy and the impersonal laws of physics. There is no personal God who created the cosmos and governs it as an act of free will. If God exists at all, he acts only through inviolable laws of nature and adds nothing to them. In consequence, all the creating had to be done by the laws and the particles, which is to say by some combination of random chance and law-like regularity (Johnson, 2000: 13). It must be kept in mind as enunciated by Simon, as quoted by Calne, that "Reason is wholly instrumental. It cannot tell us where to go; at best it can tell us how to get there. It is a gun for hire that can be employed in the service of any goals we have, good or bad" (Calne, 1999: 14).

Since faith was clearly a dimension of reality, it must therefore have a relationship to reason. The Greeks were also convinced that mathematics was the basis for rational explanation and reason and this had a great influence on early Christian philosophers (Hansen, n.d.).

Randall summarized the central ideas of the Augustinians:

> For this great tradition, the proper of science is a Logos, a rational structure or system of ideas, an intelligible realm the content of which is best illustrated by the truths of mathematics. The right method of science is the direct apprehension of intuition of these intelligible ideas and their relations or structure by nous or intellect. Experience is fragmentary and unimportant; at best it affords a dim image or illustration of the ideas which intellect perceives in their purity (Randall, 1962:27).

Augustine, for example, espoused Plato's conviction that mathematical principles were nuclear to everything in the universe and that in them lay the secret and the explanation of human existence. The certain principles of mathematics were a much more reliable and sure guide than any empirical approach. After all, the senses were part of the physical and evil body and stood in contrast to the soul or the true 'inner man'. Therefore, Augustine took the position that rationality and reason were based on abstract thought processes of the mind and not on the empirical information available to the senses. He was convinced that the way to invisible reality and eventually to God was to meditate and cogitate as a mathematical exercise. This eventually would lead to faith and reason and eventually *intellectual* processes gradually became the only basis for faith or belief (Lavine, 1989: 78-79).

Augustine, and Neo-Platonism, which was the basis of his thinking, had no place for the empirical enterprise. Natural science was a lower level activity and knowing God was the burden of philosophers and their reasoning. This eventuated in a parallel development in the various church councils of the fourth century, when creedal development became the foundation of accepted belief systems. One did not have to understand what was promulgated in the creeds, and only acceptance, blind perhaps, was required. Understanding or empiricism was not a necessary requirement.

The Neo-Platonism of Augustine was at least in part responsible for the eventual schism between the church and science which erupted in the period of the Enlightenment and which still exists today. Neo-Platonism simply rejected any empirical methodology whatsoever and to this day this remains the basis of the scientific enterprise. Neo-Platonism refused to consider any experimental approach and for Augustine the knowledge of God and human existence was achieved by introspection and free association and not by empirical examination of the world. (Kreis, 2005).

Accepting Augustine's conceptual and experiential definition of faith, Luther described the Epistle of James as "an epistle of straw" because it demanded "works," a type of empiricism, as an evidence of faith. Even today, Evangelical Christendom tends to espouse the Augustinian view of faith without works and basically ignores the words of the Apostle James that "faith without works is dead" (James 2:17).

The term "faith" has been used in a variety of additional ways with somewhat different meanings. It is frequently used as a shorthand for "the faith", that is, for a body of beliefs of a theological or religious character which forms the cognitive content, or the core of the cognitive content, of some recognizable religion. It is referred to as "the faith" because it is a set of propositions that the holders regard as trustworthy truths about God and about themselves in their relation to God. This particular use of the word faith may also be used to refer to the convictions of an atheist because the atheist also has, perhaps, a more informal body of beliefs. Naturally atheists do not include a belief in God and so lack a personal connection, but trust in something "other" is still required.

A person's faith does not consist only in the faith that he confesses and in which he trusts (the proper significance of faith) and which he understands. His faith also involves affective experience and behaviors. Nevertheless, the faith that he confesses has a core-content, a content of beliefs. Such faith involves understanding, for a person can hardly believe what he does if he does not have some degree of understanding of the content. He may not understand it, and may seek to understand it more. Increased understanding of the propositions of the faith enhances the experience of faith as a whole (Geisler and Turek, 2004: 45).

Helm opined regarding reason and understanding as follows:

> Reason, as a method towards understanding, performs a twofold role in its relation to faith. It is through reason that one understands the propositions on which faith and trust initially rely. By means of reason, faith is then transmuted into understanding and the understanding gained involves reason in a different sense, namely rational insight into God himself. Faith in "the faith" is here used in what is primarily a fiducial sense, that is, the faith is that core sense of propositions to which a person entrusts himself as embodying, in his judgment, the truth about God (Helm, 1997:11).

Helm continued:

> So reason performs a two-fold role. It is through reason that one understands the propositions on which faith initially relies. By reason faith is then transmuted into understanding, the understanding gained involves reason in a different sense, as rational insight into God himself ... 'Faith' in 'the faith' is being used in what is primarily a fiducial sense; the faith is that core set of propositions to which a person entrusts himself as embodying, in his judgment, the truth about God (Helm, 1997:11).

Another way in which faith is used does not focus on what is believed, but rather on the act of believing upon or trusting. "The faith" is what is believed, while faith is the affective and behavioral response, the personal attitude of commitment to what is believed. It is clear that the essential epistemological incompleteness of faith as belief falls short of knowledge; in addition, the incompleteness of faith is partly due to the particularity of what is believed, and the need to connect it with other matters (Helm, 1997:11).

As Helm has emphasized, faith is an evidential and psychological mediator and ultimate pontific. There is some evidence for the truth of what is believed, but not enough to think of it as rising to the level of knowledge. Faith relies on the object of faith that is denoted by the propositions which comprise "the faith", with a greater strength than the evidence might strictly warrant. In this way faith makes up for any degree of evidential deficiency based on confidence in its object. "From a strictly evidentialist point of view, belief of such strength may appear irrational, for the weight of the evidence does not warrant it" (Helm, 1997:12-13).

Another view of faith is that the certainty of faith is proportional to the evidence for the belief that is a component of faith.

> If this proportion is not maintained then faith is weaker than it ought to be; if it is exceeded then faith is hard to distinguish from credulity and foolhardiness. On this view what distinguishes trust from mere belief is not that trust makes up for evidential insufficiency but that it is an act of reliance based upon, and proportional to the evidence in support of the beliefs (Helm, 1997:13).

An additional conception of faith is where

> evidence is irrelevant to the genuineness or the appropriateness of faith. As it is sometimes expressed, faith is inherently and necessarily risky. To seek evidence in order to minimize the risk would be to misunderstand what faith is. It would be an evidence of unfaithfulness. On such a view, faith is often presented as "offensive" to reason, as an expression of trust and confidence in God which runs counter to those who must regard matters of faith as reasonable before they are credible. Just as, in the Enlightenment view of reason, there is conflict between faith and reason from the side of reason, so in this view of faith there is a conflict initiated by faith;

this type of faith disregards the claims of reason. In this view faith is inherently risky, not because there is in fact little evidence for what is believed and more would be desirable, but because whatever evidence there is in some way against the truth of the proposition believed, and this faith "contends" with evidence against it (Helm, 1997:14-15).

What each of these views of faith have in common, for all their differences, is that there is an "essential incompleteness about faith and some degree of a 'leap' is required; an evidential incompleteness which prevents faith from being knowledge, or a distance and opaqueness which prevents faith from being knowledge. Such incompleteness is usually regarded as unsatisfactory" (Helm, 1997: 15). The intellectual and evidential basis of faith is capable of being augmented by a process of reflection and investigation in which reason is appropriate. The believer looks for additional evidence that he does not at present possess. "In furtherance of faith seeking understanding the believer seeks to clarify and strengthen the grounds of the faith, grounds which nudge it in the direction of *scientia*" (Helm, 1997:15). Believers will, in fact, continue to appreciate the object-choice of personal trust.

How may faith as belief seek completeness? For the psychologically mature believer, by as much as possible having its beliefs turned into knowledge, and by gaining as much comprehension of its beliefs as possible. Faith is not necessarily antagonistic to the empirical enterprise. Either way, understanding is primarily epistemological in character. It seeks additional evidential support for what is believed in order to complete it, in order to transform faith into knowledge, or it seeks to link up the belief of faith with other beliefs of faith, or with other matters that lie outside the faith, and in this way it increases the credibility of what is believed. Faith seeks comprehension and comprehensiveness.

A common charge brought against creationists is that their approach to natural history is influenced by their faith.

At times in the defense against creationism it is pointed out that many scientists who accept evolution are also devoutly religious. This appears to be an attempt to give evolution respectability in the eyes of non-scientists. On the other hand, some scholars have opined that to reconcile evolution with religion leads to *doublethink,* which is the power of holding two contradictory beliefs in one's mind simultaneously, and accepting both of them. (Griffith, 2011).

The approach of evolutionists is also influenced by their faith. The theory of evolution is an attempt to account for the natural world without God. It is an expression of naturalism, the predetermined belief that the only form of reality is the physical dimension. Anything that is not physical, and cannot therefore be investigated and measured empirically by the scientific method, is not reality and does not exist. The theory of evolution, with its foundation in naturalism, sets out to demonstrate that the world is self-explanatory, that is, everything can be explained without God by the operation of natural laws and of chance, the random collision of atoms, and molecules and the random mutation of genes. But atheism is a faith. It is as much as act of faith to believe that God does not exist as it is to believe that he does. The reality of a spiritual being, who is not by definition susceptible to scientific investigation, must be a matter of faith, one way or the other. The atheist may unconsciously be harboring a surrogate object-choice, namely, reified science. Hasker speaks to this issue:

> A great many scientists and philosophers share a faith that when the scientific world picture is complete, they believe that man's existence will be completely explained within the framework of physics and biology and biochemistry very much along the lines of these sciences as they presently exist. I have characterized this as faith, for that is what it is. Our present science by no means provides such a comprehensive explanation of human existence, nor is it obvious that the future development of science must lead in this direction (Hasker, 1983: 99).

Scientists, whatever their faith, put aside the idea of supernatural causality when they enter the laboratory; their job is to find natural causes. But the fundamental question is precisely this: is there more to life than science can explain? To rule out the possibility of supernatural causation from the start, as naturalism does, is to make a dogmatic statement of faith, and begs the question that one is trying to answer: is the natural world self-explanatory? Evolutionists as scientists manifest the same bias. Darwin's religious doubts, which apparently began early in his life, continued waxing and waning throughout his professional career. Yet he was an honest, loving and thoughtful man and one empathizes with the quandary of his human condition, but it appears that the theory of evolution may be, in part at least, the outcome of a scientist looking for the explanation of the phenomena of the natural world without God, and in this fear he builds on a faith-based-presuppositional-assumption, namely, that a god cannot exist.

Richard Dawkins, in the promulgation of his fundamentalist faith of atheism, accuses Christians (and others) of "fundamentalism", a dogmatic belief in God and in creation that ignores the scientific evidence. But, in spite of his claims to the contrary, Richard Dawkins is himself a fundamentalist of a different stripe: for him supernatural causation is fundamentally inadmissible as an explanation of anything, because God does not exist. This is a faith-based position, and one that rests on a preconceived belief that there is no God (Dawkins, 1976: 68).

The controversy over the theory of evolution has been presented as a conflict between science and religion. This is not the case. A conflict does exist, but it is a conflict between the content of one type of faith and another, between theism and atheism, between belief and unbelief, between conceptual-affective faith on the one hand and faith in empiricism and the doctrines of science on the other. It is not an exaggeration to say that as science has advanced the gaps have become not smaller, but wider. It would not be hyperbole to say that the theory of evolution now has more gaps than theory (Woodward, 2006: 76). The Christian apologist will explain that the precision of this universe is not self-explanatory; it demands some leap of faith, either a leap of faith into believing in the probability of a multitude of other evolved universes, or a leap of faith into believing in God as the designer of this one.

At the opposite end of the spectrum, it is a commonly expressed notion among scientists who possess an idealistic view of scientific knowledge that perhaps savors of reification, that mankind is capable of knowledge but certainly not through faith or feeling. It is often stated that this fact results in the perennial conflict and incompatibility between science and religion. It is, however, suggested that all knowledge is based on faith and presupposition and trust in some object-choice which can be traced back to some faith-based-presuppositional-assumption, which cannot be proved. It is now well recognized in modern physics that there are a variety of such unproven laws which actually often constitute the foundation on which further advances depend. For example, one must start with the recognition that there is something one is aware of. It is a "something" that has a specific identity and is not a "nothing." Something exists and one is consciously aware of it. This is an assumption and it cannot be proved because it is a first axiom. It antedates anything else and is the basis from which its truth can be demonstrated. To accept the statement as true is an act of faith because its truth or falsehood cannot be shown deductively. For any metaphysical model the axioms upon which the model is based cannot be proven. Because all other knowledge must be derived from the axioms, they must, as a first step, be assumed to be true without proof. This is an example of a faith-based-presuppositional-assumption.

Poole (2001: 38) notes that some people think that they can live logically and make their decisions based exclusively on logic. Scientists consider themselves as purely rational creatures without the need for faith. However, as has been appreciated since the 18th century, everything we think and do is based on the assumption that the future will be like the past, and all beliefs in "matters of fact" are non-rational. Without the possibility of proof, we must assume many things before we can "know" anything at all. It appears to be a basic fact that the rules by which nature functions constitute a faith-based-presuppositional-assumption. This is the foundation on which science rests and yet it cannot be proven deductively. Therefore, it is a faith-based-presuppositional-assumption. In addition, every scientific finding is based on inductive, and not on deductive, arguments. Even Ockham's Razor is an assumption about nature and therefore is also based on faith. Faith cannot be eliminated from thinking and it is impossible to live by "bread" or reason alone. Our knowledge is based on induction and fundamentally on assumptions, and the basis of knowledge, whether we like it or not, is faith-trust (Poole, 2001: 38).

Faith added to trust develops into confidence that eventuates in action. Psychologically faith, as a cognitive response, produces affect, which develops into trust, which grows into confidence and eventuates in behavior. All of the sequence is directed towards the object of the faith, which results in trust and confidence.

In summary, faith is used in a number of different ways:

1. To refer to a body of knowledge that Christians believe and affirm and the object of which is God. People have been given sufficient knowledge of and information regarding God to enable them to trust Him as the object of faith.

2. A "creed" is a grouping of such statements that are accepted as true. Kreeft succinctly stated that "without propositions we cannot know or tell others what God we believe in and what we believe about God" (Kreeft, 1994:30).

3. Reference to a more advanced form of faith is found in James 2:19 where we learn that simply believing in God as a cognitive and intellectual exercise is not enough. One needs to believe actively and affectively in God as object-choice, to place one's trust in Him, and to experience the conviction affectively that He is what he says He is in his Word, and not merely true but true for one personally. In popular language this is at times referred to as information moving from the "head" to the "heart." This is a Saint Thomas phenomenon. Jesus defined this behavioral dimension of faith which goes beyond empiricism and the experiences of the senses and culminates in trust- based action (2 Cor. 5:7). This is faith that moves from the mind and intellectual understanding to a total response in ABC: Affect, Behavior and Cognition. The experience is often shrouded in an aura of insight, an epiphany of having a sudden illuminating glimpse of the obvious. This experience in Evangelical Theology is often considered to be the moment of "saving faith", which although often experienced as a crisis may also be experienced as a process (Ona, 2007: 13).

4. The enemy of such a conceptual-affective faith experience may be either evidentialism or fideism. Evidentialism is the position that everything one knows by faith must be understood or proved by reason. Fideism is the position that the only knowledge one can know and possess by gained by faith, apart from reason.

Marcus Borg, in *The Heart of Christianity,* had an interesting categorization of four types of faith using Latin terms.

1. **Assensus** -- is accepting a statement to be true on the basis of intelligence. "Head belief" is rooted in physical evidence and one accepts what can be seen and felt.

2. **Fiducia** -- is trust or reliance on God. This is trust that does not require any empirical evidence.

3. **Fidelitas** -- indicates living for God and practicing faithfulness even when one has the expectation that things may end badly.

4. **Visio** -- is a way of seeing reality and especially seeing God's grace at work. This is a whole new way of viewing life which has the effect of transforming reality (Borg, 2003).

The Christian faith is above everything else a balanced faith and is reasonable. There is no requirement that one must have a rational answer for *every* question in order to possess a valid faith. The Christian has good reason to believe that God exists. This in itself does not necessarily demonstrate that faith in God is rational or that faith requires that one prove absolutely and conclusively that God exists. Faith is built on the foundation of reason but is distinct from reason and it has a basis in fact. Paul is clear that faith is something we can know (Romans 1:19-20).

The early Church fathers also had some definite views on faith. Bickel and Jantz (2008: 41-47) outline these as follows:

1. Justin Martyr in the second century argued that Christianity should be tolerated because it was a true philosophy somewhat like Platonism.

2. Origen showed that the resurrection of Jesus, while not natural, was credible.

3. Augustine (354-430) taught that faith and reason work together to enable people to develop knowledge of God. He opined that it was foolish to believe in Christ without any proof concerning Christ. Even though Augustine did not think that it was possible to come to faith through reason, he saw the two as interactive and interdependent.

4. In the Middle Ages, Anselm (1032-1109) developed many proofs that Christianity is a reasonable faith, including the ontological argument. He wrote, "I believe in order to understand."

5. Thomas Aquinas (1225-1274) developed the cosmological and moral arguments and also the argument from design. He concluded that some truths about God are discoverable through reason and faith working together, while others are known only through faith.

6. During the Reformation, Luther (1482-1546) reflected two different views regarding faith and reason. He taught that reason had its limits in helping people come to faith. Reason knows no part in knowing God. In later life he modified his views somewhat.

7. Calvin taught that faith is always reasonable, even though it does not always appear to be so to non-believers because reason has been corrupted by sin (Bickel & Jantz, 2008: 41-47).

It is important not to confuse the idea of the relationship between faith and reason, and assume that faith and reason are always antagonistic, or potentially so. Matters of faith, for example, may be thought to conflict with human reason. Faith is viewed as authoritarian, while reason is autonomous. Faith is considered to be biased, while reason is neutral, with no axe to grind. This is an inaccurate perception.

The idea of an endemic conflict between faith and reason is particularly strong in the "Enlightenment Tradition" of philosophy, what has been called The Enlightened Age. In this tradition, "reason" is thought of as a set of truths known by the unaided intellect of any person, or by any person whose mind is not pre-disposed by dogma. These truths are thus self-evident, or at least much more likely to be true than any religious dogma, which are alleged to be the fruit of authoritarianism or escapism. In the Enlightenment view for any matter of faith to be rationally acceptable it must first pass a test of "reason" which follows this definition and description. In such thinking, any matter of faith-trust, if it is to be credible, must be self-evident, or must follow logically from truths that are self-evident, or it must be more credible than not. For any religious belief to be reasonable it must be more probable than not, given the belief that God exists.

In the eyes of many contemporary philosophers, who tend to form the mainstream of modern western philosophy from Descartes onwards, no propositions of religion pass, or could *ever* pass, the test of reason, and so all religion must be considered to be "irrational" (Britton, 1935: 21-27). Because such propositions are unreasonable, reason, it is claimed, need not spend herself further on matters of faith, which is merely another term for credulity. The *a prioris* of science need not, therefore, even be considered as a possibility. Many attempts were made to demonstrate the reasonableness of faith. These attempts were in operation long before the Enlightenment, and were based on the conviction that the propositions of faith *ought* to pass the test of reason, or ought to be required to pass it.

In the Five Ways of Aquinas, for example, he sought to offer proofs of God's existence in typical rationalist fashion and to ground the propositions of faith in matters that are obvious or evident to everyone. He stated that "From effects evident to us, therefore, we can demonstrate what in itself is not evident to us, namely, that God exists" (Helm, 1997: 4). However, Aquinas also stated that there is nothing to stop a person accepting on faith some truth that he or she personally cannot demonstrate, even if that truth is such that demonstration could make it evident.

Kuyper's Analysis of Faith

Special attention and analysis is focused on the views of Abraham Kuyper on faith. This is being done because it is felt that his views are close to the usual evangelical perception and experience that is the vantage point of the author of this research. Kuyper succeeds in integrating many of the concepts of faith just reviewed and to add concepts that are not usually understood by evangelical students. This is not to suggest in the slightest that other views of faith are less useful or less important. All the views already reviewed make useful contributions to the subject but the opinions and experience of Kuyper are considered by this author to be especially useful.

Kuyper made the significant claim that every science to a certain degree starts from faith. He, in the face of contention and disagreement in the learned world, was convinced that among or beneath these conflicts there is a primary conflict, namely, "The powerful conflict between those who cling to the confession of the Triune God and His Word, and those who seek the solution of the world-problem in Deism, Pantheism and Naturalism." Kuyper adds, "A conflict between faith and science does not exist, because every science in a certain degree starts *from faith"* (Kuyper, 1943: 131). He adds that every science presupposes faith in self; presupposes the activity of our self-consciousness; presupposes faith in the accurate working of our senses; presupposes faith in the correctness of the laws of thought; presupposes faith in something universal hidden behind special phenomena; presupposes faith in life, and especially presupposes faith in the principles, from which we proceed; all of which signify that all these indispensable axioms, needed in a productive scientific investigation, do not come to us by proof, but are established in our judgment by our inner conception and are given by the Creator with self-consciousness (Kuyper, 1943: 131).

The essence of the conflict engaged in by both sides is whether the cosmos as it exists today is in a normal condition or an abnormal condition. The normalists, that is, the evolutionists, are concerned exclusively with natural data and they believe in a slow progression from lower to higher forms of life in a way that is unorchestrated by God. On the other hand, the abnormalists believe in a primordial creation into which sin entered and which eventuated in the Fall.

It is important to note here that what Kuyper means by "faith" is not faith in a soteriological sense but what epistemologists call "belief" and which rises to the level of trust. These beliefs which Kuyper is discussing have two features:

1. They are held with certainty and conviction;

2. They are not the outcome of observation or demonstration, that is, they are not based on empirical examination.

"This places faith over against demonstration; but *not* of itself over against *knowing*" (Kuyper, 1943: 131). It therefore appears that Kuyper does not adhere to the ancient tradition according to which belief (faith) and knowledge are mutually exclusive (Hamlyn, 1978: 78-94). He takes the position that belief is not opposed to knowing and he distinguishes between two kinds of knowledge, namely, knowledge that results from demonstration and knowledge that does not, and therefore may be considered foundational or basic knowledge. Here Kuyper is in agreement with numerous philosophers, including Aristotle, Descartes and Locke, who all distinguished demonstrative knowledge from intuitive knowledge (Edvinsson & Malone, 1997:10-15).

Kuyper takes the position that faith, when understood in this way, actually permeates the very life of science. He gives a number of examples:

1. The empirical sciences involve observation which depends on trust in the faculty of perception. Belief in our senses (that is, that our senses are reliable) is foundational and is not based on some argument or proof.

2. He adds: "We actually owe all our convictions of the realism of the object exclusively to faith. Without faith you can never go from your ego to the non-ego; there is no other bridge to be constructed from phenomena to noumena ... and it is an undoubted fact that, with the exception perhaps of some

weak-minded philosopher, every man, without
thinking of verification ... is certain every moment
of the day that his surroundings are as they actually
appear; so that on the ground of this certainty he
acts and works without hesitation" (Kuyper, 1943:
133-4). The point is that scientists do not believe
in the existence of an external world on the basis
of argument or demonstration. Their belief in the
existence of the objects of their study is foundational.

3.   Kuyper also makes the point that even
demonstration, the sine qua non of science,
proceeds from foundational beliefs, and that
demonstration is always based on axioms that
cannot be proved and must be taken for granted.
He states, for example, that "They are given with
our self-consciousness ... they inhere in it ... they
are inseparable from it, and ... of themselves they
bring their certainty with them" (Kuyper, 1943: 134).
He adds that "when we have to take for granted
unproved and unprovable axioms, faith makes its
appearance and here is that mysterious bond which
binds the ego to the axioms" (Kuyper, 1943: 134).

Faith is also part and parcel of science in the belief
of general laws, which, says Kuyper, cannot be proved.
Kuyper is not claiming that the formula of the law of gravitation, for example, rests on faith. The formula is the result of
investigation. However:

The idea itself that there are such laws, and that when
certain phenomenon exhibit themselves, you are certain
of the existence of such laws, and does not result from
demonstration, but is assumed in your demonstration and
is the basis on which your demonstration rests ... Without
faith in the existence of the general in the special, in laws
which govern this special, and in your right to build a general conclusion on a given number of observations, you
would never come to knowledge of such a law. Therefore
the belief that general laws of nature exist, is a foundational one (Kuyper, 1943: 139).

In the natural sciences, faith renders the exclusively formal service of making us believe in our senses, in the reality of the phenomena, and in the axioms and laws of logic by which we demonstrate (Kuyper, 1943: 146). What Kuyper is contending is that in the life of the natural sciences the role of faith is symptomatic of foundational or basic beliefs. We proceed with the conviction that our senses are reliable and that the external world really exists.

The problem is compounded by the fact that different people have different foundational beliefs. This is not a major problem as long as the differences are simply differences in degree or in emphasis. However, some differences are not in degree or in emphasis but in principle. He elaborates as follows. A difference is a difference of principle when it is:

> a difference which does not find its origin within the circle of human consciousness, but outside of it ... The Christian religion places before us this supremely important fact. For it speaks of a regeneration, of a being begotten anew, followed by an enlightening, which changes man in his very being; and that indeed by a change or transformation which is effected by a supernatural cause ... The Christian is inwardly different from the non- Christian and consequently feels a different content rising from his consciousness; the Christian and the non-Christian therefore face the cosmos from different points of view, and are impelled by different impulses. (Kuyper, 1943: 152-4.)

This is in perfect agreement with the thinking of Philbin, a Roman Catholic theologian, who wrote of the energizing Spirit coming as a gift from God. "Just as God comes to the aid of our weakness of will by his undue grace, so he enlightens our minds and makes *faith* possible by the special gift of supernatural revelation" (Philbin, 1953: 349). Aquinas comments on the necessity of this addition of faith to the human personality as follows: "It was necessary that the unshakeable certitude and pure truth concerning divine things should be presented to men by way of faith" (Aquinas, 1998: 439).

Kuyper's position is that all science proceeds from things accepted solely by faith, that is, from foundational beliefs. Kuyper, however, adds regeneration to this process because Christians have awareness of things non-Christians do not have and so they may have some different beliefs, including foundational beliefs or basic beliefs, than non-Christians. Kuyper contends that the believer has received an addition to his personality, that is, the energizing power of the Holy Spirit. This is the Johannine *anothen* experience. Paul has reminded us that the eyes of one's understanding may be blinded by unbelief. Christians, for example, according to St Paul, have a belief that God exists, and this belief *may* be foundational. Plantinga also takes the position that belief in God is basic or foundational (Plantinga, 1997: 18). Belief in God, Plantinga notes, may be rational and intellectually honest without the necessity of "proof". Micah Cobb 2011 concludes:

> If it is legitimate to hold the belief in God is properly basic, then a Christian's belief in God can be rational without needing arguments or proofs that God exists. The Christian does not need to have a proof of God's existence to be intellectually honest. This means that the Christian does not need natural theology. In fact, if the Reformed theologians are correct the Christian shouldn't need it (Micah Cobb 2011).

In either case, belief in God makes a difference in science and this may be basic to the differences between scientists of faith and those without it, rather than an essential conflict between the two substantive corpora of knowledge.

Kuyper takes the position that in the scientific enterprise the essential difference between theists and non-theists is that because of the addition of the energy of the Spirit to their psychological functioning they are differently constituted and therefore see a corresponding difference in the constitution of all things. He points out that the sum total of the theist's beliefs, that is, the foundational set plus everything that follows from it by valid forms of inference, is very different from the sum total of the naturalist's beliefs. He is careful to add, however, that "there is a very broad realm of investigation in which the difference between the two groups exerts no influence, for in the present dispensation polygenesis works no change in the senses, nor in the plastic conception of visible things" (Kuyper, 1898: 57). There is common ground with respect to perception and empirical observations and also to reasoning. "The formal process of thought has not been attacked by sin, and for this reason polygenesis works no change in this mental task. There is but one logic, and not two" (Kuyper, 1898: 161).

Kuyper was a foundationalist and felt that some beliefs are permissible but that some are impermissible. Only those beliefs that are foundational or based on beliefs that are foundational are permissible. However, this still leaves the enigma as to which beliefs are foundational, even though there are inferential procedures that enable us to get from foundational to non-foundational beliefs, especially deduction and induction. It would appear, therefore, that faith is an element in the pre-suppositionalism which is basic to both religion and science.

Applicability of Kuyper's Integration

- There is a corpus of knowledge that is accepted as the body of faith in both science and religion.
- There must be a major element of trust either in God the creator or in the doctrine of science reified.
- The degree of conviction of rightness in both camps is a reflection of the element of faith.
- The conviction and trust combined in the faith experience will eventuate in the ABC phenomenon – changes in Affect, Cognition and Behavior.
- Everyone involved this ABC change requires the utilization of energy.
- For the non-believer the energy utilized is the natural

supply of psychic energy which is the energizing principle of psychological functioning.

- For the believer this radical change in ABC is energized by natural psychic energy augmented by the addition of the divine energy of God, generally termed the Holy Spirit.

- This energizing force of the Spirit added to the human personality often erupts in an epiphany of insight, analogous to psychoanalytic insight and best described as a sudden glimpse of the obvious, which then is the basis for the ABC metamorphosis.

- Kuyper's view of the faith experience fits in with this suggested model.

In view of the fact that the whole concept of "spirit" is nebulous and difficult for material entities to appreciate and also because in the New Testament there is a definite difference between the Holy Spirit (the person, in common Evangelical parlance) and "holy spirit" (God's energizing power), it might perhaps be permissible and useful to think of "spirit" as "life-energy" or *élan vital.* According to this analysis of Kuyper's views this, of course, would mean that there are two sources of this energy, namely natural or physical and spiritual. In addition, this would help clarify Paul's distinctions between the natural and spiritual man (e.g., 1 Cor. 2:14, 15), with the carnal man possessing the divine energy but for one reason or another not utilizing it in daily adjustment.

The hypothesis of an energizing force in the human personality has been well recognized from the work of the early psychoanalytic physicians and remains a fundamental postulate of psychoanalytic theory. Even though this metaphor has often been criticized by some analytic theorists it remains the foundation stone of Freud's economic theory, and the topographical and dynamic views imply it. Every psychic movement, in the last analysis, is linked to a phenomenon of energy. This notion of psychic energy had its source in the work of neurophysiologists at the end of the 19th century, Sigmund Exner in particular and in the psychophysics of Gustav Fechner. In psychoanalytic theory it is first discussed at great length in Joseph Breuer's *Studies in Hysteria*, in Freud's *Project for a Scientific Psychology* (1895) and in *The Interpretation of Dreams* (1900) (Freud, 1895: 281-387; 1900: 339-625; 1923: 1-66).

Spirit and Faith

More and more it is being recognized that there is something *more* and irreducible in the living organism. This has been emphasized even by such diehard pro-evolutionists as Pierre Teilhard de Chardin, who wrote:

> Modern thought is at last getting acclimatized once more to the idea of the creature value of synthesis in the evolutionary sense. It is beginning to see that there is definitely
>
> more in the molecule than in the atom,
>
> more in the cell than in the molecule,
>
> more in society than in the individual, and
>
> more in mathematical construction than in calculations and theorems.
>
> We are now inclined to admit that at each further degree of combination something which is irreducible to isolated elements emerges in a new order (de Chardin, 2008: 267-268).

De Chardin was convinced that psychological or mindlike properties exist throughout the universe in both the animate and the inanimate. This appears to be the "energy" or the "stuff" of matter and of the universe. De Chardin stated that "Physics is no longer sure whether what is left in its hand is pure energy, or, on the contrary, thought" (de Chardin, 2008: 281). In addition to the well known and measurable energy of the physical universe, de Chardin postulated the existence of a second energy which he described as "psychic energy." However, since he could not accept a fundamentalist dualism, he concluded that all energy in nature is psychic. He stated: "Without the slightest doubt *there is something or other* through which material and spiritual energy hold together and are complementary. In the last analysis, *somehow or other,* there must be a single energy operating in the world" (de Chardin, 2008: 63).

There is a possibility that de Chardin here shows some evidence of the bi-polarity of his combined theological and psychological education. When he introduces the concept of psychic energy he is regurgitating a concept as old as psychoanalysis itself, that psychological events are energy-based. Freud wrote: "Mental processes are essentially unconscious ... and those that are conscious are merely isolated acts and parts of the whole psychic entity ... The psychoanalytical definition of the mind is that it comprises processes of the nature of feeling, thinking and wishing, and it maintains that there are such things as unconscious thinking and unconscious wishing" (Freud, 1935: 22-23).

Even Freud may have been surprised to learn how he had anticipated some current ideas or that theologically the stress might be on the creativity of "holy spirit", which is often *exegeted* incorrectly as "the Holy Spirit". This is the "spirit," the energizing principle of life, which "returns to the God who gave it" (Ecclesiastes 12:7) at the death of the individual. It is the driving energy of the human personality that is the energizing force of life. It is the *sine qua non*, the essential difference, between the animate and the inanimate. It should not, therefore, be too surprising that this suggested "divine energy" implanted by God when an individual comes alive in Christ, as an addition to normal human psychic energy, is the power that makes the Christian different, as postulated by Kuyper.

Faith and Cognitive Psychology

The subject of faith is one that is of importance in any discussion of cognitive and evolutionary psychology since faith is the psychological epiphenomenon involved. In this study it has been documented that faith is the *sine qua non* of all theory building and therefore is also inherent in the conceptions of evolutionary psychology. According to Thomas Fikes (2001:340), "Combining the conceptual methods of evolutionary biology and the empirical methods of the cognitive sciences holds promise, but it appears that the rhetoric for an immature discipline, such as evolutionary theory, is excessively strong against disciplines with which it might productively co-exist."

The following is a summary of the views of Hurlbut and Kalanithi (2001), who have written extensively on cognitive science and evolutionary theory:

1. Evolutionary cognitive psychology is an attempt to explore the formation of the human mind using a set of assumptions drawn from evolutionary theory.

2. Darwin's theory assumes heritable units that carry specific adaptations between generations and natural selection which results in the preservation of advantageous traits.

3. The source of variation, the nature of the actual hereditable units and whether selective forces operate on the psychological level all remain extremely speculative.

4. The claims of evolutionary psychology have not been established scientific truths but conjectures which are more philosophical and religious in nature.

5. Evolutionary psychology claims to be a methodology and not metaphysics, but when misapplied it becomes an extreme form of naturalism.

6. Categories such as good, evil and motivation cannot be explained.

7. Reason is recognized as a ruthless adaptive tool, not a rational calculator or moral guide.

8. Evolution may be a useful tool for understanding some

dimensions of biology, but it is not the arbiter of issues of metaphysics or religion.

9. Evolution's initial set of assumptions derive not from scientific evidence but represent philosophical and theological faith-based presuppositions.

10. Evolution reduces all human behaviors to value-neutral adaptations (i.e. having no genuine reference to transcendent truths) and to deny the spiritual significance of mind and moral culture.

11. The foundational arguments of evolutionary psychology are tautological, questionable a priori assumptions. Evolutionary theory needs to be engaged as explanatory power in exploring how freedom and the capacity for moral awareness are anchored in and arise from basic biology and yet beckon beyond to issues of transcendent truth (Hurlbut and Kalanithi (2001).

The Essentiality of Faith

Whether the focus is on the orientation and viewpoints of naturalism, science or reason, it becomes apparent that the faith-based-presuppositional-assumption is the over-reaching foundational basis for both evolutionary thinking and for theological thinking and indeed for all science. Perhaps both those who worship at the altar of natural selection and chance have more in common with those who recognize a supreme being in the universe than either side would like to admit. To fail to recognize the necessity of the faith-based-presuppositional-assumption as foundational to both science and religion is to open the way for a reductionist fallacy.

Study and Review Questions for Chapter Five

1. How is naturalism related to the world being a closed system?

2. How does naturalism have theological roots?

3. Why is the use of scientific creationism a problem for Christians?

4. Why is it difficult to define the term "faith?"

5. Why did Luther describe the Book of James as "an epistle of straw?"

6. How does reason perform a two-fold role in faith?

7. In what way is the controversy over evolution not a conflict between science and religion?

Topics Discussed in Chapter Six

Intelligent Design Defined and Described

Intelligent Design in Biology

Intelligent Design as Science

Support and Antagonism

Irreducible Complexity

Accident, Design or Purpose

Intelligent Design and Information Theory

The Anthropic Principle

Study and Review Questions

INTELLIGENT DESIGN

Intelligent Design defined and described

Intelligent Design (ID) is the proposition that some features of living organisms and of the universe can best be explained by the purposeful action of an intelligent cause and not by an undirected process such as natural selection. The theory "rejects the theory of natural selection, arguing that the complexities of the universe and of all life suggest an intelligent cause in the form of a supreme creator" (Collins English Dictionary, 10th ed., 2009). The theory was criticized as a form of creationism and a contemporary adaptation of the teleological argument for the existence of God. The critics also accuse it of being an attempt to produce an evidence-based scientific theory rather than an idea that is theological in that it seeks to redefine science to permit extra-natural explanations into the scientific equation.

The central idea of Intelligent Design theory is that design is empirically detectable, just as the detectability of design in man-made objects is straightforward, non-controversial, and often intuitive. With respect to the origin and development of cosmological and biological systems, Intelligent Design theory holds that the same principles provide a logical inference of design in nature. That is, without necessarily "proving" actual intelligent design in nature, the observable material evidence provides a reasonable basis from which to infer design, and such an inference supports a legitimate scientific hypothesis of intelligent design. As such, Intelligent Design theory is a scientific disagreement with the core claim of materialistic theories of evolution such as chemical and Darwinian evolution that the design exhibited in our universe is merely apparent design, i.e., unintelligent design caused by unguided, purposeless, natural forces of physics and chemistry alone.

O'Leary explained the origin of the Intelligent Design theory:

> Modern design arguments stem from 20th century science findings about the complexity of life that Darwin and his followers did not expect. The modern case for design is based on information theory which provides a tool for distinguishing between mere order, which can occur without design, and complex order, which probably cannot (O'Leary, 2004:172).

The proponents of the Intelligent Design concept claim that it was developed out of a sense of discomfort experienced by a number of well-trained scientists who became dissatisfied with the traditional theory of evolution and the alleged phenomenon of natural selection. Bethell explained the motivation behind the development of the theory:

> The proponents of Intelligent Design say that living organisms are so complex that they could not have been generated by the long series of accidents that Darwinism relies on. All forms of life – plants, animals, and human beings – must have been designed (Bethell, 2005:199).

Behe opined that the theory of evolution was both interesting and useful, as long as it was still perceived as a theory. However, it had proved to be inadequate to explain some significant issues which are of importance in biology, namely, (1) irreducible complexity, (2) specified complexity, and (3) a fine-tuned universe (Behe, 1995:39).

Although the traditional definition of science deliberately excluded everything but the natural and physical dimension and had purposely omitted anything that might conceivably point to the possibility of a metaphysical element. It appeared to some scholars; such as, Behe and Dembski, that behind all the natural phenomena considered in the question of the origin of life, there was compelling evidence of design in the universe and that this phenomenon is worthy of scientific attention. The claim was made that evidences in nature seem to serve some function beyond their own limited makeup, and these functions are interpreted as constituting evidence of an extra-natural designing force (Sarkar, 2007: 85). Ruse has summarized this development as follows

> For instance, the bee's pollination of the flower would be seen by ID advocates as evidence for design because the bee contributes to a system far more complex and vital than it could possibly comprehend, and thus would be one part among many in a sophisticated, natural machine that assures the reproduction of the flower. Moreover, ID advocates would argue that the existence of natural "machines" that serve some purpose imply a designer, and in fact "are God's handiwork, fashioned to help organisms" (Ruse, 2003: 6).

Anthony Flew penned a new introduction to *God & Philosophy (2007),* repeating in the words of Plato's Socrates his inclination to "follow the argument where it leads" (Flew, 2007).

As has already been demonstrated, "faith" is an essential ingredient in science and in religious thinking. It is impossible to understand the issues involved in the Intelligent Design controversy without first noting the importance of the faith element in evolutionary theory *qua* science. In the same way, it would be difficult to discuss the faith element in the evolutionary dialog without noting the Intelligent Design movement and its ideas. The perennial notion of some type of intelligent design in nature is illustrated by the occurrence of the design theme that occurs in literature. The concept of intelligent design was not left exclusively to scientists but is found outside the purely scientific realm. An example is in the poetry of Joseph Addison (1672-1719), who most likely never heard of Intelligent Design. His poetic reflection still gives an excellent description of his notion of what Intelligent Design is. In his famous "Ode" his theistic basis for design is quite clearly faith-based.

> *The spacious firmament on high*
> *With all the blue ethereal sky,*
> *And spangled heavens, a shining frame,*
> *Their original proclaim.*
>
> *The unwearied sun, from day to day,*
> *Does his creator's power display,*
> *And publishes to every land*
> *The work of an almighty hand.*
>
> *Soon as the evening shades prevail,*
> *The moon takes up the wondrous tale,*
> *And nightly to the listening earth*
> *Repeats the story of her birth:*
> *Whilst all the stars that round her burn,*
> *And all the planets in their turn,*
> *Confirm the tidings as they roll,*
> *And spread the truth from pole to pole.*
>
> *What though, in solemn silence, all*
> *Move round the dark, terrestrial ball?*
> *What though no real voice nor sound*
> *Amid their radiant orbs be found?*
> *In reason's ear they all rejoice,*
> *And utter forth a glorious voice,*
> *For ever singing, as they shine,*
> *"The hand that made us is divine"*
> *(Addison, 1983: 103).*

Ode received great acclaim and was printed in *The Spectator*, co-founded by Addison, and was to be immortalized in the North Aisle of Henry VII's Chapel in Westminster Abbey. Charles Darwin was eventually to be laid to rest near a convinced believer in divine design!

Intelligent Design in Biology

The concept of speciation, (evolutionary process by which new species arise), is well recognized to be the basic foundation of all evolutionary theory. As Gould observed:

> The essence of Darwinism lies in the claim that natural selection is a creative force, and in the reductionist assertion that selection upon individual organisms is the locus of evolutionary change (Gould, 1982:380).

It is accepted that without an adequate and convincing definition of how change from one species to another occurs, the theory of evolution is bereft of significant substance. The difficulty is compounded by that fact that there is no clear cut, fully acceptable, definition of "species," a fact which was recognized by Darwin and which may explain why he never confronted the issue of speciation in a direct and forthright manner. As Dembski, Coyne and Orr pointed out that there are more than two dozen definitions of species and none of them is entirely satisfactory (Dembski, 2008: 86).

Darwinian apologists, in a defensive mode, have an answer to this rather significant oversight. They claim that the reason there are no observed instances of primary speciation is the process takes such an extended period of time, which, of course, means that they cannot anticipate that there will ever be direct evidence of such a change. Dembski opined that:

> Darwinists therefore discount the lack of observed instances of primary speciation by saying that it takes too long to observe them ... Darwinists claim that all species have descended from a common ancestor through variation and speciation. But until they can point to a single observed instance of primary speciation, their claim must remain an unverified assumption not an observed scientific fact (Dembski, 2008:93).

An advantage of Intelligent Design theory is that it does not demand speciation or ignore it but stresses that the *sine qua non* of such changes is the delivery of specific information to the living cell. No one understands how this occurs. It is clear that intelligence has the potential to produce biological changes in a manner that is compatible with Intelligent Design. Dembski deals with this issue as follows:

> The theory of intelligent design neither requires nor excludes speciation – even speciation by Darwinian mechanisms ... It holds that intelligence can itself be a source of biological novelties that lead to macro-evolutionary changes. In this way intelligent design is compatible with speciation (Dembski, 2008: 109).

The biological evidence for molecular design, in the opinion of Intelligent Design scientists, also constitutes strong evidence that there is a designer. Carrée has summarized some convincing evidences for molecular design, gleaning these points from Fazale Rana's book *The Cell's Design* (Carrée, 2010: 2):

1. Molecular Motors: William Paley's famous "Watchmaker's Argument" states that if you come across a watch on the ground, logic dictates that the mechanical complexities of the watch reveal a maker. Recent discoveries of molecular motors containing rotors, pumps, spindles, and gears all operating within the cell have revived Paley's argument.

2. Chicken and Egg Relationships: DNA cannot exist without proteins. Proteins cannot exist without DNA. Undirected evolution cannot explain how these two interdependent molecules emerged, but a designer's involvement would eliminate this dilemma.

3. Molecular Convergence: By its very nature, evolution cannot repeat results in unrelated organisms (e.g., echolocation in dolphins and bats), but a designer can repeat effective designs. There are more than 100 examples of molecular convergence in nature.

4. Preplanning: Some molecular structures, such as the flagellum's tail, need to be constructed in a specific step-wise manner, involving genetic on/off switches throughout the process. One misstep or malfunction compromises the entire structure. Such precision indicates the need for preplanning by a designer.

5. Quality Control: Internal checks guard against malfunction. Cells can identify and destroy erroneous proteins. Incorrectly spliced DNA code is corrected. Again, these systems indicate the hand of a designer.

6. Biochemical Information: Simple as it may seem, the cell wall regulates exports and imports to the cell, assists in cell metabolism and division, and regulates function. Such complexity suggests a designer's craftsmanship.

7. Minimum Complexity: In theory, the simplest life-forms could consist of just 500-600 gene products. However, each gene product is about 1,000 nucleotides (DNA molecules) in length, necessitating hundreds of thousands of nucleotides strung together. This complexity poses gargantuan problems for the Darwinian theory of evolution and for scientific researchers.

8. Fine-tuning of the Genetic Code: The odds of finding the right genetic codes for life are $1.4x\ 10^{70}$. Any conceivable change to the genetic code would be lethal to the cell, indicating the code could not have evolved. Only a designer could map and construct such an intricate system (Caree, 2010: 2).

The supporters of the Intelligent Design concept have produced strong evidence of its truth. However, for every argument for the concept, a counter-argument will also be found.

Intelligent Design as Science

For a number of scientists the theory of evolution has not proved to be satisfactory from an intellectual or from a scientific point of view. Ernest Mayr, a leading scientist in the field of evolutionary biology, expressed his dissatisfaction as follows:

> Evolution is a historical process that cannot be proven by the same arguments and methods by which purely physical or functional phenomena can be documented. Evolution as a whole, and the explanations of particular events, must be inferred from observations (Mayr, 2001: 12).

In somewhat greater detail he stated:

> Darwin introduced historicity into science. Evolutionary biology, in contrast with physics and chemistry, is a historical science – the evolutionist attempts to explain events and processes that have already taken place. Laws and experiments are inappropriate techniques for the explication of such events and processes. Instead one constructs a historical narrative, consisting of a tentative reconstruction of the particular scenario that led to the events one is trying to explain (Mayr, 2000:80).

Intelligent Design represents the work of a new group of scientists who have arisen to challenge natural evolutionary theory in a new way. These thought- provoking and highly respected individuals did not seek to dismantle sub-theories pertaining to origins, such as the big bang, primordial soup, or the survival of the fittest. Instead, they began to challenge the scientific community with new concepts such as irreducible complexity, universal probability and complex specified information. These terms reflect what appear to be non-religious and scientifically plausible concepts that forcefully explain how the blind luck so indispensable in Darwinism could never do the impossible. Poppe stated the following:

> The processes and phenomena currently operating within the universe and on earth are insufficient to produce themselves. No amount of natural evolutionary theory

can account for the complexity and compatibility that are continually observed by science. Therefore, there must be a guiding intelligence repeatedly involved in creating the complexity, but subjected to it. Such complexity must always be the result of independent information because there is a mathematical limit to what blind luck can accomplish (Poppe, 2006: 20-21).

One of the early pioneers in the field of Intelligent Design was the biochemist Charles Thaxton, who coined the term "Intelligent Design" to explain the need for intelligence behind the elaborate information found inside DNA. He stated that "just when it seemed that natural causes might suffice to account for all natural phenomena there were breakthrough discoveries in both mathematics and biology" (Thaxton, 1998: 5).

Luskin has made pertinent and illuminating observations on the positive case for design, all of which point to the acceptability of Intelligent Design theory in the scientific enterprise. He attacks the argument made by many Darwinians that the design concept is merely a negative argument against evolution. He points out that the principal characteristic of a design agency, as enunciated by Dembski, is directed contingency, or what is commonly referred to as choice (Dembski, 1998: 62). Luskin stated that "observations of the types of choices that intelligent agents commonly make when designing systems, result in a positive case for the scientific basis of Intelligent Design. Such a case is easily constructed by elucidating predictable, reliable indicators of design" (Luskin, 2008). Most importantly, Luskin points out that design can be inferred using the scientific methods of observation, hypothesis, experiment, and conclusion. Design theorists begin with observations of how intelligent agents act when designing to help them recognize and detect design in the natural world. They proceed as follows: (Luskin, 2008.)

> (1) Intelligent agents think with an "end-goal" in mind, allowing them to solve complex problems by taking many

parts and arranging them in intricate patterns that perform a specific function (e.g., complex and specific information):

"Agents can arrange matter with distant goals in mind" (Meyer, 2004a:388). "Our experience-based knowledge of information-flow confirms that systems with large amounts of specified complexity (especially codes and languages) invariably originate from an intelligent source from a mind or personal agent" (Meyer, 2004b: 213).

(2) Intelligent agents can rapidly infuse large amounts of information into systems:

"We know from experience that intelligent agents often conceive of plans prior to the material instantiation of the systems that conform to the plans – that is, the intelligent design of a blueprint often precedes the assembly of parts in accord with a blueprint or preconceived design plan" (Meyer et al., 2003:386).

(3) Intelligent agents repeatedly "re-use" functional components that work in different systems (e.g., wheels for cars and airplanes):

"An intelligent agent may reuse or redeploy the same module in different systems ... intelligent causes can generate identical patterns independently" (Nelson & Wells, 2003: 316).

(4) Intelligent agents typically create functional things (although one may sometimes think something is functionless, not realizing its true function):

"Since non-coding regions do not produce proteins, Darwinian biologists have been dismissing them for decades as random evolutionary noise or 'junk DNA'. From an ID perspective, however, it is extremely unlikely that an organism would expend its resources on preserving and translating so much junk" (Wells, 2004:55).

These observations can then be converted into predictions about what we should find if an object were designed. This, it is claimed by ID proponents, clearly makes the Intelligent design theory eligible to be considered as 'science' and makes Intelligent Design a scientific theory capable of generating testable predictions:

(a) Natural structures will be found that contain many parts arranged in intricate patterns that perform a specific function (e.g. complex and specified information).

(b) Forms containing large amounts of novel information will appear in the fossil record suddenly and without similar precursors.

(c) Convergence will appear routinely. Genes and other functional parts will be re-used in different and unrelated organisms.

(d) Much so called 'junk DNA' will turn out to perform valuable functions.

One of the fears of scientists who oppose Intelligent Design is that this theory may change the definition of science by allowing the extra-natural into the laboratory. Naturalistic scientists insist that for theists and non-theists alike, there must be a cardinal rule to limit scientific explanations to natural causes. However, this insistence is becoming more and more unacceptable to many, scientists and non-scientists alike. Most evolutionary biologists delight in the unexplained. More people are gravitating towards the alternative explanation, Intelligent Design, which claims that certain features of the natural world are of such complexity that the most plausible explanation is that they are products of an intelligent cause rather than random mutation and natural selection. Supporters of the theory claim the nature of the intelligent cause is outside the scope of the theory (Roach, 2005:198).

There can be little doubt that Darwin and his apologists in the modern scientific community have accepted a distorted and prejudicial view of science that struggles to explain and understand the universe without God or anything of a metaphysical nature. Philip Johnson wrote:

> The design position is falsifiable, since advocates of naturalism could discover a natural process capable of creating the necessary information if such a process exists. (If neo-Darwinism were true as a general theory of biological creation, it would falsify the claim that some additional information-creating mechanism is necessary). Hence, by the standard of falsifiability, the intelligent design hypothesis is scientific, and the refusal to consider it on its merits is unscientific (Johnson, 2000: 134-135).

Dembski's chief criticisms of the current scientific establishment and its refusal to consider the arguments for Intelligent Design are in no way *ad hominem*, but are directed at the philosophic basis of modern science:

> Scientific naturalism locates the self-sufficiency of nature in the natural laws of science. Accordingly, scientific naturalism would have us to understand the universe entirely in terms of those laws ... To be sure, there is no logical contradiction for the scientific naturalist to affirm God's existence, but this can be done only by making God a superfluous rider on top of a self-contained account of the world. What evidence is there of God interacting with the world? To answer this question we must look to science. The science we look to, however, needs to be unencumbered by naturalist philosophy (Dembski,1999: 103-104).

Richard Simon alleged that "the attack on naturalism is an important component of intelligent design because it represents the greatest metaphysical barrier to the re-admittance of theology into science" (Simon, 2010:4). However, Simon is quite fair and objective in his detailed analysis of the relationship between ID and science. He concludes:

> Despite the fact that theological claims on nature may in certain respects be helpful for naturalistic science, the uneasy relationship between science and religion is healthy and probably unavoidable. Even if Behe, operating within an ID framework, contributed indirectly to evolutionary understandings of biological complexity, this does not mean that

biologists would have done well to consider ID as a serious scientific pursuit. And more generally, even if naturalistic theories may benefit indirectly from religious challenges, this does not mean that naturalism is an untenable principle. The only conclusion that may be drawn is that some religiously oriented challenges to science may be stripped of their supernatural overtones and incorporated as a positive contribution to naturalistic systems ... Religious challenges have in the past proven productive for science, not because they were ultimately correct in their claims, but by suggesting new directions in research and thought that had previously been occluded or neglected (Simon, 2010:15-16).

There is a possibility that in some cases those who are adamantly opposed to the Intelligent Design idea have failed to understand that the concept is a "theory" and that by definition a theory is not written in stone as the final and unchangeable word on any question in science. This may reflect a reluctance to understand the nature of science and the fact that science is not supremely authoritative and has its limitations.

Support and Antagonism

Mario Seiglie noted:

...just as with previous scientific revolutions, this one [the Intelligent Design revolution] started when a courageous group of scientists questioned the dominant theory in a field of science and offered evidence to unseat it. They faced strong opposition from the reigning authorities, who felt their prominent position, reputation and power were being threatened (Seiglie, 2006: 18).

Such a reaction from those in positions of "scientific" authority has been documented throughout the course of the history of science. Most scientists, for example, sided with Einstein on the concept of a static universe and remained so convinced until the arrival of the Hubble telescope demonstrated otherwise. It now appears that the Intelligent Design movement, like many scientific predecessors, as it becomes more accepted, is beginning to shake the scientific establishment on the assumptions of

Darwinian evolution. As Stephen Meyer has stated, "We want to have an effect on the dominant view of culture." (As reported in Wilgoren, 2005).

The strength of this scientific revolution may be a comment from U.S. President George W. Bush that Intelligent Design should be taught in public schools along-side evolution: "I think that part of education is to expose people to different schools of thought" (Bumiller, 2005). A few days later, Senate majority leader Bill Frist, who is also a physician, made the same point. He opined that teaching both Intelligent Design and evolution in schools "doesn't force any particular theory on anyone" (Dennett, 2005).

Review of the literature and especially the public oriented rhetoric and most of the arguments against Intelligent Design, offers few valid scientific objections to Intelligent Design theory; it is more often characterized by ridicule than with factual scientific opinion. Johnson notes that "books simply refuse to take seriously any argument against Darwinism or materialism, relying heavily on carica-tures, ridicule and the strong negative implications of cre-ationism" (Johnson, 2000:126). He continued:

> Intelligent design theorists need to explain why the vast majority of evolutionary scientists refuse to consider evi-dence of intelligent design in biology, scornfully dismissing the entire concept as "religion" rather than "science." This is because they identify science with naturalism, mean-ing that only natural (i.e., material or physical) forces may play a role in the history of life (Johnson, 2000:129).

Paul Davis, an avowed evolutionist, appears to consider the evidence offered by Intelligent Design seri-ously. He opined as follows:

> [There] is for me powerful evidence that there is some-thing going on behind it all ... It seems as though some-body has fined-tuned nature's numbers to make the Universe ... The Impression of design is overwhelming" (Davies, 1984:243).

Perhaps the leading polemicist of invective against any form of design concept in nature is Richard Dawkins, popularly recognized as a strident secular proponent of Darwinism. He and his cohorts adamantly refuse to consider that a design of any type is inherent in nature. However, on the first page of *The Blind Watchman*, he indicated that he would accept the notion that there may exist "the appearance" of design in nature. He wrote, "Biology is the study of complicated things that give the appearance of having been designed for a purpose" (Dawkins, 1996:2-3). He added that the theory of evolution has made it possible for him to be "an intellectually fulfilled atheist (Dawkins, 1996: 1, 6). Dawkins is so convinced that his view is correct that he feels free to diagnose religion as a delusion. By definition, a delusion is a fixed idea, a false idea, an idea that cannot be corrected by an appeal to reality. Bordering on the cognitive impairment of a delusion is that of an over-valued idea, a notion eccentric rather than false, but likely to become a governing force in an individual's life (Ebert, 2008:50). Cutler and Marcus clarify the definition of a delusion, as follows: "A delusion is a firmly held, false belief not shared by members of the patient's culture (by definition reality testing is not intact, i.e. the patient is unable to consider the possibility that the belief is incorrect" (Cutler, 2010:11). According to the rules of psychopathology, some pro-evolutionary theory scientists may be displaying such an impairment. Of course, similar psychiatric observations may be made regarding those on the opposite side of the debate.

On the other hand, Intelligent Design proponents take the position that if evolution from a primordial soup by random change is not established by science, but is rather based on a variety of philosophic suppositions, the classic theory is inadequate and false and in fact may be just as delusional as Dawkins considers religion to be. The admission that there is some evidence that at times the appearance of design is found in nature, may be an admission that the complicated functioning of life "gives the *appearance* of having been designed for a purpose" (Dawkins, 1996:2-3). Dawkins has many supporters and antagonists, philosophers and scientists, in his anti-religion crusade. On the opposite side of the debate Daniel Dennett, for example, the author of *Darwin's Dangerous Idea* (1995), states that Darwinism is a "universal acid which eats through just about every traditional concept and leaves in its wake a revolutionized world" (Dennett, 1995:65).

Some of the critics of Intelligent Design continue to claim that postulating any type of design or designer rises to the level of magic and that the theory is unfalsifiable and unscientific. One critic of Intelligent Design, Douglas H. Erwin, a pale biologist at the Smithsonian Institute, stated to the New York Times, "One of the rules of science is, no miracles allowed. That's a fundamental presumption of what we do" (Chang, 2005). Erwin, however, appears to be oblivious to the fact that a comparable criticism can also be leveled at Darwinism. If material causes *only* are admitted, and nothing exists in the universe but molecules in motion, then evolution must be true – a logical deduction from the premise of materialism. Since there is no doubt whatsoever that we are here, then how did we get here? It would appear that materialists have a quandary. They have no choice but to accept the fact that the molecules whirled themselves into extraordinarily complex, conscious beings (Bethell, 2005:203).

Ross has summarized the most common anti-theistic arguments against Intelligent Design as follows:

1. We would not be here to observe the universe unless the extremely unlikely did take place. This is basically an argument for the reification of chance and that the evidence for design is merely coincidental.

2. Design arguments are outside the realm of science and therefore must be ignored. This is a method of winning an argument by fabricating definitions in advance.

3. As we continue to evolve we will become the creator-Designer. This is a cognitive sleight of 'mind' maneuver to predict an evolved being in the future who is so omnipotent that he/she/it has the ability to create a design appearance in the distant past (Ross, 1993:118-120).

The Intelligent Design movement also bears all the scars of an internecine denominational rivalry, with the invective too often being hurled from the Young Earth Creationist side. It may come as a surprise that there should be such affect-laden responses between the Intelligent Design group and the Young Earth Creationists because both ostensibly have the same goal in mind, namely, keeping a Creator-Designer in charge of creation. Yet, those who have been aware of the long history of denominational rivalries and friction (often those who loudly proclaim "One Faith, One Lord" and who would have to be recognized officially as evangelicals), often refuse to relate to each other in a Philadelphian fraternal way and are sometimes even kinder to naturalist humanistic evolutionists than to their own fellow-believers (Johnson, 1999).

The "young earth" theistic opponents of Intelligent Design reject the claim that "certain features" of living and non-living things were designed by an "intelligent cause" (whatever that cause may be) and do not exist as the result of natural causes. The problem and critique of these classical Young Earth Creationists with their Intelligent Design brothers is that the promulgators of Intelligent Design do not specifically state just who or what the nature or source of this postulated intelligence is. In this way, allegedly they are leaving the question of the Creator open and thus permitting evolution and natural causes to be part of the creation equation.

The traditional creationists also appear to be suspicious of the Intelligent Design position because they claim its roots lie in the natural theology movement of the 18th and 19th centuries, rather than in the Bible. They may also be skeptical because the Intelligent Design proponents use facts and arguments which are drawn from the fields of biology, chemistry and physics and which are not based exclusively on theological or philosophical arguments for a designer. What if the design is a synonym for random natural selection? On the other hand, how many young earth creationists realize that the young earth position may have been, in recent years, first promulgated in the Seventh Day Adventist theology of Mrs. Ellen White and revealed to her in a vision? (White, 1958: 107-108).

According to Karl Giberson:

> The most consistent creationist voice at the beginning of the 20th century belonged to the new Seventh-day Adventist movement, which looked to the mid-nineteenth century prophetic writings of Ellen White for guidance. What we call young-earth creationism today—as promoted by Answers in Genesis, Creation Ministries International, the Institute for Creation Research and other groups—can be traced back to one of White's visions (Giberson, 2008).

There is a possibility, however, that the "gap theory" relating to Genesis 1 may have been the impetus for the development of "old-earth" creationist theology. This exegesis of Genesis 1 was initially promulgated by William Pember in 1876 (Pember, 1975: 199).

It many ways Intelligent Design supports the biblical-creationist viewpoint in that no great leap of faith is required to see the designer as God. In spite of this, Intelligent Design has often been unfairly accused, by their Christian brethren, of agreeing with the presupposition of Darwinism that the supernatural does not exist and that this bias will influence the way one reads and interprets scientific evidence. It seems quite clear that the Designer, in the minds of the majority of the authors and proponents of the movement, is indeed the Creator portrayed in the Bible. However, it may be that it is not considered wise or good "science" or politically correct to agree. Such a conclusion is not a necessity. So when Young Earth Creationists claim that their principal objection is that according to Intelligent Design theory, people are left to decide for themselves who is the Creator – whether God, Allah, Brahman, etc., they are guilty of using a straw man strategy. It is reasonable to suspect that most of those who are familiar with creationist literature would conclude that Intelligent Design proponents are, in the main, evangelical, Bible-believing Christians. Personal analysis and observation of a number of young earth creationists who oppose the intelligent design concept leads this author to conclude that it would probably not be too severe to say that this type of cryptic straw-man strategy has the aroma of fundamentalist denominationalism and territorial protectionism.

The Young Earth classical creationists, such as Morris and Mortenson, also criticize the Intelligent Design movement because it does not offer any solution to the evil in the world. (Morris, 1996:6; Mortenson, 2009:25-29)

Surely an omnipotent designer would have done a better job at designing. Intelligent Design. Proponents are accused of refusing to acknowledge God as Redeemer. If there is no solution to the problem of evil and if "the Fall" is not recognized as a reality, then perhaps there can be no solution to the problem of sin and thus no hope of redemption from its effects. They are accused of being so naïve as to think that knowledge of God can come through general revelation, that is, through nature alone. They stress that there must also be the Bible as the source of special revelation to answer these philosophical and religious enigmas.

The Roman Catholic Church has looked with some degree of favour on the Intelligent Design concept. Cardinal Schönborn of Vienna wrote an article for the *New York Times* in which he stated unequivocally that evolution in the sense of an unguided, unplanned, random process is not true. He wrote:

Scientific theories that try to explain away the appearance of design as the result of "chance and necessity" are not science at all, but as [Pope] John Paul put it, an abdication of human intelligence (Schönborn, 2005: 4).

A correct scientific approach to this type of problem is to follow the evidence wherever it may lead, in spite of preconceived notions and emotional biases.

Irreducible complexity

Dr. Michael Behe, who describes himself as an evolutionist, advanced the idea of Intelligent Design in his book, *Darwin's Black Box*. He recalls that the concept of natural selection was accepted as the explanation for evolution until the development of the electron microscope, at which time it became possible to examine the structure of single cells. Each cell has thousands of enzymes in which Behe perceives "irreducible complexity" that determines the development of the cell into the final organism. It has been established, based on scientific observation, that the concept of natural selection is no longer appropriate and is merely the unscientific speculation of how life might have developed.

The issue of "irreducible complexity" has proved to be of major concern and significance to Intelligent Design proponents. This is a term that was introduced by biochemist Behe in his 1996 book *Darwin's Black Box.* Behe defined Irreducible Complexity as "a single system which is composed of several well-matched interacting parts that contribute to the basic function, wherein the removal of any one of the parts causes the system to effectively cease functioning".(Behe, 1997).

Behe used the now famous mouse-trap analogy to make his point, but critics point out Behe's basic assumption, namely that the required parts of a system have always been necessary and therefore could not have been added sequentially. They state that something that is at first merely advantageous may later become necessary as other changes in the system develop (Ussery, 2000).

A number of scholars in the mathematical and scientific communities have discredited Demski's computations. Wilkins and Elsberry, for example, state that Demski's "explanatory filter" is *eliminative,* because it eliminates explanations sequentially: first regularity, then chance, finally defaulting to design. They argue that this procedure is flawed, as a model for scientific inference, because the asymmetric way it treats the different possible explanations renders it prone to making false conclusions (Wilkins & Elsberry, 2001).

Richard Dawkins, in his criticisms of the Intelligent Design concept, argued in *The God Delusion* that allowing for an intelligent designer to account for unlikely complexity only postpones the problem (Dawkins, 2006: 88). Paul Marks has argued that evolution through selection is better able to explain the observed complexity, as evident from the use of selective evolution to design certain electronic, aeronautic and automotive systems that are considered problems too complex for human "intelligent designers" (Marks, 2007).

On the other hand, Behe gave detailed descriptions of examples of irreducibly complex systems, including vision, the blood clotting cascade, and most famously the bacterial flagellum, a feature resembling a motorized paddle which some kinds of bacteria use for motion. Because in all of these examples the removal of one element makes the entire system non-functional, Behe claimed they could not have evolved by slight successive modifications to precursor systems, as those non-functional systems give the organism no advantage in natural selection. Importantly, Behe does not stop at his critique of evolution, but offers Intelligent Design as an alternative to interpretation of irreducible complexity. "Clearly," Behe wrote, "if something was not put together gradually, then it must have been put together quickly or even suddenly" (Behe, 1996:187). In Behe's opinion, this sudden appearance of an intricate and complex system is compelling evidence for an extra-natural power.

As previously noted, one of the world's most renowned atheists, Sir Antony Flew, renounced his atheism because of the compelling evidence of the DNA molecule. He stated:

> It seems to me that the findings of more than fifty years of DNA research have provided materials for a new and enormously powerful argument for design ... Biologists' investigation of DNA has shown, by the most unbelievable complexity of the arrangements which are needed to produce life, that intelligence must have been involved (Flew, 2004).

The structure of the cell has been proved to be so amazingly complex that it requires a gargantuan edifice of "faith" to imagine that it came about as the result of chance. Is it conceivable that omniscience and chance can co-exist? Since God is infinite, omniscient, omnipresent and omnipotent, would His character and attributes permit Him to use such methods? Arthur Eddington thought not:

> Chance does not and cannot exist in any divine omniscience since chance is a finite concept which belongs to finite beings (Eddington, 1930: 672).

Critics (Gould, for example) point out that the argument from irreducible complexity makes sense only if one assumes that the present function of a system must have always been the one for which it was selected. He wrote that the concept of co-optation or expatiation, in which existing features become adapted for new functions has long been a mainstay of biology (Gould, 1991:43). Behe took an opposing position and accepted the possibility of co-optation but considers it unlikely; his critics claim that this dismissal is unwarranted (Luskin, 2012). Darwinians have pointed out that Intelligent Design proponents have failed to appreciate that *the necessary parts of a system have always been necessary, and therefore could not have been added sequentially.* However, something which is at first merely advantageous may later become necessary. For example, one of the clotting factors that Behe listed as part of the clotting cascade may be absent in whales (Hanson, n.d.)

Microbiology has shown that the deeper a single cell is explored the more complicated it is. A single cell has so many thousands of elements so intricately related to each other, each serving a specific function, that it contains an "irreducible complex structure." In other words, if one or more of these elements are missing, the development of the cell is warped. Chance mutations wreck the delicate balance system built into each cell with the result that it cannot reproduce itself or the resulting organism is an abnormality (Popper, 1992:199).

In *The Origin of Species,* Darwin acknowledged that "if it could be demonstrated that any complex organ existed which could not possibly have been formed by numerous, successive, slight modifications, my theory would absolutely break down" (Darwin, 1859:84). Intelligent Design theorists have demonstrated that living creatures are full of such examples at the molecular level. Behe coined the term "irreducible complexity" to explain that complex systems will work if all the components operate at once. He explains that you could not get an intricate, interrelated system from successive and slight modifications, as Darwin proposed. He gives a number of examples of molecular "machines" inside living beings that could not have appeared in a step-by-step evolutionary process. He concludes that they are obvious evidence of intelligent design (Carrée, 2010:2).

While the irreducible complexity argument holds that evolutionary mechanisms cannot account for the emergence of some complex biochemical cellular patterns, Intelligent Design advocates argue that the systems must therefore have been deliberately engineered by some form of intelligence.

According to the classical theory of evolution, genetic variations occur without specific design or intent ... Most ID advocates accept that evolution through mutation and natural selection occurs, but assert that it cannot account for irreducible complexity, because none of the parts of an irreducible system would be functional or advantageous until the entire system is in place (Wikipedia contributors, 2012).

In response, proponents of Intelligent Design argue that the irreducible complexity of protein machines provides convincing evidence of actual design in biology. Dembski wrote:

> By and large critics have conceded that Behe got his facts straight. They have also conceded his claim that detailed neo-Darwinian accounts for how irreducibly complex protein machines could come about are absent from the biological literature ... The fact is that for irreducibly complex biochemical systems, no indirect Darwinian pathways are known (Dembski, 2008:156-157).

As the evidence mounts for irreducible complexity, it appears to be becoming increasingly difficult to deny the possibility of design and its appropriateness as a scientific enterprise.

Accident, Design or Purpose

Another flaw in evolutionary theory has been pointed out by proponents of Intelligent Design. Darwinian theory depends on the concept of natural selection, but this phenomenon does not begin to play any role until self-reproducing organisms are already in existence. This explanation is, therefore, inadequate for the origin of self-starting organisms. William Dembski has stated that this is merely "attributing the power to choose, which properly belongs only to intelligent agents, to natural causes, which inherently lack the power to choose" (Dembski, 1999:229).

In this connection, Behe, in *Darwin's Black Box*, makes another significant criticism of evolutionary theory. He has struggled with the issue of how complex biochemical systems could have come into existence in the first place. These are essential to life and, in his opinion, there is no possibility that their appearance could have occurred by chance. There is no answer to this question in evolutionary literature (Behe, 1996:32).

Just how tenuous and unsatisfactory is the attribution of the evolutionary process to chance is underlined in speculations by Francis Crick, co-discoverer of the structure of DNA, when in 1978 and again in the 1990s he made the highly improbable suggestion that the earth had been "seeded" by spores engineered on a distant planet, a process he called "directed panspermia." It appears that he made this proposal only because he understood the insurmountable difficulty of accepting the idea of undirected life. To avoid invoking the mind of someone or something supernatural, he was forced to introduce the idea of some type of intelligent designer, even if this happened to be fantastic aliens from space (Bethell, 2005:212).

Previously evolutionists could take refuge in ignorance. They too had a "god of the gap" and they too required faith. Since molecular structures were not understood, scientists could conveniently make the faith-based assumption that the organization of matter at the sub-microscopic level was straightforward. Therefore, as Behe was quick to note, all insolvable problems in evolution theory could be relegated to a "black box," which forbade any inspection, examination or even discussion (Behe, 1996:110).

Johnson made the point that critics fail to appreciate that the real issue is information creation, not simply chance:

> Design theory says chance, law and design all operate in the world and that it is possible to distinguish between innovative changes that require design and variations which can be produced by some combination of law and chance (Johnson, 2000:131).

Johnson also made the point:

> Laws produce simple repetitive order, and chance produces meaningless disorder; when combined, law and chance work against each other to prevent the emer-

gence of meaningful sequence. The issue is whether scientific evidence indicates that law and chance alone can accomplish biological creation or that an intelligent cause is also required (Johnson, 2000: 127, 134).

Schönborn wrote:

Alfred North Whitehead's ironic remark about those Darwinists who disavow any form of directedness toward an end is well known: "Those who devote themselves to the purpose of proving that there is no purpose constitute an interesting object of study." Human action is not conceivable as anything other than as oriented toward a goal, and there is hardly an example of any activity more goal-oriented than scientific activity. (Schönborn, 2007).. Schönborn is quoting from Whitehead's 1929 work, The Function of Reason [Princeton, N.J.: Princeton University Press, p.12.)

Astronomers and physicists had a harder time buying into the random-chance scenario. Knowing what they know, they have not made the best Darwinists, because of the weak philosophic argument that everything just fell into place without intelligence. The following are pertinent observations from leaders in the fields of science who, as noted by Poppe, have lucidly expressed their views on accident and chance. Werner von Braun, an astrophysicist of no small repute, stated:

I find it as difficult to understand a scientist who does not acknowledge the presence of a superior rationality behind the existence of the universe as it is to comprehend a theologian who would deny the advances of science (Poppe, 2006:141-142).

Astronomer Alan Sand age expressed his views:

I find it quite improbable that such order came out of chaos. There has to be some organizing principle. God to me is a mystery, but it is the explanation for the miracle of existence, why there is something instead of nothing (Poppe, 2006:141-142).

In like manner, Professor Freeman Davis, professor of physics at Princeton University, expressed his opinion almost poetically:

As we look out into the universe and identify the many accidents of physics and astronomy that have worked together for our benefit, it seems almost as if the universe must in some sense have known we were coming (Poppe, 2006:141-142).

Intelligent Design and Information Theory

On both sides of the divide, many are agreed that macro-evolution has occurred and does occur. Johnson has opined:

Evolution has occurred, if evolution simply means the change of any degree or kind, and so in that trivial sense evolution is necessarily "right." But evolution is a much more dubious concept if it means massive increase in genetic information produced by chance variation and differential reproductive success. By that definition, evolution is very wrong (Johnson, 2000:133).

Evolutionists have claimed that instead of a designer adapting earth to accommodate life, life adapted to the pre-existing conditions it found on the planet. Poppe points out that those who make such claims seldom realize the depth of this assumption. He avers that the finely tuned features of the majority of these factors are not a matter of alterations but eradications – not just conditions to adjust to, but conditions that bring death under any circumstance (Poppe, 2006:138). O'Leary wrote that modern design arguments stem from 20th century science findings about the complexity of life that Darwin and his followers did not expect. The modern case for design is based on information theory that provides a tool for distinguishing between mere order, which can occur without design, and complex order, which probably cannot (O'Leary, 2004:172).

Seiglie noted:

In the 1960s, some scientists began to look at information as something different from matter and energy. For example, a book contains information, but the ink and the paper are not the information itself and can only transmit it … Information does not have mass or charge or length in millimeters. Likewise, matter does not have bytes ... This dearth of shared descriptors makes matter and information two separate domains of existence, which have to be discussed separately, in their own terms (John Brockman, The Third Culture: Beyond the Scientific Revolution, 1995, p. 43).

Interestingly, matter, energy and information all unite in living things. Without information an organism cannot live. In fact, at death, all the biochemical ingredients are still there, but the information is no longer being effectively relayed to the trillions of cells in the body, so the complex biological machinery shuts down.

Another biologist, Jonathan Wells, also was incensed with the faulty information being perpetuated by Darwinian evolutionists in schools and universities. He wrote Icons of Evolution (2000), which exposed how some of the major "scientific" examples used to teach Darwinian evolution are in fact fraudulent or misrepresented.

One of the main points of the intelligent design revolution is that evolution has not been able to explain either the origin of life or the information in our cells ... So not only the problem of the origin of life but also the dilemma of the information inside the DNA molecule defies Darwinian explanation and argues powerfully for intelligent design (Seiglie, 2006:18).

The Anthropic Principle

Since 1970 a number of significant articles have appeared, related to the Anthropic Principle; such as, Carter's *"Large Number Coincidences and the Anthropic Principle in Cosmology,"* which have focused on the way in which the universe is fine-tuned for life, "ranging from the strength of the gravitational constant to the values of the resonance levels of carbon nuclei to the frequency of supernovae" (Dembski, 1999:11). The Anthropic Principle enunciates that the universe has all the necessary and narrowly defined characteristics to make human life possible (Ross, 1993:87). In astrophysics and cosmology, this principle is the philosophical consideration that observations of the existence of human beings placed constraints on the evolution of the universe.

Arno Penzias, commenting on the extremely delicate balance of those factors that permit life on earth, stated:

> Astronomy leads us to a unique event, a universe which was created out of nothing, one with the very delicate balance needed to provide exactly the conditions required to permit life, and one which has an underlying (one might say "supernatural") plan (Penzias, 1992:83).

The argument for Intelligent Design rests primarily on the existence of complex genetic information and the absence of a natural mechanism for creating it (Johnson, 2000:130). Since the days of Darwin, many scientists continued to claim that the earth is a planet with no special characteristics and that the conditions in the universe simply allowed life to evolve from natural processes. Carl Sagan, for example, has opined that "our posturing, our imagined self-importance, the delusion that we have some privileged position in the universe, are challenged by this point of pale light. Our planet is a lonely speck in the great enveloping cosmic dark" (Sagan, 1994:7).

Now, the scientific evidence has apparently revealed that we occupy a privileged position in the universe. It was to explain this cosmic fine tuning that scientists coined the term "Anthropic Principle," which describes a universe designed for life, and in particular, human life. This principle states that all the constants in physics are *precisely* the values required to have a universe capable of supporting life. O'Leary has taken note of the opinion of astronomer Fred Hoyle, an agnostic, who reluctantly admitted that the universe appears to be delicately tuned for life. "A common sense interpretation of the facts suggests that a super-intellect has monkeyed with the physics, as well as the chemistry and biology of the universe … The numbers one calculates from the facts seem to me so overwhelming as to put this one conclusion almost beyond question" (O'Leary, 2004:41).

Anthropic coincidences appear to indicate that all the prior conditions that need to be present and precisely satisfied and correlated for human life to be possible are actually present in the universe. Often this phenomenon is referred to as the "fine-tuning of the universe." Impressed with this finding, Ross opined:

> ... the fundamental forces of nature have to fall within very precise tolerances for the basic constituents of the universe to support life (Ross, 1991:121-122).

Barrow and Tippler, convinced evolutionists, confessed:

> The early investigations of the constraints imposed upon the constants of Nature by the requirement that our form of lifer exist produced some surprising results, It was found that there exist a number of unlikely coincidences between numbers of enormous magnitude that are, superficially, completely independent; moreover, these coincidences appear essential to the existence of carbon-based observers in the Universe (Barrow & Tipler, 1988:5).

Ross (1993:111-114) points out that in the last thirty years more characteristics of the universe appear to indicate a careful and designed fine-tuning in support of life. Presently, researchers have uncovered twenty-five characteristics that must exist within narrowly defined values for any kind of life to exist. Some of these required constants are:

1. Strong nuclear force.

2. Weak nuclear force.

3. Gravitational force.

4. Electromagnetic force.

5. Ratio of electromagnetic force to gravitational force.

6. Ratio of electron to proton mass.

7. Ration of protons to electrons.

8. Expansion rate of the universe.

9. Entropy level of the universe.

10. Mass density of the universe.

11. Velocity of light.

12. Age of the universe.

13. Initial uniformity of radiation.

14. Fine structure constant.

15. Average distance between stars.

16. Decay rate of the proton.

17. Carbon to Oxygen energy level ration.

18. Ground state energy level of Helium.

19. Decay rate of Beryllium.

20. Mass excess of the neutron over the proton.

21. Initial excess of the nucleons over anti-nucleons.

22. Polarity of the water molecule.

23. Supernovae eruptions.

24. White dwarf binaries.

25. Ratio of exotic to ordinary matter.

Ross adds as a subscript to this list:

The list of finely tuned characteristics for the universe continues to grow. Parameters 23, 24 and 25, for example, were added in the last several months. The more accurately and extensively astronomers measure the universe, the more finely tuned they discover it to be. Also, as we have seen for many of the already measured characteristics, the degree of fine-tuning is utterly amazing – far beyond what human endeavors can accomplish (Ross, 1993:111-114).

Many scientists have now come to the conclusion that the Anthropic Principle argument is perhaps the most

powerful argument for intelligent design. It is an appreciation of this concept that has resulted in many scientists
coming to the conclusion that "the universe cannot reason-
ably be explained as a cosmic accident. Evidence for an
intelligent designer becomes more compelling the more
we understand about our carefully crafted habitat" (Walter
Bradley, *The Mystery of Life's Origin* [1984], quoted by
Seiglie [2006] relying on a quote found in Lee Strobel
[2004], *The Case for a Creator,* p. 127).

As a footnote to the antagonism against the concept of
the Anthropic Principle, it is worthy of mention that Barrow
and Tipler, point out that the beginning of the Anthropic
Principle concept perhaps lies in the expulsion of humanity
from a self-assumed privileged position at the center of the
universe. They add that this does not mean that humans do
not have something special in this connection. However, it
is fascinating to note that these two renowned and highly
regarded scholars and scientists see in the Anthropic
Principle a support for evolutionary theory.

Although the Intelligent Design movement is often
portrayed by its critics as a variant of Bible-based creationism, many Intelligent Design arguments are formulated
in secular and acceptable scientific terms and do not
depend on biblical fundamentalism. The theory does not
explicitly state or demand that Intelligent Design adherents accept the Bible's accounts of God as the designer,
but the designer appears to be implicitly hypothesized in
some form or another. In this connection, Behe was careful
to point out that the most important difference between
modern Intelligent Design theory and Paley's arguments,
is that Intelligent Design is limited to design itself (Behe,
2001:165).

Conclusions

Common criticisms of Intelligent Design theory may be
summarized as follows:

1. It is merely an attempt to revive a contemporary of natural theology and it can end up leading down the path to semi-deistic thinking.

2. Some investigators such as Michael Behe believe that biological diversity derives from common descent, but are skeptical that the postulated Darwinian processes of natural selection are sufficient to generate such complexity.

3. Some scientists do not hold to Young Earth Creationism but yet believe that there are irreducibly complex systems in cellular chemistry that can be explained only by invoking some mechanism of design.

4. Dembski, a mathematician, believes that it is possible to infer that "some systems, for example in biology, display ... 'specified complexity'. Such a designation can only be justified by first excluding the possibility that the system has been generated by ... 'natural processes'." These are considered to fall into one of three categories: chance, necessity, or the joint action of chance and necessity. (Alexander, n.d.)

If it can be shown that the system of the object in question could not possibly have been brought about by one of these three types of explanations, then they display "specified complexity" and must, therefore, be the product of Intelligent Design.

Finally, review of the past and current literature on Intelligent Design reveals the following:

1. For centuries it was the generally accepted view that nature had been designed.

2. Eventually rationalism with its metaphysical axioms constrained the sciences to naturalism.

3. Today's naturalism, minus all metaphysical entities, has been proclaimed by *fiat* to be the authoritative word of science.

4. The supporters of the Intelligent Design approach claim that it is an example of "empirical thinking."

5. Intelligent Design has not stepped into a "God of the Gaps" blunder because it is not predicating religious faith on scientific results.

6. The evidence for design is overwhelming and it recognizes the evidence and pursues it wherever it may lead.

7. No *a priori* assumptions are made about what solutions are and what are not allowed, in marked contrast to naturalism-dependent science.

8. Intelligent Design is not opposed to all naturalistic explanations.

9. Intelligent Design is not about proving religion. It is about analyzing the workings of nature without religious constraints.

In spite of overwhelming proof by the highest scientific standards, it will remain a struggle to transcend and be free from strongly held and possibly erroneous academic beliefs, wrongly identified as science. This is accurately and clearly demonstrated in a candid but unabashed admission of Harvard zoologist Richard Lewontin, as recorded by O'Leary:

> We take the side of science in spite of the patent absurdity of some of its constructs, in spite of its failure to fulfill many of its extravagant promises of health and life, and in site of the tolerance of the scientific community for unsubstantiated just-so stories, because we have a prior commitment to materialism ... we cannot allow a divine foot in the door" (O'Leary: 2004:222).

It appears that in spite of such a fox-terrier commitment there remains little objective and compelling scientific evidence against Intelligent Design theory, except for the manufactured definition of science. For the present, the Intelligent Design research and findings constitute a strong argument for the "intelligence behind design" concept and for the theistic position. This will remain so until other reasons for the important constants in nature are discovered.

Study and Review Question for Chapter Six

1. Describe Intelligent Design in writing to a friend?

2. How did Joseph Addison's poetry aid the development of Intelligent Design?

3. Explain the chicken and the egg relationship.

4. How did a breakthrough in mathematics and biology assist coining the term Intelligent Design?

5. Describe how the "gap theory" of Genesis 1 figures into the ages of the earth.

6. Explain how the compelling evidence of the DNA molecule influenced Sir Antony Flew to renounce atheism?

7. How does the Anthropic Principle effect evolution?

Topics Discussed in Chapter Seven

Creation Defined

Theistic Evolution Defined

Theists for Theistic Evolution

The Attraction of Theistic Evolution

Problems with and Criticism of Theistic Evolution

Ictic *versus* Processive Creation

Consequences of Ignoring Ictic *versus* Processive

Creationists Oppose Theistic Evolution

Study and Review Questions

THEISTIC EVOLUTION

Creation Defined

Creation is a theological term that refers to the belief that God's actions constitute a framework within which all empirical data are to be interpreted. It is of importance to appreciate that the term "creation" does not refer exclusively to a single methodology used by the Creator in producing biological diversity. The concept of creation is therefore not the nemesis of all hypotheses of evolutionary theory. White and White speak to this issue:

> Within this biblical framework the term "creation" refers not to a particular mechanism for explaining the origins of biological diversity, but to the relationship between God and everything that exists ... The concept of "creation" is not therefore in any sense a rival to the biological theory of evolution ... "Creation" is not therefore a scientific term at all and makes no pretense to be – rather it is a theological term expressing an a priori belief about God's actions, a framework within which all of our scientific observations and descriptions are then interpreted (White & White, 2004: 9).

Christians must be careful in their eagerness to uphold the authority of what God has revealed in His Word, they must face without obscurantism the known and proved facts in the realm of nature. As Verduin stated:

> They (Christians) also share with each other the duty of giving the Bible such right of way as rightfully belongs to it. To do violence knowingly to the data of either of the two "books" (the written book or the book of nature), of which the Belgic Confession speaks in its Art. 2, is serious sin. And to

be complacent in the presence of seeming contradictions between the two is extremely irreverent, to say the least (Verduin,1956:2).

It is obvious that the definition of creation offered and favored by any individual will depend on the worldview of the individual concerned and in particular, whether science by definition excludes anything that has even a taint of the supernatural. Thompson described this situation:

> There are two fundamentally different, and diametrically opposed, explanations for the origin of the Universe, the origin of life in that Universe, and the origin of new types of varying life forms. Each of these explanations is a cosmogony – an entire world view, or philosophy, of origins and destinies, of life and its meaning. One of the cosmogonies is known as evolution (often referred to as organic evolution, the theory of evolution, the evolution model, atheistic evolution, etc.). The second and opposing view is creation (often referred to as special creation, the theory of creation, the creation model, etc.) (Thompson, 2001a).

Theistic Evolution Defined

A plethora of publications and source material articles are available on evolution and its associated branches and interpretations but few scientists or Christians appear to be familiar with the term "theistic evolution" (Van Till, 1999:161; Ross, 2006:186; Behe, 2007:229). On the Google search engine, for example, there was only one mention of theistic evolution for every ten about creationism and for every 140 about intelligent design (Collins, 2006: 199).

Theistic Evolution is essentially the position in which an individual believes evolution to be true and at the same time believes that evolution is the method God used in creation It is the belief that God is the Creator but that in His creation He has used the evolutionary process of natural selection to accomplish His ultimate purpose for the human family. The theistic evolution viewpoint is essentially a collection of positions that share some degree of reconciliation of Christian faith with evolutionary biology. It is an attempt to reconcile the blind contingencies of random variation and natural selection with divine purpose by offering what might be termed a "free-will defense" of God as Creator (Van Till, 1999:161; Ross, 2006:186; Behe, 2007:229).

A theistic evolutionist believes in evolution and in God at the same time. However, because so many concepts in theistic evolution are personalized and developed to answer personal needs and queries, it is difficult to formulate one single definition of what it is and what it represents. Some of the definitions in the literature illustrate this difficulty. Willard Young has suggested:

> ...many Christians, including men of science as well as theologians, accommodate the discoveries of their science to their religion by suggesting that God did not create the world (in its present form) supernaturally. Rather, he used natural processes as His "method of creation," and guided evolution to the final realization of man. In this view, Adam's body was produced as a result of the process of evolution, and God then completed His creation of man by giving him an eternal soul. The creation of life as described in Genesis is thus recognized to be essentially poetic, or at least to be flexible enough to permit God wide latitude in His method of creation. This interpretation is generally referred to as "theistic evolution" (Young, 1985:46).

Baxter noted:

> ... the theistic evolutionist holds a position between that of the absolute evolutionist and the creationist. He believes that God created the materials of our universe and then guided and superintended the process by which all life has evolved from the very simplest one-celled form up to the sophisticated forms which we know today. Evolution was God's method of bringing about the present development, though originally the materials were created by God (Baxter, 1971:159).

Theists for Theistic Evolution

Theistic evolution has been accepted by numerous serious, scholarly and well respected Christian believers, such as Asa Gray, a close friend of Darwin, and

Theodosius Dobzhansky, who has been called the twentieth-century architect of evolutionary theory. A number of well-respected, present-day scholars who are Christians also favour the theistic evolution viewpoint. Many Christians, including Pope Paul II, and scholars in non-Christian religions, such as Hindus and Moslems, accept this view and in all likelihood it was also the view of Maimonides, the highly respected twelfth-century Jewish philosopher, and also the view of Saint Augustine (Numbers, 2006: 34-38; Augustine, 1982). As Jason Dulle pointed out:

> Many Christians have come to adopt some form of evolutionary theory as set forth by naturalistic science. Because the very nature of evolutionary theory excludes the idea of God, those Christians who accept it as scientific fact have to find a way to reconcile their faith in God as creator with a view that completely excludes God's involvement with the cosmos, if not the very existence of God Himself. How can a Christian reconcile a view of origins in which God is creator with a view that claims God is not creator? They have done so by baptizing the theory of evolution with God in an attempt to wed the two together. Rather than believing that purely natural, random, chance processes brought our cosmos into existence and "shaped" it into its present form over billions of years, the process of evolution is said to be guided by God (requiring the intelligent guidance of a spiritual being (Dulle, n.d.).

Although there are numerous variations in the theistic evolution perspective, Francis Collins has given a useful summary of the main tenets:

1.　The universe came into being out of nothingness approximately 14 million years ago.

2.　Despite massive improbabilities, the properties of the universe appear to have been perfectly tuned for life.

3.　While the precise mechanism of the origin of life on earth remains unknown, once life arose, the process of evolution and natural selection permitted the development of biological diversity and complexity over very long periods of time.

4. Once evolution got under way, no special supernatural intervention was required.

5. Humans are part of this process, sharing a common ancestry with the great apes.

6. But humans are also unique in ways that defy evolutionary explanation and point to our spiritual nature. This includes the existence of the Moral Law (the knowledge of right and wrong) and the search for God that characterizes all cultures throughout history. (Collins (2006:200)

Werner Gitt (2006) summarized the basic tenets of theistic evolution and is in agreement with Collins. Another example is Neal Buffaloe, professor of biology at the University of Central Arkansas and a member of the Christian Church (Disciples of Christ). He is on record as having taught his students as follows:

> It is simply a fact that it [evolution] produced that wonder which we know as the human species ... We have sought to show that evolution is not in itself the enemy of Theism, as the creationists mistakenly assume, but rather can reasonably be interpreted as providing support for the doctrine of divine creation (Buffaloe and Murray, 1981:20, as quoted by Thompson, 2001).

The scientist Francis Collins gave what amounts to a "testimony" that has the flavor of Evangelical zeal. It would be difficult for any non-biased individual to doubt the reality of Collins' convictions!

> Theistic evolution is entirely compatible with everything that science teaches us. It is also compatible with the great monotheistic religions of the world. The theistic evolution perspective cannot, of course, prove that God is real, as no logical argument can fully achieve that. But this synthesis has provided for legions of scientists believers a satisfying, consistent, enriching perspective that allows both the scientific and spiritual world views to coexist happily within us. This perspective makes it possible for the scientist-believers to be intellectually fulfilled and

spiritual alive, both worshipping God and using the tools of science to uncover some of the awesome mysteries of His creation (Collins, 2006:210).

Theistic evolutionists have attempted to find a way to reconcile their faith with the Darwinian model of evolution. Willard Young provided a startling example of this trend: in 2005 an open letter circulated among clergy in North America called the "Clergy Letter Project." Coming in short of a full-fledged theological position, the clergy letter sought with success to collect 10,000 signatures from clergy. It attempted to persuade school boards that the creationists and the Intelligent Design voices were not the only religious voices. The letter lucidly demonstrated antagonism to the concept of "creation science" favored by fundamentalist Christians, and argued that a Bible-based Christianity could still endorse the best science. The letter is considered important to the present issue that it is reported in full:

An Open Letter Concerning Religion and Science

Within the community of Christian believers there are areas of dispute and disagreement, including the proper way to interpret Holy Scripture. While virtually all Christians take the Bible seriously and hold it to be authoritative in matters of faith and practice, the overwhelming majority do not read the Bible literally, as they would a science textbook. Many of the beloved stories of the Bible - the Creation, Adam and Eve, Noah and the ark – convey timeless truths about God, human beings, and the proper relationship between Creator and creation, expressed in the only form capable of transmitting these truths from generation to generation. Religious truth is of a different order from scientific truth. Its purpose is not to convey scientific information but to transform hearts.

We the undersigned, Christian clergy from many different traditions, believe that the timeless truths of the bible and the discoveries of modern science may comfortably coexist. We believe that the theory of evolution is a foundational scientific truth, one that has stood up to rigorous scrutiny and upon which much of human knowledge and achievement rests.

To reject this truth is to treat it as "one theory among others" is to deliberately embrace scientific ignorance and transmit such ignorance to our children. We believe that among God's good gifts are human minds capable of critical thought and that the failure to fully employ this gift is a rejection of the will of our Creator. To argue that God's loving plan of salvation for humanity precludes the full employment of the God-given faculty of reason is to attempt to limit God, an act of hubris. We urge the school-board members to preserve the integrity of the science curriculum by affirming the teaching of the theory of evolution as a core component of human knowledge. We ask that science remain science and that religion remain religion, two very different, but complementary, forms of truth.

This is certainly an unusual document and is pregnant with the animosity and the hubris that it decries. Consider, for example:

1. This declaration was made by a group of people allegedly trained in theology and religion but without any claim to expertise in the scientific enterprise;

2. They made a public announcement of their belief in a theory in a field of great scientific complexity;

3. They have already made the judgment that those who disagree with their position have embraced ignorance;

4. Their statement implies that they have knowledge of what constitutes a theory;

5. They have depreciated and attributed ignorance to numerous biologists and scientists who today have expressed doubts about evolution as a credible scientific theory;

6. They imply that anyone who disagrees with them may be guilty of intellectual child abuse;

7. They pontificate that anyone who disagrees with them is lacking in critical thought and acting outside of God's will.

This *amicus curiae* propaganda has the flavor of denominational rivalry and intolerance. It would perhaps have been more appropriate if the authors of this declaration had acted in accordance with their own stated dictum, namely, "Let science remain science, and religion remain religion." What is perhaps even more surprising is that some of those who were convinced by the scientific claims and validity of the Intelligent Design thesis have expressed approval of the theistic evolutionary position. According to Cookson (2005:38), "*The Economist* expressed this phenomenon as follows: 'But if God has a plan for the world and everyone in it … then it is much easier to imagine evolution occurring under divine guidance than as a result of random mutation and the survival of the fittest." This is surprising because one of the major criticisms of the Intelligent Design position is that its advocates are in fact cryptic biblical fundamentalists who are afraid to show their true colors.

Cornelius Hunter pointed out that the philosophic basis of theistic evolution may not be whether God exists, but whether He has an active role in nature. In the evolution theodicy, the creator must be disjoint from creation. For those who find this sort of God acceptable, theistic evolution may be an attractive possibility. Theistic evolution is conceptually diverse, the spectrum stretching from classical theism to the metaphysically diluted theology of Teilhard de Chardin. As Hunter explained:

> Theistic evolution is, if anything, diverse. Thinkers have tried to unite theism and evolution using just about every variety of the two domains. In most cases, however, there is a trade-off between the two. Toward one end of the spectrum the evolution is nearly orthodox and the theism is diluted, while toward the other end the theism is orthodox and the evolution is diluted (Hunter, 2001:166).

An example of this diversity is Theodosius Dobzhansky, who was one of the leading evolutionists of the 20th century. He took the position that evolution is a proven fact, that variation is unguided and random and that there are no final causes. He believed that "evolution does not strive to accomplish any particular purpose or to reach any specific goal except the preservation of life itself. Evolution did not happen according to a predetermined plan" (Dobzhansky, 1955:374).

At the other end of the spectrum stands Benjamin Warfield (1851-1921), an aggressive defender of the Christian faith and perhaps the most surprising supporter of evolutionary theory. He was a 19th century Princeton theologian who declared himself to be a "Darwinian of the purest water." He advocated a theistically directed evolutionary process that included the "constant oversight of God in the whole process, and His occasional supernatural interference for the production of new beginnings by an actual output of creative force, producing something new, i.e., something not included even *in posse* in preceding conditions." (unpublished Lectures on Anthropology, Dec. 1888, cited in Livingstone, 1987:146).

Warfield felt evolutionary theory was probably accurate and merely represented the concept of the evolutionary process being used by God as an instrument in the creative process. He was not only a classical theist but his concept of inspiration strongly influenced fundamentalism and the production of the "Five Fundamentals" of 1910, which has remained the bedrock of the fundamentalist creedal position in America. He stated that "the Scriptures are the joint product of divine and human activities ... The whole Bible is recognized as human ... The whole Bible is recognized as Divine..." (Warfield, 2000:56-57). It is startling that Warfield, as one of the most important influences in the development of fundamentalist theology, was a Darwinian!

Presently Howard Van Till, a supporter of orthodox Reformed doctrine, has taken up the defense of theistic evolution; he feels that evolution aggrandizes the Creator for creating the world using natural laws. He prefers to call his views "the optimally gifted creation" rather than theistic evolution. He is excited about the satisfaction experienced "in celebrating the astounding giftedness of the creation as a manifestation of God's unfathomable creativity and unlimited generosity." He asked his readers to join him "in experiencing the Creator's lordship and transcendence over the creation, not in exceptions to the creation's giftedness, not in claims for evidence of gifts withheld, not in discontinuities, but in every gift of being that God has given to the remarkable creation of which we are an integral part" (Van Till, 1999: 246-247).

Bernard Ramm, a leading and well-respected evangelical apologist, apparently accepted theistic evolution without hesitation. He wrote:

> To this point we have shown that evolution with all necessary qualifications has been adopted into both Catholic and Protestant evangelical theology and has not meant the disruption of either. To charge that evolution is anti-Christian, and that theistic evolution is not a respectable position, is very difficult to make good in view of the evidence we have given (Ramm, 1954: 289-290).

Danish theologian Niels Henrik Gregersen is another example of a theistic evolutionist. He argued for the central idea of theistic evolution, namely, that God created the world to be self-organizing, and supports nature's self-creativity. God designed nature to be self-creative and His self-creativity includes human beings. "We are living in a world which is so designed that we are enabled to live beyond design. The world is graciously designed for the freedom of self-development and co-evolution" (Gregersen, 2002:79).

The Attraction of Theistic Evolution

Many people in the world of religion have come to accept the theory of evolution as part of their personal worldview. Such theologians and scholars include, John Haught, Robert Pennock, Wesley Elsberry and Kenneth Miller Presently this acceptance is the common view in

Europe, and in the United States it appears to be more common (NCSE, 2008a; Miller, 2009).

White and White made the point:

> The adoption of a robust biblical theism ... evacuates evolutionary theory of any kind of philosophical pretensions, least of all any claim to be an argument for a materialistic philosophy. Science is about truth-telling and, if Darwinian evolution is currently the best explanation we have to explain how biological diversity came into being – and biologists think that it is – then we should be at the forefront in telling the truth about God's world (White & White, 2004: 99).

It is true that many Christians, even devout Christians, have been convinced that God created all living organisms by a long process of evolution. The British historian James Moore stated that "with but a few exceptions, the leading Christian thinkers in Britain and America came to terms quite readily with Darwinism and evolution" (Moore, 1979:92).

The American sociologist, George Marsden added that "with the exception of Harvard's Louis Agassiz, virtually every American Protestant zoologist and botanist accepted some form of evolution by the early 1870s" and Asa Gray, an orthodox Presbyterian in belief and professor of natural history at Harvard, had long been a Darwinian confidant, and was one of the privileged few to receive complimentary copies of The Origin of Species (Marsden, 1984:101).

Some Christians appear to have found a degree of refuge from the *angst* of the science-creation dilemma by classifying themselves as 'theistic evolutionists.' Smith reflects that this was the path chosen by the Roman cleric, Teilhard de Chardin.

> They see the whole world of development of life from the amoeba type of cell to homo sapiens, which from the outside looks as if it were spontaneous, as a development which has taken place under the hidden guiding hand of God. Mutations and natural selections are, in their way of thought, God's method for producing His creation. This means that

viewing the whole realm of nature developing upward by mutation followed by natural selection to man and beyond (perhaps point Omega with Teilhard de Chardin) is simply to watch the Creator at work (Wilder-Smith, 1968:167).

A bipolar approach to creation is by no means a novel idea. Even though it is becoming increasingly popular, it goes back as far as Augustine and Aquinas. Wysong noted:

Theistic evolution has been advocated in the past by men like Augustine and Aquinas. Today it is in vogue. It is downright hard to find anyone who does not believe in evolution in one form or another, and it is also difficult to find anyone who does not believe in a creator in one form or another. This hybrid belief has given reprieve to those not wishing to make a total commitment to either side (Wysong, 1976:63).

On this phenomenon, Morris pontificated:

The sad fact is that evolutionism has also deeply affected evangelical schools and churches. After all, even modern ultra-liberal theological schools (e.g., Harvard, Yale) and denominations (e.g., Methodist, Episcopalian) were once orthodox and zealous for the Scriptures. These institutions have traveled down the road of compromise with evolutionary humanism farther than most, but many evangelicals today seem to have embarked on the same icy road, unaware of the dangers ahead and impatient with those who would warn them. Evangelicals (meaning those who accept the inerrant authority of the Bible and believe in the deity of Christ and His substitutionary death and bodily resurrection) generally "dare not call it compromise." And perhaps are not even aware of it. But compromise they have, in many instances. Some have accepted full- blown theistic evolution, but many more believe in either "progressive creation" or "reconstructive creation" (i.e., the so-called Gap Theory) ... The sad truth is that many evangelical leaders, who profess to believe in biblical inerrancy and authority, have also compromised with evolution (Morris, 1989:101,104).

In this theological scourging of those who disagree with him on the question of origins, Morris revealed his lack of knowledge of the significance and ramifications of the so-called "Gap theory." That the pontificating of Morris, however, is not mere personal hyperbole but an accurate representation of the disparities demonstrated in the current creation-evolution schism is clearly reflected in the words, although in themselves mainly inaccurate, of Stanley Beck, of the American Lutheran Church:

> To call himself reasonably well educated and informed, a Christian can hardly afford not to believe in evolution. Evolution, including human evolution, is no longer in contention. Evolution has been demonstrated so thoroughly...even produced experimentally, that it has ceased to be a matter of opinion. And to announce that you do not believe in evolution is as irrational as to announce that you do not believe in electricity (Beck, 1963:316-317).

Many appear to accept the evolutionary hypothesis because they have been convinced that the scientific evidence is strong. Nobel laureate George W. Beadle, for example, stated "One must accept all of evolution or none. And the evidence for organic evolution is overwhelmingly convincing ... Belief in evolution, including the spontaneous origin of life from non-living antecedents, need in no way conflict with religion" (quoted in Buffaloe, 1969:17, 20, 21).

In a symposium at Wheaton College, a school that historically has been a bastion of Fundamentalism or at least Evangelicalism, Walter Hearn stated:

> ... surely we know that processes have been involved in bringing us into existence. Why shudder, then, at the idea that processes were involved in bringing Adam into existence? Granted that we do not know details of the processes, why may we not assume that God did use processes? (Hearn, 1961:42).

Some Christians who accept theistic evolution because they are convinced it is compatible with the Word of God. Albertus Pieters, a well recognized Bible expositor wrote the following in his Notes on Genesis:

> If a Christian is inclined to yield as far as possible to the theory of organic evolution, he can hold that man's body was prepared by God through such a natural process ... In such a conception there is nothing contrary to the Bible (Pieters, 1947: 201).

Other sincere Christians believe the concept of evolution actually glorifies God. Such are apparently convinced this makes God more credible because the evolutionary process is more credible than *ictic* creation. Paul Moody's viewpoint is that it is as possible to worship a God who works though natural laws, slowly evolving life on this planet, as it is to worship God who creates by sudden command (Moody, 1970: 496).

Finally, others believe that it simply does not matter whether one believes in citric creation or theistic creation. Thomas reviewed this position in his book *Facts and Faith*:

> In connection with the study of evolution it is important that we consider the question of theistic evolution or "religious" evolution, which question is a real problem to some people. The reasoning is, that inasmuch as so many people do believe in evolution, what is the use of "making a big fuss about it"? They feel that we might accept some basic principles about evolution and yet hold for the existence of God and for creation in some way – that perhaps God simply used evolution as a means of getting man here (Thomas, 1965:30).

Analysis of the reasons why the concept of theistic evolution appears to be popular and attractive reveals some salient features:

1. Evolution is what many students, including Christian students, have been taught is a scientific fact. Marshall and Sandra Hall, in their book *The Truth: God or Evolution,* conclude:

> In the first place, evolution is what is taught in the schools. At least two, and in some cases three or four generations, have used textbooks that presented it as proved fact. The teachers, who for the most part learned it as truth, pass it on as truth. Students are as thoroughly and surely indoctrinated with the concept of evolution as students have ever been indoctrinated with any unproven belief (Hall, 1974: 10).

2. It is often assumed that to believe in evolution is a sign that you are intelligent and well educated and not a

blue-collar "Funny Fundy." Morris asserts that "the main reason most educated people believe in evolution is simply because they have been told that most educated people believe in evolution" (Morris, 1963:26).

3. Paul Ricci and the Halls emphasize that *ex cathedra* pronouncements by ego ideals support the notion:

> The reliability of evolution not only as a theory but as a principle of understanding is not contested by the vast majority of biologists, geologists, astronomers, and other scientists (Ricci, 1986:172).

> How, then, are people with little or no special knowledge of the various sciences and related subjects to challenge the authorities? It is natural to accept what "experts" say, and most people do (Hall, 1974:10).

4. To believe in theistic evolution may be a useful rationalization when the underlying unconscious motivation is a desire to minimize the claims of God and His moral injunctions. Osborn opines that "in truth, from the earliest stages of Greek thought man has been eager to discover some natural cause of evolution, and to abandon the idea of supernatural intervention in the order of nature" (Osborn, 1918:ix).

5. The idea of special creation is unthinkable and incredible to any intelligent person. "Evolution is unproved and unprovable. We believe it because the only alternative is special creation, and that is unthinkable" (Keith, 1972:73).

6. Some respected Christian thinkers of integrity have examined the evidence and have concluded that evolution is the correct answer to the origins question.

Problems with and Criticism of Theistic Evolution

A number of problems regarding theistic evolution were highlighted by other evangelicals who were antagonistic to its tenets, but often these were not expressed in a Philadelphian spirit. Some of these criticisms included:

1. The concept of theistic evolution is not widely known. It appears that believing scientists on occasion may be reluctant to air their views lest they become the objects of criticism from their fellow scientists or fellow Christians. In addition, few theologians appear to be adequately familiar with the details of theistic evolution. (Sigmund, 2012).

2. Many of the nouns and adjectives used in such a discussion are already loaded with negative connotations. Examples include the words "intelligent," "fundamental," or "designer." (Pigliucci, 2001).

3. Often theistic evolution, not necessarily accurately, is interpreted as doing violence to science or religion or both (Wilkins, 2001: 711–724).

4. Some believers have a difficult time imagining that God would have carried out creation using such an apparently random, potentially heartless, and inefficient process as Darwinian evolution. After all, evolutionists claim that the process is full of "chance" and "random" outcomes. How could God take such chances in producing a human being in His image? (Collins, 2006:205; Rusbult, 2006).

5. The charge has been made that theistic evolution reflects a misrepresentation of a loving God and instead presents a god who utilizes destruction and death.

6. Theistic evolution reintroduces the "God of the Gaps" elements. In evolutionary theory the concept of God is left for those areas which the theory cannot explain. As Jantsch noted:

    > In this way He is reduced to being a "god of the gaps" for those In theistic evolution the only work-place allotted to God is that part of nature which evolution cannot "explain" with the means presently

at its disposal phenomena about which there are doubts. This leads to the view that "God is therefore not absolute, but He Himself has evolved – He is evolution" (Jantsch, 1974: 412).

A similar observation was made by Gitt (1995).

7. The claim is made by Biblical literalists that theistic evolution reduces the words of the Bible to imagery, mythology and poetic license so that what is meant is not what is said. Literalists are adamant that the Biblical account of creation should not be regarded as a parable, poetry, a myth or an allegory, but as actual historical narrative and that the concept of Theistic Evolution undermines the basic way of reading the Bible, as vouched for by Jesus, the prophets and the apostles. Theistic evolution reduces events reported in the Bible to mythical imagery with the result that an understanding of the message of the Bible as being true in word and meaning is lost (Gitt, 1995).

8. Opponents of theistic evolution are convinced that it obliterates the doctrine and experience of sin and the Moral Law. The result is basically that people may do whatever is right in their own eyes (Noebel, 2001:110).

9. Theistic evolution is considered an assault on the doctrine of the Incarnation, a foundational doctrine of the Christian faith, in that it reduces the need for the appearance of a redeemer from sin. "Consideration of evolution inevitably forces us to a critical review … of Christian formulations. This clearly holds for the central Christian concept of the "incarnation" of God (Von Ditfurth, 1984: 21-22).

10. Theistic evolution mythologizes the redemptive work of Christ. Gitt lamented:

> The Bible teaches that the first man's fall into sin was a real event and that this was the direct cause of sin in the world ...Theistic Evolution does not acknowledge Adam as the first man, nor that he was created directly from "the dust of the ground" by God (Genesis 2:7) ...Thus any theological view which mythologizes Adam undermines the biblical basis of Jesus' work of redemption (Gitt, 1995).

11. Theistic evolution marginalizes biblical chronology. The Bible gives a time-scale for history and this underlies a proper understanding of the Bible. Supporters of theistic evolution disregard the biblically given measures of time in favor of evolutionist time-scales involving millions of years, both past and future, for which literalists claim there are no convincing physical evidences (Von Roeschlaub, 1998).

12. Theistic evolution denies purpose. The Bible is an account of purpose. For example:

- Humanity is God's purpose in creation (Genesis 1:27-28).

- Humanity is the purpose of God's plan of redemption (Isaiah 53:5).

- Humanity is the purpose of the mission of God's Son (1 John 4:9).

- We are the purpose of God's inheritance (Titus 3:7).

- Heaven is our destination (1 Peter 1:4).

As Werner Gitt (1995) wrote, "the very thought of purposefulness is anathema to evolutionists." "Evolutionary adaptations never follow a purposeful program, they thus cannot be regarded as teleonomical" (Penzlin, 1987:19).

A basic question remains, namely, can one believe both the Bible and evolutionary theory and concepts? Cookson has noted that "the Vatican, which has often appeared ambivalent in the past, has recently gone out of its way to affirm the compatibility of evolutionary science with the Bible" (Cookson, 2005:28). However, this has not become a required belief for Roman Catholics, and some senior prelates have not accepted this position.

The rage for the acceptance of the theory of evolution is widespread, in spite of the fact that many leading scientists and biologists currently are openly expressing doubts about its scientific validity. Denton, a highly respected molecular biologist and physician, who openly admits his agnosticism, has expressed his doubts that "evolutionary theory is still, as it was in Darwin's time, a highly speculative hypothesis entirely without direct factual support and very far from that self-evident axiom some of its more aggressive advocates would have us believe" (Denton, 1986:77). This popular acclaim and acceptance is perhaps not so much due to scientific validity as it is to the popularizing evangelism of some of its advocates. As has been demonstrated, this was certainly true in the early history of Darwinism.

For the biblical fundamentalist, the problem with theistic evolution is clear. The Bible states that "God said, Let us make man in our image, according to our likeness; let them have dominion over the fish of the sea, over the birds of the air, and over the cattle, over all the earth" (Genesis 1:26). In the biblical text, it appears that there is a clear distinction drawn between the human and the animal world. Earlier statements clearly indicate that mammals, birds and fish were not created in the image of God (verses 20-25). It therefore appears that there is something different about humankind. Taken as a literal statement the biblical narrative, as interpreted by fundamentalists, does not support the notion of evolution as a creator that has shaped dust into people. The text, in addition, carefully points out that sex came from the hands of the Creator and not by an evolutionary process (Genesis 1:28).

An additional difficulty with theistic evolution is that it simply accepts, some would claim rather naïvely, materialistic evolution without giving adequate consideration and weight to all the compelling objections to materialistic science, which includes evolution. For this reason, some Christians who believe the Bible, reject the theistic evolution position because they believe its materialistic presuppositions undermine the Scriptures by (1) destroying the meaning of language, and (2) accepting fallible human science as the arbiter of what the Scriptures mean, or when they are to be considered to be in error. Science, rather than the Holy Spirit, has become the yardstick of hermeneutics. (Larson, 2006: 202; De Young, 2012).

McGrath wisely stated that Augustine was proleptical and anticipated the objections of theists, in order to preserve their theological positions, might fall into the trap of squeezing the biblical text in order to preserve their theological positions. Such exegesis is an attempt to make the text fit ongoing current scientific theory, and, indeed, history reveals that such an attempt was to occur during the Copernican controversies of the late 16th century. Augustine emphasized that in one's approach to the biblical text it is appropriate to consider a variety of interpretations and such must not be a mere reconciliation of biblical revelation with current scientific views. In this way, Christians could consider and learn from the findings and interpretations of science, but still have the freedom to consider other traditional exegetical perspectives. McGrath, reviewing the views of Augustine, puts it beautifully when he adds that the church continued to believe in the infallibility of Scripture and not the infallibility of the interpreters of the text (McGrath, 2009:40).

Gary Schwartz, by no means a fundamentalist evangelical, was convinced that the evidence leads at least to a reasonable hypothesis of theistic evolution. He stated that "at the present time, there is sufficient empirical (evidential) and conceptual (theoretical) reason to hypothesize the existence of 'theistic evolution'" (Schwartz, 2006:234).

David DeWitt is the Director of the Center for Creation Studies and Associate Professor of Biology at Liberty

University, Lynchburg, Virginia, a well regarded bastion of fundamentalist creationist interpretation. As may be expected, he is an ardent classical creationist. In a 1994 article, he explains the reasons why he cannot accept theistic evolution. His explication, summarized below, falls rather short of convincing and sounds more exhortational than exegetical:

1. Theistic evolution is a significant threat to the Christian church and undermines the Christian faith.

2. The Bible says that God created all things by the word of His power in six days.

3. If death and evolution were what God used to create then death is not the "last enemy" (1 Corinthians 15:26), nor is it the wages of sin. If this is the case then what becomes of Jesus Christ, whose very purpose in coming was to break the power of death and pay the penalty for our sins?

4. The question, "Did God really say that He created man from the dust of the ground and not through a process of molecules to man evolution?" sounds very much like the serpent's question, "Did God really say...?"

5. The Bible does not teach the notion of death before sin (DeWitt, 2004).

Jason Dulle pointed to what he believed was the inconsistency of attempting to reconcile evolutionary theory with Christian theology. He concluded his argument by speculating that behind the acceptance of theistic evolution by Christians was the desire to appear academically respectable, and asked how a merging of biblical theology and science can be attempted until there is first of all irrefutable evidence for the validity of the theory of evolution.

> The only reasons to wed evolution and theism is because we find evolution to be an irrefutable fact of science, or have a desire to be accepted as intellectually credible among the scientific community. That evolution is not irrefutable is evi-

denced by the many criticisms leveled against it by philosophers, paleontologists, mathematicians, and even Darwinian scientists themselves (Dulle, n.d.).

Dulle also listed the basic difference between classical evolution and theistic evolution. In Darwinian evolution, nature does the selecting, and such selecting is random and pointless. In theistic evolution, God does the selecting, and such selecting is particular and meaningful. Dulle supported his comparison with a number of quotes from recognized authorities, including Darwin:

> The view that each variation has been providentially arranged seems to me to make Natural Selection entirely superfluous, and indeed takes the whole case of the appearance of new species out of the range of science (Darwin, 2004: 200).

> Darwin in a letter to Sir Charles Lyell, the leading geologist of his day:

> If I were convinced that I required such additions to the theory of natural selection, I would reject it as rubbish ... I would give nothing for the theory of natural selection, if it requires miraculous additions at any one stage of descent (Darwin, 1959: 6-7).

> Richard Dawkins commented on Darwin's remarks as follows:

> In Darwin's view the whole point of the theory of evolution by natural selection was that it provided a non-miraculous account of the existence of complex adaptations ... For Darwin, any evolution that had to be helped over the jumps by God was not evolution at all (Dawkins, 1991: 248-249).

For the fundamentalist literalist the greatest deficit in the theistic evolutionary concept has been enunciated by Wayne House, who expresses concern that the theory of evolution tacitly gives credence to scientific naturalism:

> Theistic evolution plays into the hands of the secularists by making peace, not with evolution, but with the theory of knowledge at the root of the conflict: the only kind of knowl-

edge allowed is scientific ... By adopting theistic evolution and methodological naturalism, one implicitly affirms scientism and its limits on knowledge and thereby contributes, even if unintentionally, to the marginalization of Christianity in the culture (House, 2008:56).

Ictic *versus* Processive Creation

Verduin made extensive use of the terms "ictic" or "irruptive" and "processive" in his discussions of creation. He pointed out that the word "irruption" comes from the Latin *in* and *rumpere,* and literally means an invasion or a breaking into. The word "ictic" comes from the Latin *icere,* and has a history of being used in American theological controversy, but is now used as a synonym for "irruptive" (Verduin, 1956:14-15). McGrath has also pointed out:

> that all involved in these divergent viewpoints could learn from St. Augustine and his refusal to worship at the altar of new scientific theory or to squeeze the biblical text into an acceptable mould or the ex cathedra homilies of the high priests of secularism and their gospel of an excluded Supreme being (McGrath, *2009).*

McGrath also noted that Augustine believed that God brought everything into existence by His creative power instantaneously in a punctiliar fashion and also at the same time, *ab initio* began a process of ongoing creation. Initially God created *ex nihilo,* but at the same time blessed the products of that creation with the capacity to develop. Augustine was adamant that this did not include any idea of random or arbitrary changes within the creation process. He was convinced that the ictic act was indicated in Psalm 33:6-9 and the processive endowment in John 5:17 (McGrath, 2009).

> *By the Word of the Lord the heaven were made,*
> *And all the host of them by the breath of His mouth.*
> *He gathers the waters of the seas together as a heap;*
> *He lays up the deep in storehouses.*
> *Let all the earth fear the Lord;*

Let all the inhabitants of the world stand in awe of him.

For he spoke, and it was done;

He commanded and it stood fast. (Psalm 33: 6-9)

Augustine also saw Processive Creation in the words of Jesus:

But Jesus answered them,

"My Father has been working until now,

And I have been working." (John 5:17)

According to the processive view, God's creative power was not limited to one initial creative act, and God continues to work developmentally in the world. In this way creation continues to unfold its God-given potential. Augustine would not have accepted the notion of random or lawless process in the universe. Darwinian concepts of random variation would have been anathema to Augustine. (McGrath, 2009:39-41.)

In evaluating the theistic evolutionary concept, it is important to recognize, first, that not everything that has been labeled as *creationism* is acceptable to Christian thinking, and second, that not everything that has been called *evolutionism* is objectionable. Evangelical Christians generally have assumed that when the word "creation" is used it must mean *ex nihilo* or "to make something out of nothing." It is true that this is the sense that is often used in Scripture. For example:

In the beginning God created the heaven and the earth (Genesis 1:1).

Through faith we understand that the worlds were framed by the word of God, so that things which are seen were not made of things which do appear (Hebrews 11:3).

The Bible indicates that the creation was not a simple punctiliar and static event and that on occasion the Creator took recourse to materials that were already in existence:

And the Lord formed man out of the dust of the ground, and breathed into his nostrils the breath of life: and man became a living soul (Genesis 2:7).

A number of respected Bible expositors now feel that in order to be in complete agreement with Scripture it is necessary to expand the common definition of creation to include the activity of God with already existing materials and creature-hood. This is what has been termed by theologians as "primary" and "secondary" creation or as "immediate" and "mediate" creation. This distinction between immediate and mediate creation, has often been ignored by evangelicals. In fact, the language of the Reformed Creeds appears also to manifest this confusion and could be improved in this area. Article II of the Belgic Confession could be recast in such a way that it would no longer be possible to construe the "of nothing" with "all creatures" but only with "heaven and earth." As it now stands this Article can be read to conflict with Article XIV, which states that the creature Adam was *not* created "out of nothing." A similar improvement could be made in Lord's Day IX of the Heidelberg Catechism (Verduin, 1956:14).

One of the problems of failing to appreciate the difference between immediate and mediate creation is the treatment given to the concept of time. Following Augustine, who wrote that God created the world *non in tempore sed cum tempore* (not *in* time but *with* time), evangelical theologians generally have tended to treat time as a dimension that began after creation had ended. It appears that here Augustine was wrong, when he considered creation to be an activity that ante-dated time. This is not consistent with biblical revelation, which clearly demonstrates that God's creative activity and the passing of time were contemporary. It is clear that mediate creation continued *in tempore.*

Consequences of Ignoring *Ictic versus Processive*

There is no doubt that, according to biblical revelation, creation also had a processional dimension as well as an ictic or irruptional event. This differentiation clarifies the controversy regarding evolution, because orthodox evangelicalism has focused on the ictic dimension while those who are unorthodox and/or scientific have tended to focus on creation as a process. In this connection Verduin opined, that the controversy between "liberalism" and "fundamentalism" in America may best be understood as a tug-of-war between a theology in the signature of process and a theology in the signature of irruption. He wrote:

> Horace Bushnell (1802-1876), often and rightly called "the father of American religious liberalism," wrote Christian Nurture (1847), a book that is a well reasoned attack upon the ictic theology of his times, and also an equally well reasoned defense of the processional dimension of God's redemptive work. Although the forces of ictism resisted Bushnell valiantly, so that Bushnell was deposed, the new theology in the signature of process gradually won out. American fundamentalism in turn is a rebellion against processionalism and a return to the old ictism of pre-liberal times (Verduin, 1956:15).

Another example of this bias is in the evangelical church today. In fundamentalist groups, there is an intense and firm conviction that the moment of being "born again" or "coming alive in Christ" is a moment of irruption of God into the life of an individual. (Ona, 2007:10; Philpott. 2012: 2). This is a moment that the individual will forever remember as the beginning of a new life in Christ. This moment of irruption and the memory of it is so important to many evangelicals that unless one can recall "the day and the hour" of the experience there will be doubts as to the authenticity of their salvation. It is difficult for some in these groups to appreciate that there are some individuals, who are obviously devoted Christians, who cannot point to a specific minute in time and place as the moment when they accepted the Lord. That there are many such individuals is clear and there can be no doubt about their genuine conversion. It becomes clear on reflection that their attraction to Christ involved a process in which they were gradually nearing the point of acceptance and yet they cannot specify a particular moment as the moment of their arrival. This is a clear example of the processive process in regeneration. Personal experience and observation of this author indicates at sometimes the more pertinent issue is ignored, namely, whether such an individual is presently demonstrating evidence of life in Christ, and such evidence may be seen in how one relates to someone who may hold a different theological perspective. (Ona, 2007: 15). Verduin wrote on this "regeneration" phenomenon:

> Theologians who have a predilection for the ictic have insisted that regeneration is immediate, i.e., that it has nothing to do with process and the processional. Happily Reformed theology has refused to go wholly in this direction. While granting that regeneration has a genuinely irruptive dimension and that in it we encounter a divine activity the end result of which is a human being who is like the wind of which we know neither the whence nor the whither, yet authentic Reformed thought has just as certainly kept its eye open for the processional dimension in which exploitation of potential inherent in creaturality was not ruled out. This shows a fine theistic intuition on the part of the Reformed thinkers. (Verduin, 1956:9)

It appears that God is as willing to exploit inherent potentiality in the process dimension as He is in all *Opera dei*. He placed the potential there and it should not surprise us to see God using in mediate creation as He does in the ictic event. The exaltation of the ictic at the expense of the processive has had some dastardly consequences. The derogation of the processive and the exaltation of the irruptional may have resulted in reactions that encouraged the rise of atheistic evolutionism. Verduin (1956:5) notes that Goethe, the great German poet, was an immanentist who appears to have had an eye open for what is processional. However, in Goethe's development and education it appears that his primary exposure was to the ictic. His distaste engendered by this exclusive perspective may have been a factor in his attraction to pantheism. His outrage at the ictic may be seen in his poetry and especially in his poem *Gott, Gemüt und Welt* (Goethe, 1827:1-4):

Was wär' ein Gott, der nur von aussem stiesse,

Im Kreis das All am Finger laufen liesse!

Ihm ziemt's, die Welt im Inneren zu bewegen.

Natur in sich, sich in Natur zu hegen,

So dasz, was in ihm lebt und webt und ist

Nie seine Kraft, nie seinen Geist vermiszt!

My translation:

What was a God who only pushed from outside into the orb;

He let the universe run with the snap of His finger!

It was appropriate for Him to set the world moving

in the inside of nature itself, to maintain His presence in nature,

so that whatever exists intrinsically in Him and "weaves" will

never lack His power or His spirit.

The probability is that in his developmental years, Goethe had been instructed in the orthodoxy against which he rebelled - that we are dealing with a matter of *entweder-oder* and that a choice must be made between the ictic and the processive. His religious milieu stressed the irruptional that then led to a reaction favorable to the processive.

An understanding and appreciation of the different perception of the ictic and the processional raises the possibility that a genuine theistic and biblically- based creationism does not necessarily and exclusively favour the irruptional. The possibility is that God may have created only in installments and that process and potential are both involved in God's handiwork. God could have created an Eve *ex nihilo* but instead He too had recourse to potential. It appears that, in the United States at least, the fundamentalist evangelicals have not yet appreciated the difference between "crisis" and "process" conversion!

In considering the issue of evolution, the question is whether God chose to use advanced forms of plant life as raw material when he created low forms of animal life. Then did He use low-form plant life to create low-form animal life? To date, according to some well trained and recognized scientists, the evidence produced by classical evolutionists remains unconvincing, and a place for the ictic action of God remains. (Denton,1986:77).

Creationists Oppose Theistic Evolution

Many staunch fundamentalist evangelicals take a dim view of theistic evolution, believing that it represents compromise with the enemy and with basic truth. Henry Morris, for example, has claimed that there are always some who "seek to ease the tension by yielding up some of the distinctive aspects of the Bible-founded separation to which they were called. Neither is it surprising then that the same spirit of compromise is moving strongly today among erstwhile Bible-centered Christians" (Morris,1966:6).

Ken Ham, who presently is a foremost apologist for the young earth creationist position, declared that theistic evolution is a compromise belief that God used evolutionary processes to create the universe and life on earth over billions of years. His complaints are as follows: (Ham, 2008: 33-38):

1. "In the theistic evolutionary system God is not the omnipotent Lord of all." This statement is incorrect because many theistic evolutionists are devout orthodox Christians.

2. "Theistic evolution denies the Incarnation." This is another incorrect accusation. Niels Gregersen, for example (Gregersen, 2002), accepts the classical doctrine of the incarnation, as do many other theistic evolutionists.

3. "Theistic evolutionists deny biblical authority." This in many cases is an unfair accusation and

tends to ignore the fact that creationist and theistic evolutionists may simply have a different methods of exegesis and interpretation of the biblical text (Ham, 2008:33-38).

Werner Gitt followed this same path when he enumerated ten dangers of theistic evolution. Unfortunately, the list of reasons he formulated does little to advance the dialog in an intellectual or even spiritual direction. Most of his opinions appear to be built on a polemical 'straw-man' technique which is less than convincing. (Gitt, 1995).

1. <u>Theistic evolution misrepresents the nature of God</u>.

Theistic evolution gives a false representation of the nature of God because death and ghastliness are ascribed to the Creator as principles of creation. (Progressive creationism, likewise, allows for millions of years of death and horror before sin (Gitt, 1995).

A more representative depiction of God is that since He is Sovereign, every methodology He chooses will be righteous. Surely, any competent observer without a cryptic agenda will understand that this righteous and holy sovereign God, in Old Testament history, on occasion permitted and used that which appears to us to be ghastly, cruel and even barbarous. His Word recorded His character and methods, "I am the Lord, I change not" (Mal 3:6).

2. <u>God becomes the God of the Gaps</u>.

In theistic evolution the only workspace allotted to God is that part of nature which evolution cannot "explain" with the means presently at its disposal. In this way He is reduced to being a "god of the gaps" for those phenomena about which we have doubts. This leads to the view that "God is therefore not absolute, but He himself has evolved – He is evolution" (Jantsch, 1979:412).

This is blatantly incorrect. The Bible-believing theistic evolutionist could counter this by pointing out that God as Sovereign is the Creator of all life; who are we to insist that He do this our way? The Creator is He "who quickens all things" (1 Tim 6:13) and to exegete this as indicated that God himself was quickened is the apogee of eisegesis.

3. Denial of central Bible teachings

The doctrine of theistic evolution undermines this basic way of reading the Bible, as vouched for by Jesus, the prophets and the Apostles. Events reported in the Bible are reduced to mythical imagery, and an understanding of the message of the Bible as being true in word and meaning is lost.

This is true only if one majors in concretism and there is denial of different genres in the inspired Word and in particular if figures of speech are not recognized.

4. Loss of the way for finding God

However, evolution knows no sin in the Biblical sense of missing one's purpose (in relation to God). Sin is made meaningless, and that is exactly the opposite of what the Holy Spirit does – He declares sin to be sinful. If sin is seen as a harmless evolutionary factor, then one has lost the key to finding God, which is not resolved by adding "God" to the evolutionary scenario.

From a purely psychological point of view, sin is the practice of narcissism. There is a sense in which the theory of evolution may give a more lucid explanation of the existence of narcissism as a universal character trait than does the theological doctrine of the Fall.

5. The doctrine of God's incarnation is undermined.

The idea of evolution undermines the foundation of our salvation. Evolutionist Hoimar von Ditfurth discusses the incompatibility of Jesus' incarnation with evolutionary thought: "Consideration of evolution inevitably forces us to a critical review ... of Christian formulations. This clearly holds for the central Christian concept of the 'incarnation of God" (von Ditfurth, 1984: 21-22).

Is this not limiting God in the method He would choose to prepare the vessel in which He would choose to be manifested?

6. The biblical basis of Jesus' work of redemption is mythologized.

Theistic evolution does not acknowledge Adam as the first man, nor that he was created directly from "the dust of the ground" by God (Genesis 2:17). Most theistic evolutionists regard the creation account as being merely a mythical tale, albeit with some spiritual significance. However, the sinner Adam and the Saviour Jesus are linked together in the Bible in Romans 5:16-18. Thus any view which mythologizes Adam undermines the biblical basis of Jesus' work of redemption.

Does seeing Adam as a representative of the human race rise to the level of mythology? Is this literary methodology not found in many places in the inspired Word?

7. Loss of biblical chronology

The Bible provides us with a time-scale for history and this underlies a proper understanding of the Bible.

The history of the Old Testament period is at times difficult to unravel. However, to do so involves the genius and results of ongoing historical research and few would state that all problems in this area have been solved. As historical research continues, further modifications of the current views of biblical chronology will change as new knowledge is gained. The Bible was never intended to be a mere history textbook and so the biblical timeline will always be somewhat tentative.

8. Loss of Creation Concepts

Certain essential creation concepts are taught in the Bible. God created matter without using any available material ... Theistic evolution ignores all such biblical creation principles and replaces them with evolutionary notions, thereby contradicting and opposing God's omnipotent acts of creation.

God formed Adam out of the dust of the earth, which was already in existence, and made Eve out of a previously existing Adam!

9. Misrepresentation of Reality

The Bible carries the seal of truth, and all its pronounce-ments are authoritative – whether they deal with ques-tions of faith and salvation, daily living, or matters of scientific importance.

Even theistic evolutionist Christians may be convinced that His Word is truth but this does not necessarily apply to all the interpreters of the Word!

Conclusion

For many Christians, it appears that it would be difficult to conceive of a scenario in which the Bible would support evolution as an alternative creator. This is the reason many Bible-believing Christians, who adhere to a particular world-view, see theistic evolution as impossible or even idolatrous.

> The doctrines of creation and evolution are so strongly divergent that reconciliation is totally impossible. Theistic evolutionists attempt to integrate the two doctrines; how-ever, such syncretism reduces the message of the Bible to insignificance. For the fundamentalist and literalist the conclusion is inevitable that there is no support for theistic evolution in the Bible (Gitt, 1995).

...or, for that matter, in science._

A commonly asked question that naturally follows these various viewpoints in discussions is whether one can be a Bible-believing Christian and an evolutionist at the same time. As might be expected, Neil Marsden, in Creation Magazine, published by Answers in Genesis, proclaimed a resounding negative:

> Christians who try to marry evolutionary teaching, with the billions of years of deep time, to the teachings of the Bible have a problem – the two just do not fit … All these contra-dictions show that evolution and the Bible cannot both be true. If evolution is true and God inspired the Bible, then God got it wrong – He becomes the 'father of lies', which is a total reversal and mockery of truth! Christians need to contend for the faith as never before (Jude 3) and defend the integrity of

God's word, for He is the truth and no liar. There can be no compromise (Marsden, 2006: 36-37).

The whole question of sin, the fall and the existence of evil remains a challenge for the Bible believer, when the question of evolution is considered. Domning cogently referred to this issue:

Of all the puzzles of existence that challenge our religious ideas, none causes more anguish and more crises of faith than suffering, death and evil. From the dawn of human sensibility these have resisted what Leibnitz called theodicy – vindication of the justice of God. Even today, many thinkers and mystics confronted by the suffering of the innocent can only fall silent like Job before the inscrutable mystery of God's ways. (Domning, 2001).

What should be kept in mind in the creation-evolution dialog is the need for absolute integrity by all parties on both sides the divide. Scientists must be willing to accept the standards and canons of pure scientific methodology and Bible believers must be willing to accept facts confirmed by science, and both without rationalization, subterfuge or denial. White emphasized this most important perspective:

The adoption of a robust biblical based theism, however, evacuates evolutionary theory of any kind of philosophical pretensions, least of all any claim to be an argument for a materialistic philosophy. Science is about truth-telling, and, if Darwinian evolution is currently the best explanation we have how biological diversity came into being – and biologists certainly think it is – then we should be at the forefront in telling the truth about God's world. Occasionally writers, even Christian writers, suggest that evolutionary theory is under some kind of crisis within the scientific community ... this is not true. In recent years the theory has been enormously strengthened by the advent of molecular genetics. The theory is so powerful because it links together disparate data from a wide range of scientific disciplines, including zoology, anatomy, biochemistry, molecular biology, geology, paleontology, anthropology and ecology. There is no alternate rival theory to offer at the present time. Christians should therefore be truth-tellers when it comes to accurately describing the convictions of the current generation of bio-logical scientists (White & White, 2004: 99).

White and White are both to be commended for delivering a message that all scientists need to hear, namely, that acceptance of proven facts is an evidence of intellectual integrity and honesty. One must ask, however, if they both lived up to their canons of integrity without noting the following points:

1. Many excellent and well respected scientists do not believe that we do not presently have the best explanation of how diversity came into being.

2. Are there not a significant number of scientists who presently believe that evolutionary theory is presently "under some kind of crisis within the scientific community"?

3. Is it true that recent findings of molecular genetics have "enormously strengthened" evolutionary theory in the understanding of all respected molecular geneticists?

4. Do these authors not accept the fact that there does exist an "alternate rival theory," such as, for example, Intelligent Design, which is worthy of consideration in the minds of some respected scientists?

5. Would it not be more accurate and honest to state that scientists as well as Christians "should therefore be truth-tellers when it comes to accurately describing the convictions of the current generation of biological scientists?"

The evidence reviewed indicates that there are many devout Christian thinkers on both sides of this issue and that because one has a different method of exegesis this should not be used as *ad hominem* fodder in any conceptual disagreement.

Study and Review Questions for Chapter Seven

1. Define creation as a theological term.

2. What is the basic problem in theistic evolution for Christians?

3. From your personal perspective answer the question, "How does the spontaneous origin of life from non-living antecedents, conflict with religion?"

4. What impact does the assault by theistic evolution on Incarnation have on personal salvation?

5. In what way is purposefulness anathema to evolutionists?

6. What are the dangers in attempting to reconcile classical evolution and theistic evolution?

7. Enumerate Gitt's ten dangers of theistic evolution.

Topics Discussed in Chapter Eight

Characteristics of Religion

Evolutionary Theory and the Origin of Religion

Religion and Evolutionary Psychology

The Domain of Religion

Science Defined

Similarities and Contrasts

Study and Review Questions

CREATIONISM AND EVOLUTIONARY THEORY

COMPARED AND CONTRASTED

Precision and specificity in the definition of the terms "religion" and "science" are essential. However, it is not an easy task to achieve precision and specificity in definition for either of these words. In this characteristic, both fields of science and religion manifest similarities. In the present attempt to develop a "compare and contrast" review, the principal focus is on the Christian religion, with a frequent focus on biblical evangelicalism, in order to narrow the concept of religion to workable parameters. As Barbour emphasized:

> Science seems to provide the only reliable pathway to knowledge. Many people view science as objective, universal, rational and based on solid observational evidence. Religion, by contrast, seems to be subjective, parochial, emotional, and based on traditions or authorities that disagree with each other. (Barbour, 1990).

Characteristics of Religion

Personal observation and experience indicates that religion, especially the Christian religion, is characterized by a number of elements usually considered by the adherents to be essential.

1. Belief in God without the necessity of empirical proof.

2. Experimentation is not required.

3. It is a faith-trust system.

4. Refusal to accept the conclusions of the group of believers may result in shunning or excommunication.

5. Has the power to reduce existential angst.

6. There is no dependence on falsification.

7. Often a willingness to accept *ex cathedra* pronouncements by leaders as authoritative.

8. Acceptance of revelation from a supreme being through a sacred text.

9. Belief in what has not been physically demonstrable, through the agency of the hypostasis of faith.

10. Conviction that the message offered has the power to be lifesaving and to result in salvation.

11. Conviction that there is a metaphysical dimension in the universe.

12. May crystallize into obsessive-compulsive fundamentalism with denial of any alternate viewpoint.

13. Some members of the peer group may become a *magisterium or* (teaching authority).

Evolutionary Theory and the Origin of Religion

In understanding the origin of religion, one must seek to understand the origin and development of religious thinking and practice within the parameters of evolution theory. Boyer asked:

> Is religious belief a mere leap in irrationality as many critics assume? Psychology suggests that there may be more to belief than the suspension of reason (Boyer, 2004:28.2).

Spiegel reflected on this development and has considered whether an answer to this query may lie in understanding religion within the parameters of evolutionary theory.

For decades the intellectual descendants of Darwin have pored over the ancient bones and bits of fossils, trying to piece together how fish evolved into men, theorizing about the evolutionary advantage conferred by physical change. And over the past 10 years, a small group of academics have begun to look at religion in the same way: they've started to look at God and the supernatural through the eyes of evolution. (Spiegel, 2010).

Heather Eaton took the position that religion developed from evolutionary roots. She stated that she integrated:

religion into an evolutionary framework, rather than the reverse. The level and type of consciousness out of which religions have come should be considered as a potential within the evolutionary process. Religions are a part of the evolutionary development of humans as a symbolic species, emergent phenomena within human conscious- ness, and later cultural formations. Such an approach affirms that religions, and what they represent in terms of consciousness, are more, rather than less, inherent to humans as a species (Eaton, 2008:41).

Nancey Murphy took the same position and stated:

In short, human brains have evolved to work in various ways that suited us for survival in our early environments. Religious concepts, belief systems, practices, and the rituals are the natural by-products of these cognitive pro- cesses (Murphy, 2008:11).

Vernon Reynolds noted that religion is a universal phenomenon and therefore it may have a survival-friendly basis. He stated:

Religion is a true cultural universal. All known social groups have religious beliefs and practices, and it ap- pears likely that religion is as old as Homo Sapiens. Although the content of particular religions exhibits great diversity cross-culturally, religion as a phenomenon seems to be a fundamental part of the cognitive equip- ment of all modern human populations. It may therefore be worthwhile to consider, as Edward O. Wilson and oth- ers have done, the evolutionary biological basis of religion as a human characteristic (Reynolds, 1986: 105).

Steven Mithen suggested that a principal issue in the development of religion may be the capacity of symbolism, which he considered to be a universal human trait. He wrote:

> The capacity for symbolism is, as far as we know, a unique characteristic of humans; other animals, including the other social primates, do not appear to have the cognitive capacity to mentally process objects and events which are not physically present ... Although the human monopoly of symbolic thought is not above question, it is widely accepted, and no conclusive evidence has yet been found to discredit it. Symbolism is omnipresent in religion, both in the form of mental symbols for religious concepts and in the form of physical representations of supernatural beings or concepts. (Mithen, 1999).

A summary question is whether religion might be in the genes and could be the result of natural selection. It is easily understood that religion may be "survival friendly" because the existence of religious beliefs may provide some advantages for the individuals or groups that hold them. The evidence, however, for such an opinion is still lacking and such opinions are meaningful only if the basic faith-based presuppositions are recognized and accepted as the foundation stones of evolutionary theory as a whole.

Religion and Evolutionary Psychology

Another attempt to understand the origins and development of religion has been through the principles of evolutionary psychology. Since the brain and cognition are influenced by genetics, they must be influenced to some degree by natural selection in a way that has an impact on issues of survival and reproduction. This would explain the development of religion and religious experience early in the history of humanity. This may have occurred by some process of adaptation, although there is no agreement whether this would be by direct genetic linkage or through the modification of other evolved traits (Sois, 2003: 264).

Gould noted Freud's notion that large brain development eventuated in consciousness led to the realization of personal mortality. Religion may have developed to deal with this existential concern (Gould, 1991: 43).

Dawkins postulated the existence of memes [traditions, traditions, ideas, behavior, or style that spreads within a culture] which are cultural in nature and which are similar to genes in that they are influenced by natural selection. These are similar to modules in the brain developed to deal with issues of survival and reproduction. Eventually these modules may have eventuated in concepts of the supernatural and for personal protection (Dawkins, 1996:225).

Dean Hamer, on the basis of psychological, genetic and neurobiological studies, has postulated the existence of a 'God' gene which predisposes an individual towards mystical and or religious experience. There is some evidence that individuals, in which this gene is operative, have a higher degree of optimism which favors continuing survival. Such individuals will possibly be healthier and more likely to have children (Hamer, 2004:211-212).

The Domain of Religion

In the study of religion, as in all other subjects, as a wise Greek has said, "not to know what was done in the world before we were born is always to remain a child" (Oman, 1926:263). For this reason, in order to make any comparison between religion and any other field, it is first necessary to have some clear ideas as to what currently exists in the life and consciousness of humankind. The reaction and attitude toward religion is extremely complicated because there are few areas of cognitive content in which there is more ambivalence. Religion tends to elicit strong affective, even passionate, responses and operates similar the 'all-or-none law' in human physiology. One tends to be either 100% in favour of religion or 100% against it. When it comes to the subject of religion, few have a neutral response. The role and domain of religion cannot be understood without an appreciation of the psychological function it fulfils and, as much as is possible, without the pollution of subjective psychological impediments. As Oman stated:

> We cannot know an environment without interest in it, and we cannot know it is a reality without that interest being concerned to know the truth about it. Moreover, a study which lacks interest in its own sphere exposes us to the still more serious danger of confusing the subject with the things in which we are interested, because, not being able to occupy ourselves long with what does not interest us, we must introduce what does, however irrelevant it may be (Oman, 1926:263).

Even a cursory examination of religion reveals that **religion** is often confused with **ritual**, rather than cognition and affect dimensions. For many people the immediate association to the concept of religion is that it is some type of Aeonian (everlasting) fire insurance related more to a perceived afterlife than to present day needs, experiences and functioning. There can be no doubt that this is a significant and legitimate part of religious experience, but the immediate behavioral and social responses demanded by religion cannot be ignored. To recognize the behavioral responses demanded by religion, however, in no way permits religion to be treated as though it were purely an intellectual exercise or inference from the visible to the invisible or supernatural information made known by certain revelations in the past.

On the other hand, religion has been considered to be essentially conservatism and reaction, which immediately raises the question of the origin of its conservatism. It is true that religion is often conservative in nature; that is, it may be a method of conserving values, ideals, practices and traditions of the past, but religion, as Oman noted:

> ...is also the most revolutionary of all forces. In history, the latter aspect has been at least as prominent as the

former, because it is religion which has produced the faith and courage and self-sacrifice which have combated traditional ideas and customs, and dared, in the face of every kind of social ostracism, to stand alone in defense of what seemed truer and higher (Oman, 1926:263).

It is clear that the conception of what constitutes religion is as wide as the multitudes of its adherents, and in order to understand and appreciate its domain and functions one's conception must be wide enough to include them all. It is therefore necessary to keep in mind the various serious theories of religion, including the possibility of evolutionary factors. The latter possibility will be difficult for biblical fundamentalists to accept even as a possibility.

These theories may be summarized:

1. Religion as belief in gods or observance of cults.

2. Religion as a special type of thought or feeling or acting.

3. Religion as a form of illusion.

4. The factors of experience.

5. The sense of the holy.

6. The judgment of the sacred.

7. The existence of the supernatural.

8. The evolutionary antecedents.

Science Defined

Science may be defined as a system of acquiring knowledge based on empirical procedures or methods in order to organize a body of knowledge gained through research. This enterprise remains a continuing effort to discover and increase knowledge through research. Scientists make observations, record measurable data related to their observations, and analyze the information at hand in order to construct theoretical explanations of the phenomena involved. It may be considered as the cumulative acquisition of knowledge. In these ways science appears to be the antithesis of religion, although the areas of interest for both frequently overlap.

Similarities and Contrasts

The following in summary form is an attempt to compare and contrast a variety of features in both fields of evolution and religion that have already been dealt with in this work. Under the designation (a) will be the characteristics of evolutionary theory and under (b) the characteristics of religion.

1a An important aim of science is to understand the world.

1b An important aim of religion is to understand the meta-physical world.

2a In science knowledge is accrued progressively and developmentally.

2b In religion knowledge is accrued by additional study, insights, archaeological findings, linguistic discoveries, etc.

3a Science is influenced by personal bias, cultural issues and personal subjectivity.

3b Religion is influenced by personal bias, personal psychological needs, cultural background, etc.

4a In science, there must not be confusion between historical studies and material studies.

4b In religion, there must not be confusion between sola scriptura and extra-biblical revelations.

5a Science specifically excludes a metaphysical dimension.

5b Religion specifically includes a metaphysical dimension.

6a Science is composed of structured knowledge based on the intellect as the medium of thought.

6b   Religion is composed of revealed knowledge as interpret-
     ed by the intellect and divine assistance.

**7a   Evolution, as a subdivision of science, must be
     considered historical science and not operational
     science.**

**7b   Religion is a revelational branch of knowledge sup-
     ported by historical science.**

8a   Assumptions and presuppositions are foundational in the
     historical sciences.

8b   Assumptions and presuppositions are foundational in
     religion.

**9a   Changes in sciences are often based on conceptual
     changes.**

**9b   Changes in religion are often based on conceptual
     changes.**

10a In science cultural and personal beliefs influence both
     perception and interpretation of natural phenomena.

10b In religion cultural and personal beliefs influence
     hermeneutics.

11a The methodology of science is as follows:

  1. Examination of the object to be empirically studied.

  2. Development of a theory that explains the data gained by
      observation.

  3. Examination of the theory with knowledge already
      verified.

  4. Continued observations to learn more facts.

  5. Results are rarely absolute because additional
      knowledge may be gained.

  6. Much of scientific theory remains tentative.

11b The methodology of religion is as follows:

  1. A sacred text, human experience and narratives are col-
      lected, studied and analyzed.

2. Observations and findings are collated to develop a hermeneutic.

3. The product of the hermeneutic is then compared to other parts of scripture, history and community narrative.

12a Additional study of the text and sources are continued.

12b Only in cases of specific revelation is a conclusion considered absolute, and even this has to interpreted through a human filter.

13a Much of scientific theory remains tentative.

13b Much of theological interpretation remains tentative.

14a In science, no one can ever be absolutely sure about anything, but there is faith in continued investigation.

14b In religious interpretation, no one can ever be absolutely sure of anything, but there is complete confidence in faith and revelation.

15a In science, it requires faith to be absolutely certain there is no creator.

15b In theology, it requires faith to be absolutely certain there is a creator.

16a Science assumes that the universe is governed by a set of laws.

16b Religion assumes that the universe is governed by a set of laws.

17a There are questions which science will never be able to answer.

17b There are questions which religion will never be able to answer without faith.

18a A motivation for the scientific enterprise is the alleviation of existential angst.

18b A motivation for the development of religion is the alleviation of existential angst.

19a **A motivation for the scientific enterprise is the desire to control the environment so that human genes will propagate, resulting in continued existence.**

19b **A motivation for the development of religion is the desire to find assurance of a continued existence in the afterlife.**

20a In science the need for personal security is sometimes manifested by the fox-terrier-like defensive rigidity of a particular theory or view.

20b In theology the need for personal security if sometimes manifested by the fox-terrier-like defensive rigidity of a particular view or interpretation.

21a **Science looks to an unending continuous acquisition of new information in this physical world.**

21b **Theology looks forward to an unending and continuous experience of bliss in a metaphysical world.**

22a The knowledge gained in science is often based on intuition.

22b The knowledge gained in religion is often based on intuition.

23a **The evolutionary process has never been observed phenomenologically and, therefore, faith and presupposition are required.**

23b **The spiritual dimension has never been observed phenomenologically and, therefore, faith and presupposition are required.**

24a Often the foundation of scientific materialism is the presupposition that naturalism is true, regardless of the scientific evidence.

24b Often the foundation of religious ideas is the presupposition that religious views are true, regardless of the scientific evidence.

25a **A major motivating force in science is the desire for intelligibility in understanding the physical world.**

25b A major motivating force in religion is the desire for intelligibility in understanding both the physical and the metaphysical world.

26a Subjectivity in science will interfere with the epistemic value of those involved.

26b Subjectivity in religion will interfere with the epistemic value of those involved.

27a Criteria useful in evaluating the adequacy of scientific concepts in the search for authentic knowledge:

- Competence
- Integrity
- Sound judgment
- Predictive accuracy, i.e., the ability to explain the current state of affairs
- Internal coherence - does not contain elements that are logically inconsistent with other elements.
- Unifying power - the ability to unify previously considered unrelated findings and integrate them into a comprehensive framework.
- Fertility - the stimulus to further investigation and interpretation.

27b Criteria useful in evaluating the adequacy of religious concepts in the search for authentic knowledge.

- Competence.
- Integrity.
- Sound judgment.
- Predictive accuracy, i.e., the ability to explain the current state of affairs.
- Internal coherence - does not contain elements that are logically inconsistent with other elements.
- Unifying power - the ability to unify previously considered unrelated findings and integrate them into a comprehensive framework.

- Fertility - the stimulus to further investigation and interpretation.

28a In science, denial is a frequent defense of investigators.

28b In religion, denial is a frequent defense of adherents.

29a Science is at times held in the bondage of *ex cathedra* control.

29b Religion is at times held in the bondage of *ex cathedra* control.

30a Science proceeds within the parameters of a chosen world view.

30b Religion proceeds within the parameters of a chosen world view.

31a A unique and final methodology of investigation does not exist in science.

31b A unique and final methodology of hermeneutics does not exist in religion.

32a Science makes statements about the domain of nature.

32b Religion makes statements about the domain of nature.

33a Science seeks knowledge based on the sure foundation of logic and sense.

33b Religion seeks knowledge which is based on or in agreement with infallible Scripture.

34a Science fails to observe the appropriate boundaries of science.

34b Religion fails to observe the appropriate boundaries of science.

35a The scientific materialist starts from science and ends up making broad philosophical claims.

35b The religious biblical literalist starts from theology and ends up making scientific claims.

36a Science claims to be the only reliable path to knowledge of the physical world and to be objective, universal, rational and based on solid observational evidence.

36b Religion claims to be the only reliable path to knowledge of the metaphysical world and to be based on traditions, revelation, human experience, formative scriptures, communal rituals and ethical norms.

37a Science alone is objective, open-minded, universal, cumulative, and progressive.

37b Religion is subjective, closed-minded, parochial, uncritical, resistant to change.

Perhaps one of the most important similarities between evolutionary theory and religion is that both are built around a nucleus of questions regarding origins. This is an issue important in Christianity and is an initial and recurring theme throughout the sacred text of the Hebrew-Greek scriptures. From the beginning to the end, there is an emphasis on the origin and creation of the universe and how this is foundational to the Christian religion and even to religious experience. On the other hand, science in general and evolutionary theory in particular, while recognizing the importance of the issue, generally are reluctant to confront the question of origins. In addition, there is usually a reluctance to admit that science cannot provide any answer to the question. Attempts are often made to deal with the issue by the method of rationalization of 'black-box' provisos and at times with outright hostility (Horgan, 1996:30).

> An additional parameter is that scientific materialism stands at the opposite end of the theological spectrum from biblical literalism (Barbour, 1990).

Both these positions share some of the same characteristics. Both, for example, believe there are serious conflicts between contemporary science and classical religious beliefs. In addition, both seek knowledge with a sure foundation: science, that of logic and sense data, and religion, that of infallible/inspired scripture. Scientific materialism, a fundamental component of science today, makes two basic assertions:

1. The scientific method is the only path to knowledge. This is an epistemological assertion about the characteristic of inquiry and knowledge.

2. Energy/matter is the only fundamental reality in the universe. This is a metaphysical ontological assertion about the characteristics of reality. (Barbour, 1990).

These two assertions are linked by the assumption/ presupposition that the only entities and causes with which science deals are real and that only science can disclose the nature of what is real. In addition, many forms of materialism express reductionism; that is, the claim that the laws and theories of all science are in principle reducible to the laws of physics and chemistry and that the component parts of any system constitute its most fundamental reality. The materialist scientist takes the position that all phenomena will eventually be explained in terms of the actions of material components.

This reductionism is another example of a marked contrast between scientific and religious thinking. Within a Christian worldview, phenomena such as moral behavior cannot be completely reduced to the laws of cellular physiology, chemistry, or physics. If they were (that is, if there were no room for purposive action), it would be difficult to argue that a just God, or anyone else, could hold individual humans morally responsible for their actions. Discussions about evolutionary processes in Christian circles still focus on issues of reductionism. If scientific descriptions of evolutionary causes (for example, genetic and selective) are the only possible levels of description, then it would be hard to argue that God works purposefully in redemption and providence in creation. In both cases, there is no reason to believe that lawfulness at lower levels of explanation precludes genuine agency at higher levels.

Another major distinction between the two fields is the importance of a sacred text of some kind. Even when a 'sacred text' is not officially recognized, the *ex cathedra* pronouncement of a senior well-recognized individual in a leadership position is often common to both fields. This acquiescence is more often than not cryptic rather than explicit and may be the unconscious molding of an individual in the image of another. This to some degree will mean acceptance of the views of the model of identification.

The purposiveness of human behavior, so basic to biblically-based religion, is obvious only from a subjective, first-person point of view; from a more objective standpoint, purposiveness in human agency must be inferred. Evolutionary psychologists (such as Cosmides & Tooby, 2005: 598, 616; Bjorkland, 2008: 180; Mesoudi, 2011:109) as with others in the cognitive sciences, see no compatibility problems between descriptions at neural, cognitive (intentional), and behavioral/functional levels. As with human intentionality, the discovery of more proximal laws of evolution (for example, natural selection) does not preclude the truth or utility of more ultimate levels of explanation (God's agency). Although evolutionary psychologists eschew neurobiological reductionism in favor of a multi-level analysis, when it comes to questions of anthropology, many seem to have opted for a one-level evolutionary reductionism related to questions of cosmology. Such a treatment hardly seems warranted within the evolutionary theory framework, and is ruled out within any theistic worldview. This review and contrast of the two fields of religion and evolutionary theory makes it clear that while there are many important differences and distinctions, both fields often share similar perspectives.

Conclusions

It may be of value to summarize opinions and assertions made in an examination of the contrasts and comparisons between evolutionary theory and religion. An important aim of science is to understand the physical world, while an important aim of religion is to understand the metaphysical world. In science, knowledge is accrued progressively, while religious knowledge is developed by additional study, insights into revelation, archaeological findings and linguistic discoveries. Science is influenced by personal biases, cultural issues and personal subjectivity, while religion is also influenced by personal bias, personal psychological needs and cultural background.

In science, one must be wary of possible confusion between historical studies and material studies. On the other hand, in religion there must not be confusion between *sola scriptura* and extra-biblical revelations. Science specifically excludes a metaphysical dimension while generally religion includes such a component. Science is based on structured knowledge of the intellect as the medium of thought, while religion is composed of revealed knowledge as interpreted by the intellect and divine assistance.

Evolution, as a subdivision of science, is an operational science and not historical science. Religion is a revelation-based branch of knowledge supported by historical science. The methodology of science differs from that of religion in that in science there is an examination of an object to be studied empirically. This leads to the development of a theory that can explain the data gained by observation. The theory is then examined against knowledge that already has been verified. Observation to gain additional facts is continued. The results of these methodological steps are never absolute because new and conflicting knowledge may be gained in the future. For these reasons, much of scientific theory remains tentative. In religion, human experience and narrative are collected, studied, analyzed and compared with a sacred text. Observations and findings are collated to develop a hermeneutic that continues to be compared with other parts of scripture, history and community narrative.

The tentative nature of scientific theory is well recognized. It is also true that much of theological knowledge is also tentative in the sense that as new methods of hermeneutics are developed and new archaeological discoveries are made, changes in the understanding of doctrine may occur. This is not to suggest that changes in basic biblical doctrine do occur, but rather that on occasion new interpretations are developed. An illustration of such a change is the current modification of rigidly formulated dispensational theory into progressive dispensationalism in which scholars, who favour a dispensational hermeneutic, are more easily able to converse with covenant theologians (Blaising & Bock, 1993:9).

The dictates of science rigidly demand the presence of faith to be certain that there is no creator, while religion demands faith to be certain that there is a Creator. On the other hand, both science and religion are in agreement that the universe is governed by a set of laws. It is recognized that without such laws the enterprise of science would be impossible. A difference exists as to the origin of such laws. Another similarity between both fields is that both recognize that there are questions that can never be answered by either discipline.

From a psychoanalytic perspective, it appears that on occasion both science and religion share a similar motivation; namely, the alleviation of the angst of non-being. Secular science proclaims that there is nothing to be anxious about, while religion claims to have the answer to existential angst in the revelation of the hope of the gospel. Faith is mandatory in both fields – in science because the evolutionary process has not been observed phenomenologically, while religion admits that the metaphysical dimension has never been empirically observed and so faith is required. In a similar vein, the foundation of scientific materialism often reflects a presupposition of naturalism regardless of the scientific evidence. A major motivating force in science is the desire for intelligibility in understanding the physical world. A similar motivating force exists in religion; namely, the desire for intelligibility in the understanding of the physical world and the metaphysical world.

Psychological factors, such as subjectivity, are present in both fields and will tend to interfere with the epistemic values of those involved in both enterprises. Another major psychological issue is the appearance of the mechanism of denial in both fields. This tends to result in the ability and reluctance to see what they do not wish to see, because it does not fit their *a priori* notions and favored worldview.

One of the major differences between science and religion is that science concentrates on what can be sensually observed. Science proceeds in an attempt to explain reality by objective, public and repeatable data. Religion proceeds further and asks questions about the existence of beauty and order in the world and the inner experience of life, such as shame, guilt, anxiety and lack of meaning on the one hand and forgiveness, trust and wholeness on the other. Science tends to explain 'how' questions, while religion more often is concerned with 'why' questions related to origins, purpose, meaning and destiny.

In science, the basis of authority is logical coherence and consistency while in religion the final authority is God and revelation, mediated through individuals with understanding who have a gift of enlightenment and insight, all of which are validated in personal experience. Science makes quantitative predictions that can be tested experimentally. On the other hand, because God is transcendent, religion must use symbolic and analogical language to recommend a way of life, to elicit a set of attitudes, to encourage allegiance to particular principles, which are connected with ritual and practice in a worshipping community and which may lead to personal religious experience. (Barbour, 1990).

Study and Review Questions for Chapter Eight

1. Name the basic characteristics of religion.

2. Why is symbolism important to religion?

3. What are "memes?"

4. Define science.

5. This chapter compares and contrasts religion and evolution, chose three (3) sets from the 37 sets, and explain why they were selected.

6. Discuss how evolution is an operational science and not historical science.

Topics Discussed in Chapter Nine

The Definition of Religion

Examples of Definitions

Religion and Health

Non-Religious Religion

Religion and the Ancient Greeks

Freud's and Jung's Views of Religion

Characteristics of Religion

The Essence of Religion

Quasi-religious Dimension of Evolutionary Theory

Study and Review Questions

EVOLUTION AS A SECULAR RELIGION

The Definition of Religion

The most difficult and frustrating experience in religion is the fact that hundreds of definitions have been formulated and none are entirely satisfactory. The following are selections of such definitions culled from the plethora of material found in the literature. The multitude of problems with these definitions is related to the lack of precision in the definition of "religion". Most people entertain their personal favorite definition that they believe is the correct one and are convinced that all other definitions are inadequate or simply wrong. Unfortunately, there does not exist anything approaching a consensus. Therefore, to formulate any definitive answer to the question as to whether evolutionary theory may accurately be labeled as a "religion" it is first necessary to find a satisfactory definition of religion.

Examples of Definitions

Arthur Wickenden (1948:18) admitted that attempts to define religion have been legion and that little is gained from attempting additional definitions. He notes that some authors attempt to base religion in the affective processes of the personality while others focus on the intellect or the will. He concludes that the essence of religion will not found exclusively in one of these areas, but in a synthesis of them. He stated:

> Religion cannot be defined adequately in terms of emotional reactions alone, nor as a system of beliefs alone, nor as a way of life alone. All of these are valid and essential expressions of the religious impulse, and religion at its best unites

them all in a harmonious and balanced whole (Wickenden, 1948:18).

The following are some examples of definitions of religion by academics and others reported in primary and secondary sources.

1. Irving Hexham of the University of Calgary in Alberta, Canada, has assembled a useful list of definitions of religion from various authors and theologians, including quotes from James, Hegel and Whitehead (Hexham, 1993:186-187).

William James (1902): "the belief that there is an unseen order, and that our supreme good lies in harmoniously adjusting ourselves thereto."

Alfred North Whitehead (1926): "what the individual does with his own solitariness."

George Hegel: "the knowledge possessed by the finite mind of its nature as absolute mind" (quoted by Schaub, 1923:652).

2. In 1995, subscribers to the newsgroup alt.memetics attempted to define religion. A few of their formulations are summarized as follows:

Scott Hatfield: "a behavior, process or structure whose orientation is at least partially supernatural."

Jerry Moyer: "Religion is a system of beliefs by which a people reduce anxiety over natural phenomena through some means of explication."

3. H. L. Mencken, a celebrated atheist, opined:

Religion's sole function is to give man access to the powers which seem to control his destiny, and its single purpose is to induce those powers to be friendly to him (Mencken, 1946:20).

4. Clifford Geertz defined religion as a cultural system as follows:

A religion is a system of symbols which acts to establish powerful, pervasive, and long-lasting moods and motivations in men by formulating conceptions of a general order of existence and clothing these conceptions with such an aura of factuality that the moods and motivations seem uniquely realistic (Geertz, 1973:90).

5. B. Malinowski opined (in *The Role of Magic and Religion*, 1965) that religion

...relieves anxiety and enhances social integration.

6. Anthony Wallace described religion as:

...a set of rituals, rationalized by myth, which mobilizes supernatural powers for the purpose of achieving or preventing transformations of state in man or nature (Wallace, 1966:107).

7. Hall, Pilgrim, and Cavanagh (1985:11) opined:

Religion is the varied, symbolic expression of, and appropriate response to that which people deliberately affirm as being of unrestricted value for them.

8. Karl Marx (1844) famously stated:

Religion is the sigh of the oppressed creature, the heart of a heartless world, and the soul of soulless conditions. It is the opium of the people ... [Religion is] the self-conscious and self-feeling of man who has either not found himself or has already lost himself again ... the general theory of the world ... its logic in a popular form ... its moral sanction, its solemn completion, its universal ground for consolation and justification. It is the fantastic realization of the human essence.

9. Donald Swenson defined religion in terms of the sacred:

Religion is the individual and social experience of the sacred that is manifested in mythologies, ritual, ethos, and integrated into a collective or organization (Swenson, 1999:69).

10. Paul Connelly also defined religion in terms of the sacred and the spiritual:

Religion originates in an attempt to represent and order beliefs, feelings, imaginings and actions that arise in response to direct experience of the sacred and the spiritual. As this attempt expands in its formulation and elaboration, it becomes a process that creates meaning for itself on a sustaining basis, in terms of both its originating experiences and its own continuing responses. (Connelly, 1996).

Connelly also gives definitions of the terms he uses; the sacred is:

...a mysterious manifestation of power and presence that is experienced as both primordial and transformative, inspiring awe and rapt attention. This is usually an event that represents a break or discontinuity from the ordinary, forcing a re-establishment or recalibration of perspective on the part of the experiencer, but it may also be something seemingly ordinary, repeated exposure to which gradually produces a perception of mysteriously cumulative significance out of proportion to the significance originally invested in it. (Connelly, 1996).

He defined the spiritual as:

a perception of the commonality of mindfulness in the world that shifts the boundaries between self and other, producing a sense of the union of purposes of self and other in confronting the existential questions of life, and providing a mediation of the challenge-response interaction between self and other, one and many, that underlies existential questions. (Connelly, 1996.

11. **Michael York of Bath Spa University College, Bath, UK, defined religion as:**

A shared positing of the identity of and relationship between the world, humanity and the supernatural in terms of meaning assignment, value allocation and validation enactment.(York, 1995).

12. Peter Berger defined religion as:

...the human enterprise by which a sacred cosmos is established *(Berger, 1967:25).*

13. Emile Durkheim (2001:46) stated that religion was:

a unified system of beliefs and practices relative to sacred things. (

14. James Frazer stated that religion was:

...a propitiation or conciliation of powers superior to man which are believed to direct or control the course of nature and human life. (Frazer, 1922:49).

15. Immanuel Kant (1788) opined that religion was:

...the recognition of all our duties as divine commands.

16. Friedrich Schleiermacher (1799) stated that religion was:

..."a feeling for the infinite" and "a feeling of absolute dependence."

17. The members of the Agnosticism/Atheism section on About.com use a different approach; rather than attempting to define religion, they describe some of the factors that are typically found in religion. They developed the following list of characteristics of religion in their search for an acceptable definition:

- Belief in something sacred (for example, gods or other supernatural beings).
- Distinction between sacred and profane objects.
- Ritual acts focused on sacred objects.
- A moral code believed to have a sacred or supernatural basis.
- Characteristically religious feelings (awe, sense of mystery, sense of guilt, adoration), which tend to be aroused in the presence of sacred objects and during the practice of ritual.
- Prayer and other forms of communication with the supernatural.
- A world view, or a general picture of the world as a whole, and the place of the individual therein. This picture contains some specification of an over-all purpose or point of the world and an indication of how the individual fits into it.

- A more or less total organization of one's life based on one's world view.

- Religion is characterized by the development of a social bonding stimulated by a combination of these factors. (Cline, 2012).

The fascinating aspect of these erudite attempted definitions is that, while they all seek to define and explicate religious phenomena, they are so different. However, it should not be surprising that such differences occur, since the formulated definitions reflect personal psychological aspects of the designer –each individual's religion is intensely personal and individually tailored. It is relatively easy to describe religious behavior phenomenologically, but to understand what has produced the affect, behavior and cognition involved is a much more difficult enterprise. James, for example, focuses what for most people is an obvious meaning of religion, namely, that one's behavior reflects one's perception of something supreme in the universe to which humans are related in some mysterious way. The next step is to mollify the anguish of "not-knowing" by creating a defense that results in a sense of comfort and reduction of angst. To say that the *telos* of life is "the supreme good" for one personally is comforting and will also have some impact on others in one's physical or social setting.

Mencken (1946, *vide supra*) took a much more narcissistic perspective and sees religion as that which benefits the devotee's personal life by means of applying to a supreme power for personal benefits. Blessings or advantages for others are not seen as primary or of much importance. Malinowski (1961:25) tends to focus his emphasis on the external effects and the impact of religion on the social milieu and vice versa. Hall *et al.* (1985, *vide supra*) likewise focus on purely intrinsic motivation and on what is exclusively of value to the devotee. This perspective would tend to irritate the sensitivities of biblical Christians whose emphasis in their religion is largely on how they relate to their neighbor. The most promising approach in the understanding of religious phenomena, in the opinion of this student, is the consideration of the unconscious factors operative in the production of myth and ritual and how these are used to express the yearnings of *la condition humaine*.

Religion and Health

One of the fascinating aspects of religion and one that recently has been looked at from a research perspective, is that in some situations religion may have significant impact on an individual's emotional and physical health (Batson *et al.*, 1993:240). It is important to note that, since religion is such a vague concept and almost impossible to define with any degree of precision, religion *qua* religion cannot be tied to any particular influence on health. Many phenomena which some might classify as "religious" may have no effect whatsoever on health, while others, still labeled as "religion", may have a significant effect. Batson *et al.*, for example, in their research focused on three types of religiosity:

1. Extrinsic religiosity – those who use religion as a means to an end.

2. Intrinsic religiosity – those who see religion as an end, for example, as an answer to the problems of life.

3. Quest religiosity – those who think, search and ask questions regarding life and its meaning (Batson et al., 1993:240).

In their research, Batson and his co-workers found a negative relationship between religion and three components of mental health.

- Personal competence and control.
- Self-acceptance and self-actualization, and
- Open-mindedness and flexibility.

On the other hand they concluded:

Intrinsic and quest oriented individuals tend to see mental health benefits from their religious involvement. Extrinsically oriented individuals find that their religious involvement results in a negative influence on their mental health (Batson et al., 1993: 288).

Mueller, *et al.* at the Mayo Clinic also have studied the relationship of religious involvement and spirituality with physical health, mental health, health-related quality of life, and other health issues. They stated:

Most studies have shown that religious involvement and spirituality are associated with better health outcomes, including greater longevity, coping skills, and health-related quality of life (even during terminal illness) and less anxiety, depression and suicide. (Mueller, 2001).

Koenig at Duke University made similar findings. In his research, he has discovered the following:

- Religion influences the rate of recovery from depression in a positive manner.
- Religious attendance increases life expectancy.
- Religion assists in the experience of dying.
- Religion serves as an indicator of mortality.
- Religious participation results in lower systolic blood pressure.
- Religious convictions reduce hospital admissions (Koenig, 1998; Koenig & Larson, 1998; Koenig et al., 1998 a-d; Koenig et al., 1999).

McKevitt went a step beyond, claiming that religion may be beneficial to health. He claims that when religious sentiment dies there is a corresponding increase in psychopathology (McKevitt, 1961:318).

There does not appear, in the personal clinical experience of this researcher or in the relevant literature, to be any claim of a positive effect on either personal physical or psychiatric functioning in those who espouse evolutionary theory.

Non-Religious Religion

Some people do not consider their personal spiritual path to constitute a religion. Some conservative Christians seem to prefer to refer to Christianity as a personal relationship with Christ, rather a religion. In all probability, this is a reaction against the common confusion of relationship and ritual in religious dialog. Those who profess to be agnostic or atheistic often do not regard their convictions to constitute a religion – certainly in any formal sense – but a statement of the lack of belief in a supreme being. Another example is the New Age movement which is sometimes referred to as a "religion." However, it appears to be more a collection of diverse beliefs and practices, from which anyone may choose what gratifies their particular appetite. Another interesting question in this regard is whether there are advantages in being officially labeled as a "religion." If a lifestyle is considered officially to be a religion there may be, for example, tax advantages and other social benefits, which would not be available if the institution in question were considered a lifestyle, even though both "lifestyles" may be essentially similar (Drury, 2004: 8).

Religion and the Ancient Greeks

In any attempt to review the elements of religion, it is of value to consider the ancient Greeks, who in their own way, conscious of a metaphysical dimension. Plato may be considered an example of views during this period. When Plato considered religion, he seemed to focus his ire on those without any religion or those who espoused atheism. In this connection, Drake noted that Plato considered all such impious individuals as members of one of three possible classes. He quoted Plato:

> It is with genuine zeal that Plato deals with the impious, of whom there are three classes. There are atheists who

disbelieve in the gods; those who acknowledge the gods, but think they have no regard for man; and those who imagine that the gods may be bribed by gifts (Drake, 1958:93-94).

Drake believed that Plato had a strong attitude against the impious because they cause serious trouble, and because their impiety arose out of conceit of wisdom. This conceit is actually erroneous beliefs concerning deity. In refutation of the atheists, the argument is advanced that both the order in the universe and the general belief of humans confirm the existence of God and the gods   (Drake, 1958:93-94). Plato obviously had no time for conceited atheists whose self-importance may have prevented them from seeing the obvious! Ancient Greek concepts certainly fulfilled the characteristics already identified as the *sine qua non* of religion!

Freud's and Jung's Views of the Elements of Religion_

It is impossible to engage in an adequate review of the origin and elements of religion without scrutiny of the dynamic psychologists; such as, Freud and Jung. Freud tended to minimize the psychological significance of social and cultural influences and concentrated on analyzing the psychological experiences reported by his patients into the elements of projection and introjection, based on early experiences with the father (Freud, 1961:22).

Pals noted this focus on the part of Freud:

We would rather face things as we did in the sunnier days of our childhood. Then there was always a father to reassure us against the dangers of the storm and the darkness of the night. Then there was always a voice of strength to say that all would be well in the end. As adults, in fact, we all continue to crave that childhood security, though in reality we can no longer have it. Or can we? The voice of religion, says Freud, makes us think that indeed we can. Following the childhood pattern, religious beliefs project onto the external world a God, who through his power dispels the terrors of nature, gives us comfort in the face of death, and rewards us for accepting the moral restrictions imposed by civilization (Pals, 1997:71).

Among behavioral scientists, Jung in his clinical practice has had extensive familiarity with religious issues and has written widely on the subject of religion and religious experience. Mullahy, referring to Jung's *Modern Man in Search of a Soul,* gave a summary of Jung's views:

> Jung regards religion or rather a religious attitude as an element in psychic life the importance of which can hardly be overestimated. He claims that all the patients over thirty-five who consulted him during the last thirty years had the same problem, that of finding a religious outlook on life. Religion for Jung does not mean a dogma or creed. The truly religious person has a kind of deep respect for facts and events and for the person who suffers from them; hence, a respect for the "secret of such a human life." Healing or psychotherapy can also be called a religious problem. The patient needs faith, hope, love and insight. His attitude towards religion, he says, is one of the points of difference between himself and Freud.

> [Jung wrote:] I do not, however, hold myself responsible for the fact that man has, everywhere and always, spontaneously developed religious forms of expression, and that the human psyche from time immemorial has been shot through with religious feelings and ideas. Whoever cannot see this aspect of the human psyche is blind, and whoever chooses to explain it way, or to "enlighten" it away, has no sense of reality (Mullahy, 1948: *149).*

Pals noted:

> For Jung, religion draws on a deep fund of images and ideas that belong collectively to the human race and find expression in mythology, folklore, philosophy, and literature. Religion, like these other endeavors, draws on the resources of this "collective unconscious" not as a form of neurosis but as a healthy expression of true and deep humanity (Pals, 1997:77).

It is clear that Jung considered religion to be part of the human condition, and much broader than the product of a mere libidinous drive. He also stressed that the presence of religion in an individual is not necessarily a product of psychopathology. In fact, denial of the significance of religion may be evidence of religious awareness!

Characteristics of Religion

Although it is virtually impossible to formulate a precise and satisfactory definition of religion, it is less difficult to describe its phenomenological characteristics. Personal observation and clinical experience has demonstrated that some of the salient characteristics of religion are as follows:

1. Belief in the existence of some type of supernatural being or beings.

2. The *koinonia* of like-minded believers.

3. Participation in some type of rituals which assist in focusing on transcendent values.

4. Differences between sacred and profane objects and/or places.

5. The affective response of awe, mystery or religious feeling in certain situations.

6. A world view which provides structure for living.

7. Development of a moral code which comes from a supernatural entity and which becomes a life compass.

8. Conviction that there is a basic order in the universe which, when recognized and respected, results in harmony in one's life.

9. Reduction of existential *angst* by providing credible answers to the unknown.

10. Enables some degree of personal communication with the higher power/s believed to exist.

11. Makes extensive use of symbols and myths to express the inexpressible and to elevate

unconscious concepts and feelings to the level of consciousness.

12. The practice of *agape* as the model for interpersonal relations.

The Essence of Religion

As previously emphasized, before one would ever be able to deal with the question of the secular but quasi-religious nature of any theory or practice it is first necessary to ask just what religion is and what constitutes its essence. The quintessence or essence of religious experience and practice is closely related to why religion developed in the first place. The usual explanation for the origin of religion is that it provides comfort in the face of stress, explanations of reality that would otherwise be inscrutable, helps to maintain social order and morality, and is a response to the ignorance and superstition that is an attribute of the human condition.

Some scholars in the materialist camp, such as Boyer, see religion as related to evolved neuro-cerebral functioning without the need for any social or additional concepts to produce religious experience (Boyer, 2001:187). Other theorists, such as Freud, view religion as the product of the inner experience of the child, modified by the effects of society and the social milieu in which the individual develops (Freud, 1961).

Christian believers may have some degree of accord with some of these concepts, but they will also see in religion much greater and more important elements. Religion, in the words of the Shorter Catechism, is related to the human purpose in the world, which is "to bring glory to God." This phrase itself needs clarification and explanation.

A common element in both Christian and non-Christian religious experience and practice is that in some way it is a search for a close relationship or communion with the deity. There is an entering into the devotee of some aspect of the deity that formalizes and cements this relationship. In Christian theology, this is the experience of being "born again", or more accurately being born "from above", that is, by an energizing power "from above" (*anothen*, John 3:3). This is the experience of being made or becoming whole. A communal aspect of this religious entering in of God into the human psychic structure is perhaps hinted at in the fact that this "born again" experience described in John 3 as a personal and individual experience, is a reference to an anticipated recrudescence of spiritual life in the Hebrew community. Nicodemus, who was speaking to Jesus not simply as an individual but as a representative of Israel, should have known from Ezekiel, the prophet, that Israel could not enter the kingdom without a new energizing power or spirit (Ezekiel 36:26).

Etymology may assist in understanding just what religion is and what it does. The word "religion" is actually a medical word, at least etymologically. It comes from the Latin infinitive *religare* that also gives us the English word "ligament". A ligament in anatomy is a structure that joins one structure to another. In this context, I am suggesting that the notion implied in the word is that of an individual being joined or re-joined to something or someone else. Thus, in Freudian psychoanalysis maturity or wholeness is closely related to an individual being joined to his own projections and reintegrating these within his psychic apparatus (Pals, 1997:71). In the analytic psychology of Jung, the ultimate of wholeness is the rejoining of an individual with his own unconscious, especially his collective unconscious (Pals, 1997:77). Within the social theory of Fromm, maturity and health are related to the rejoining of an individual to others within the social matrix (Fromm, 1941:36). In each of these cases, the idea is that of a disruption which has required some type of rejoining. This is the essence of the religious experience. It appears that the "essence" of religion involves a basic element, namely the existential angst associated with the threat of non-being.

This thought appears to be universal in human experience and is demonstrated not only in the idea of death but also in much of human psychopathology. It is fair to say that the most prized possession humans possess is the experience of consciousness. In consciousness, "I" resides and exists and this is entirely different and separate from one's physical body. It is not uncommon in human psychopathology, to see patients with ego difficulties, who are afraid to go to sleep because they are unsure if they will wake up again and regain consciousness.

This experience in the human occurs in all ages, even in children, who frequently call for numerous drinks or make a variety of excuses to postpone the feared moment of loss of consciousness. It is, therefore, reasonable to suggest that "religion" cognitively and behaviorally has been adapted as a defense to deal with and control this dysphoria. Then developmentally from this foundation of religious practice and experience a multitude of additional psychological and cultural elements will be added later as modifications of the original defense and this in turn helps to explain the plethora of different religious beliefs and practices found among humans historically and contemporaneously.

An additional element in this defense against existential angst is the necessity for outside assistance in the resolution of the problem. At this point, the need for a superintending and powerful figure becomes important. This notion of "G/god" first arises in the child whose initial experience of a powerful and nurturing image is the mother that will begin to be introjected, even as the infant swallows a part of the mother, namely her milk. My suggestion is that this figure then becomes the model and prototype of the concept of "G/god" which will develop throughout the years of childhood and which at about the age of four will begin to be modified in many significant ways through the absorption of the image of the father.

It is clear, at least in the opinion of this researcher, that many additional factors and steps occur in this process. It is fascinating to note that even if the mother is a security provider the infant later may find it difficult to deal with the experience of a harsh paternal figure, as he proceeds along additional developmental steps. If this should occur in an individual who, for example, grows up in a fundamentalist Christian environment, he probably will have a predilection to being attracted to Armenian theology rather than that of the Calvinist variety, and vice versa. Thus depending on the particular experience in the life of the individual in question, a whole plethora of beliefs and rituals may develop to augment the basic defense. In this connection it would be fascinating to explore why humanists turn out as they do and what specific psychological influences and experiences may have been formative.

Wickenden examined the essential motivating forces in the development of religion. He points out that many people engage in religious activity because it is the commonly accepted "thing to do" in their particular culture or community. Religion is used to give a sense of belonging and to gain a feeling of social approbation. He points out that as narcissistically oriented creatures we all tend to worship to some degree "at the shrine of the God of Recognition" in a search for personal recognition. For others, especially in former generations, religion is akin to an "insurance policy" which deals with the fear of consequences of behavior. At times religion is a manifestation of expediency in moments of severe stress and difficulty. At such times, it is comforting to be in a positive relationship with those superhuman forces that could come to our assistance and provide help to deal with the immediate crisis. Another motivating factor in some adherents to religion is that religion is seen as a possible escape from the intolerable realities of life. Escape into some dream world or cloistered protection appears to offer comforting advantages (Wickenden, 1948:18).

Quasi-religious Dimension of Evolutionary Theory_

In evolutionary literature, there exist a plethora of admissions by evolutionists and, on the other hand, assertions by anti-evolutionists, regarding the secular religious nature of evolutionary theory (Huxley, 1903:241; Matthews, 1971: x, xi; Birch & Ehrlich, 1967). One of the claims of anti-evolutionists is that Darwinian theory has become a type of secular religion and is presently more than just a scientific theory (Bahnsen, 1974:89). Harrison makes a lucid assertion in this regard. "Evolution is sometimes the key mythological element in a philosophy that functions as a virtual religion" (Harrison, 1974:1007; Lipson,1980:138) Supporters of evolutionary theory, however, refuse to accept this criticism and claim it is simply another rhetorical trick practiced by anti-science biblical literalists (e.g., Gefter, 2009:22-35). It may be surprising that support for the notion that evolutionary theory is a type of secular religion comes not only from committed biblical literalists, but also from a number of prominent evolutionary scientists.

There are a number of statements in the professional literature that suggest the evolutionary theory is faith-based and rises to the level of a secular religion. It is suggested, that the following questions should be asked before any answer to the question as to whether evolution is a secular religion is proposed. These questions have been raised in response to specific statements made in the literature.

1. Is it a reasonable suggestion that evolutionary theory is science or faith?

The idea that evolutionary theory is a faith was expressed by Matthews in the introduction to no less an authoritative tome than Darwin's *The Origin of Species*. He stated that the theory of evolution:

> ...forms a satisfactory faith on which to base our interpretation of nature ... The fact of evolution is the backbone of biology, and is in the peculiar position of being a science

founded on an improved theory ... is it then science or faith? (Matthews, 1971: x, xi, xxii).

A reasonable question that may be asked is: Did More go too far when he claimed that faith is actually the very foundation of Darwin's evolutionary theory?

The more one studies paleontology, the more certain one becomes that evolution is based on faith alone... exactly the same sort of faith which is necessary to have when one encounters the great mysteries of religion (More, 1925:160).

2. Is Evolution more than a theory?

Ruse made the following unambiguous statement:

In major respects, this is precisely what it is. It is a silly claim that a naturalistic theory of origins leads straight to sexual freedom and other supposed ills of modern society. But, if we wish to deny that evolution is more than just a scientific theory, the creationists have a point (Ruse, 2003: 1523).

3. Is Darwinism an ecumenical religion?

[Evolution] ... is a full-fledged alternative to Christianity... Revolution is a religion. This was true of evolution in the beginning, and it is true of evolution today (Ruse 2000, May 13: B 3).

In fact subsequent to the publication of Darwin's book "Origin of Species" evolution became, in a sense, a scientific religion; almost all scientists have accepted it and many are prepared to "bend their observations to fit with it ...
To my mind, the theory does not stand up at all ... If living matter is not, then, caused by the interplay of atoms, natural forces, and radiation, how has it come into being?...
I think, however, that we must go further than this and admit that the only acceptable explanation is Creation. I know that this is anathema to physicists, as indeed it is to me, but we must not reject a theory that we do not like if the experimental evidence supports it (Lipson, 1980:138).

Huxley and Spencer, who were both very instrumental in the proclamation of the new gospel of evolution, felt that the theory would be useful in the developing opposition to the established church regarding social issues and that even new "cathedrals", namely natural history museums, of this secular religion would be advantageous.

> Evolution had no immediate payoff. Learning phylogenies did not cure the belly ache, and it was still a bit too daring for regular classroom instruction. But Huxley could see a place for evolution. The chief ideological support of those who opposed the reformers – the landowners, the squires, the generals, and the others – came from the Anglican Church. Hence, Huxley saw the need to found his own church, and evolution was the ideal cornerstone. It offered a story of origins, one that (thanks to progress) puts humans at the center and top and that could even provide moral messages. The philosopher Herbert Spencer was a great help here. He was ever ready to urge his fellow Victorians that the way to true virtue lies through progress, which come from promoting a struggle in society as well as in biology – a laissez-faire socioeconomic philosophy. Thus, evolution had its commandments no less than did Christianity ... he even aided the funding of new cathedrals of evolution, later known as natural history museums (Ruse, 2003:1523-1524).

4. Is Evolutionary Theory a Powerful Myth?

A more contemporary but major evolutionary theorist is Edward O. Wilson, who opined that even though evolutionary theory was a myth, it was ready to take over Christianity and demonstrate that religious experience is a totally materialist phenomenon.

> The final decisive edge enjoyed by scientific naturalism will come from its capacity to explain traditional religion, its chief competition, as a wholly material phenomenon. Theology is not likely to survive as an independent intellectual discipline (Wilson, 1978: 192).

On this same issue, Eiseley opined as follows:

> With the failure of these many efforts, science was left in the somewhat embarrassing position of having to postulate theories of living organisms which it could not demonstrate.

After having chided the theologian for his reliance on myth and miracle, science found itself in the inevitable position of having to create a mythology of its own (Eiseley, 1957:199).

5. Did Evolutionary theory fabricate a deity?

Roszak points out the irony in evolutionary theory:

The irony is devastating. The main purpose of Darwinism was to drive every last trace of an incredible God from biology. But the Theory [of evolution] replaces God with an even more incredible deity – omnipotent chance (Roszak, 1975: 101-102).

6. Does Darwinism make nature the creator of life?

Biogenesis is the theory that life originated from nonlife one day when some sand and seawater changed itself into a living being. It is accepted by faith, for there is no evidence to support such an idea. It is therefore a matter of faith, on the part of the biologist, that biogenesis did occur and he can choose whatever method of biogenesis happens to suit him personally; the evidence of what did happen is not available   (Kerkut,1960: 150).

7. Does evolution have the power to reduce existential anguish, as does religion?

[Evolution] is a religion of science that Darwinism chiefly held, and holds over men's minds (*Grene*, 1959: 48).

8. Does Darwinism have its own dogma?

Our theory of evolution has become…one which cannot be refuted by any possible observations. Every conceivable observation can be fitted into it…No one can think of ways in which to test it. Ideas without basis or based on a few laboratory experiments……have attained currency far beyond their validity. They have become part of an evolutionary dogma accepted by most of us as part of our training (Birch, 1967: 349).

The theory of evolution is impossible. At base, in spite of appearances, no one any longer believes in it … Evolution is a kind of dogma, which they believe (Lemoine, 1937: 6).

I agree that Darwinism contains wicked lies; it is not a "natural law" formulated on the basis of factual evidence, but a dogma dominating social philosophy in the last century (Hsu, 1986: 730).

In this connection, it is worthy of note that Karl Popper warns of the danger of an entrenched dogma:

A theory, even a scientific theory, may become an intellectual fashion, a   substitute for religion, an entrenched dogma. This has certainly been true of evolutionary theory (Patterson, 1977: 150).

9. Are miracles an accepted but cryptic part of Darwinian lore?

If complex organisms ever did evolve from simpler ones, the process took place contrary to the laws of nature, and must have involved what may rightly be termed the miraculous (Clark, 1943: 63).

In the same vein, Sullivan has pointed out that the continuum of inorganic material to life remains a faith-based presupposition and is essential to evolution: "The hypothesis that life has developed from inorganic matter, is, at present, still an article of faith" (Sullivan, 1933:95). Compare this with Kerjut's assertion: "It is a matter of faith, on the part of the biologist, that biogenesis did occur" (Kerkut, 1960:150).

10. Has Darwinism made a claim for its own ecclesiastical status?

Darwinism has also claimed its own ecclesiastical status as an ecumenical religion. Lipson wrote, "In fact, subsequent to the publication of Darwin's book *Origin of Species*, evolution became, in a sense, a scientific religion" (Lipson, 1980: 138). Does this "religious" body insist on orthodoxy?

The modified but still characteristically Darwinian theory has itself become an orthodoxy, preached by adherents with religious fervor, and doubted, they feel, by only a few muddlers imperfect in scientific faith (*Grene*, 1959: 49).

11. Does Darwinism evoke cognitive rigidity that prevents adequate hermeneutics?

What is at stake is not the validity of the Darwinian theory itself, but of the approach of science that it has come to represent. The peculiar form of consensus the theory wields has produced a premature closure of inquiry in several branches of biology, and even if this is to be expected in "normal science", such a dogmatic approach does not appear healthy (Brady, 1982:79, 96).

12. Does Darwinism evoke intense religious-like affect?

The facts must mould the theories, not the theories the facts ... I am most critical of my biologist friends in this matter. Try telling a biologist that, impartially judged among other accepted theories of science, such as the theory of relativity, it seems to you that the theory of natural selection has a very uncertain hypothetical status, and watch his reaction. I'll bet you that he gets red in the face. This is "religion" not "science" with him (Burton, 1957: 2).

13. Does Darwinism demand adherence to a sacerdotal elite?

Darwinism is a creed not only with scientists committed to document the all purpose role of natural selection. It is a creed with masses of people who have at best a vague notion of the mechanism of evolution as proposed by Darwin, let alone as further complicated by his successors (Bird, 1991: 108).

14. Was Darwin elevated to a sacerdotal position?

By the 1870s, Darwin was an international celebrity. Even if people did not believe that they descended from apes, they talked about it – and about Darwin. And for many of those who did believe, Darwin became a kind of secular prophet or high priest ... Total strangers, uninvited and unannounced, would peer from beyond the gate or be turned away by servants at the door. Surveying the scene, Huxley sent Darwin a sketch of a kneeling supplicant paying homage at the shrine of Pope Darwin (Larson, 2006:105).

15. Does Darwinism use the reification of chance, matter and energy in an attempt to remove all belief in God and take over?

The main purpose of Darwinism was to drive every last trace of an incredible god from biology. But the theory replaces God with an even more incredible deity – omnipotent ... Evolution is a sacred object or process in that it becomes endowed with *mysterious and awesome powers (Lessl, 1985:178).*

16. Can Evolutionary theory provide moral impetus?

Darwinism is too cut throat to be the source of moral convictions that bind society together (Holloway, 2006:53).

In view of all these opinions and assertions, it would be quite reasonable to ask how much weight should be given to Huxley's opinion that evolutionary theory is a "religion without revelation."

Wysong has made such an excellent and almost poetic summary of the significance of faith and pre-supposition to evolutionary theory that it is of value to quote it here in full.

Evolution requires plenty of faith;

- A faith in L-proteins that defy chance formation;
- A faith in the formation of DNA codes which, if generated spontaneously, would spell only pandemonium;
- A faith in a primitive environment that, in reality, would fiendishly devour any chemical precursors to life;
- A faith in experiments that prove nothing but for intelligence in the beginning;
- A faith in a primitive ocean that would not thicken, but would only haplessly dilute the chemicals;
- A faith in natural laws of thermodynamics and biogenesis that actually deny the possibility for the spontaneous generation of life;

- A faith in future scientific revelations that, when realized, always seem to present more dilemmas to the evolutionists;
- A faith in improbabilities that treasonously tell two stories – one denying evolution, the other confirming the Creator;
- Faith in transformations that remain fixed;
- Faith in mutations and natural selection that add to a double negative for evolution;
- Faith in fossils that embarrassingly show fixity through time, regular absence of transitional forms and striking testimony to a world-wide water deluge;
- A faith in time which proves to only promote degradation in the absence of mind; and
- Faith in reductionism that ends up reducing the materialist's arguments to zero and forcing the need to invoke a supernatural Creator.

(Wysong, 1976:455).

If one were to collect the testimony of religious people concerning the practical contributions which religion has made to their lives there would soon be an extended and imposing list. There would be, however, no general agreement. In fact, there would be a great deal of disagreement as to what things should be listed as to the credit of religion.

Wickenden, in spite of this lack of consensus, has developed an imposing list of the advantages of religion as a practical and useful contribution to life. He notes that religion:

- Provides comfort in a time of sorrow.
- Affords guidance in meeting the issues of life.
- Releases from fears.
- Ministers hope.
- Increases the joy of living.
- Refreshes drooping spirits.

- Affords moral cleansing.
- Illuminates the problems of life.
- Challenges to adventure.
- Increases personal power.
- Affords superhuman help in a time of human insufficiency.
- Sustains in events of crisis.
- Contributes to poise.
- Induces serenity.
- Ministers to health and healing.
- Increases wealth.
- Makes friendship richer.
- Enables one to live in rich fellowship with the divine.
- Heightens aesthetic appreciations.
- Stimulates the quest for truth.
- Undergirds morality with spiritual sanctions.
- Promises eternal life.
- Provides a scale of values.
- Invests life with meaning.
- Integrates personality around a high purpose.
- Enables one to live with a sense of mission.
- Affords redemption from evil habits and appetites.
- Stimulates unselfishness.
- Breaks down barriers between nationalities, races, and classes.
- Inspires movements for the relief of human misery and suffering.
- Serves as a spur to advancing human culture.
- Increases moral sensitivity.
- Makes people aware of sins and evils to be combated.

(Wickenden, 1939:24-25)

If evolutionary theory has a religious dimension, it would appear reasonable to expect that some of the same or similar advantages might accrue to the adherents of Darwinian theory. What is striking is that it is difficult to discover any specific personal advantages that accrue to individuals from the theory of evolution. Whereas many such benefits are seen to result from religion, it is difficult to find any definitive emotional experience that comes to adherents of evolutional theory. Evolution has brought advantages to the human race through its focus on biological issues such as genetics and ecology. Artificial selection has assisted genetic engineering, in antibiotic development and in computer science (Jäckel *et al.*, 2008:153-157; Fraser, 1958:208-298). All of these have brought significant benefit but do not bring the experience of comfort, unselfishness or moral sensitivities that accompany religion.

Conclusion

This review of definitions, comparisons and contrasts provides convincing evidence that there is no definition of "religion" which is entirely satisfactory, especially for the purpose of research. The definition by any individual or group tends to reflect more the psychological makeup and theological conviction of those involved. In order to achieve a satisfactory answer to the initial question it would, at least in theory, be necessary to administer the same series of questions to each individual or group that proclaims the rightness of their chosen definition of religion. This is consistent with the psychological makeup and needs of individuals. All such needs are intensely personal and in most instances reflect a psychological defense.

Study and Review Questions for Chapter Nine

1. From the definitions of religion presented in this chapter, select the one that best expresses your understanding.

2. From the definitions of religion presented in this chapter, select the one that least expresses your understanding.

3. How does religion produce emotional and physical health?

4. What were the three classes in which Plato placed the impious?

5. Of the 12 characteristics of religion in this chapter, select the four (4) that best expresses your understanding.

6. From Wickenden's list of the advantages of religion, choose the four (4) you consider the most important.

Topics Discussed in Chapter Ten

Conclusion

Study and Review Questions

TENTATIVE DEFINITIONS

Conclusions

This text has offered some answers, many still incomplete and tentative, to the questions initially raised in Chapter One, and at various times throughout the text. In the opinion of this author, continued research in the dimensions of faith and science may be expected and required to continue in the future. As a separate entity, the psychological examination of religious experience remains a work in process. Even a definitive and satisfactory definition of religion remains tentative. Science is also changing by the hour and newer discoveries may well cast light on the complexities of the faith-religion-science dialogue. (Schroeder, 177:55). It should also be kept in mind that any such search for understanding involves knowledge at the level of theory and, therefore any definition, should not be considered complete or static (Theocharis & Psimopoulos, 1987:595).

Just as it is important to define science and religion as specifically as possible, it is also important to scrutinize faith. Here, too, difficulties are evident. It is extremely difficult to explicate just what faith is and to elucidate its metaphysical, epistemological and ethical implications. The concept of faith has a nebulous consistency and different thinkers have different understandings of the powers of human reason, and of the exact role that reason plays in articulating its elements.(ch.4:75,96).

As generally used, the word faith implies a strong belief in a supernatural power that controls human destiny and a conviction of the trustworthiness of such a belief. However, it is something more than a mere formal assent to highly speculative dogma about the nature of a god and a divine purpose. It also has an affective component and effect while not violating the believer's intellectual integrity.

Since faith is clearly a dimension of reality it must have a relationship to reason. How does faith accord with reason? Augustine had a conceptual and experimental definition of faith and took the position that rationality and reason were based on abstract thought processes of the mind and not on the empirical information available to the senses. (Randall 1962: 27). Reason may be considered as the human ability to determine what is real by thinking. The Augustinian view is that science involves a rational structure, a system of ideas constituting an intelligible realm. The right method of science is the apprehension of these intelligible ideas. For Augustine the empirical method always takes second place to the cognitive. This was the reason that Augustine espoused Plato's conviction that mathematical principles contained the explanation of human existence. Meditation and cognition would lead to faith and reason and eventually to God. The term 'faith' is also used in a variety of additional ways with somewhat different meanings. It is, for example, used to indicate a body of theological beliefs or a set of propositions that the holders regard as trustworthy truths about God and about their relationship to God. However, an atheist may also have beliefs and convictions that rise to the level of faith. Basic assumptions, for which there is no proof, regarding the nature of the universe may correctly be termed faith.

An essential element of faith, whether in the theological or scientific arena, is its incompleteness. As mentioned above, this lack of completeness mandates a leap of some degree to overcome the distance and opaqueness that prevent faith from becoming knowledge. The result is that the intellectual and evidential basis of faith is capable of being augmented by a process of reflection and investigation in which reason is appropriate. The method of turning beliefs into knowledge involves work, investigation and study in order to gain as much comprehension as possible of the beliefs involved. Faith is not necessarily antagonistic to the empirical enterprise. (Helm. 1997:11)

It has been established that faith does play a role in both religion and science. As a part of the corpus of science, evolutionary theory is built on a foundation of assumptions which are essentially an expression of faith. This is a position that has been established. Religion and evolutionary theory have been compared and contrasted and many similarities and differences have been noted as well as the many areas which tend to overlap.

Whether the focus is on the orientation and viewpoints of naturalism, science or reason, it becomes apparent that the faith-based-presuppositional-assumption is the over-reaching foundation for both evolutionary thinking and for theological thinking, and indeed for all science. Thus those who worship at the altar of natural selection and chance have more in common with those who recognize a supreme being in the universe than either side would like to admit. To fail to recognize the necessity of the faith-based-presuppositional-assumption as foundational to both science and religion is to open the way for a reductionist fallacy.

The final conclusion in this study is that while science and evolutionary theory share many of the same features and characteristics it is presently not appropriate to claim that evolutionary theory is a secular religion, and when this claim is asserted it is worthwhile to analyze the motivation, conscious and unconscious, involved. Scientific and evolutionary theories are ephemeral in nature, and because of the nature of theory, the same is true in the scientific field. It is, therefore, to be expected that research in both areas will continue as a work in progress.

- In the area of the relationship between evolution as a branch of science and religion there are areas in which research would probably prove to be of benefit. Such are as follows:

- Is there any type of personality type which appears to be attracted to this type of research? Findings in this area might help explain questions of bias and subjectivity.

- Which personality characteristic influence the interpretation of observed empirical findings? It should never be assumed that hermeneutics is separate from the personality structure of the interpreter. In this author's experience, this has been amply demonstrated in the theological field.

- Does the researcher approach his or her task with a world view or metaphysical orientation that demands that the definition of science must exclude anything of an extra-natural nature?

- Questions of biblical anthropology and the nature of man as well as the nature of science and knowledge should prove fruitful for further examination.

- The role of and importance of intuition versus the faith experience is a worthwhile area for further study.

- Continued exegesis of Scripture must always be the foundation stone of any dialogue involving religion and any other field, with constant careful observation that *eisegesis* not be mistaken for *exegesis*.

Accepting the fact that there are significant differences of opinion between many of the highly respected workers in this field, it is appropriate to state that it is recognized that scientists on both sides of the divide will tend to engage in apology, in the original sense of the term, for their personal perspectives. The approach for in this work has been a Philadelphian spirit. The views of others with whom one disagrees were respected and considered with few recriminations and hostile accusations. Such an approach is to be considered an essential ingredient of pure science and most certainly the characteristic of those who aspire to be Christ-like. The fact that in spoken and written word both sides have on occasion failed in this regard is not a reason to refuse the high road.

Many highly respected individuals in the academic and scientific communities would claim that the Darwinian theory represents one of the most significant intellectual revolutions in human history. It must be kept in mind that the term 'evolution' is used in a number of different ways and that failure to be clear in how the term is being used may aggravate the differences in any attempted discussion. Darwin did much more than postulate the remarkable biological adaptation of organisms; he continued in the steps of the Renaissance in proposing an explanation that does not rely on any supernatural powers. To a large degree, he succeeded in this Endeavour and effected the secularization of science. However, many highly respected scientists and academicians would not agree with his theoretical conclusions; they point out that while Darwinism is a fascinating theory it remains a theory in that many of its tenets remain faith-based assumptions. However, this difference should not be a hindrance to respectful and diligent dialogue in the interest of the advancement of knowledge. Even though evolutionary theory may be an unproved speculation, it has stimulated much original thinking and still may provide a variety of advances in the general science corpus.

This text considered whether or not adherents of religion and the theory of evolution were dependent on a faith-based presupposition and assumption. The central theoretical argument of the thesis was that belief in the scientific theory of evolution is as dependent upon faith-based assumption and commitment as is religion, though the type and quality of the two respective faith systems may be different and, therefore, worthy of comparison and contrast. The following are the initial questions formulated and the conclusions reached in the review of the literature and the analysis of the various opinions expressed therein.

1. Is it possible to determine whether the essence of the scientific theory of evolution is also based on faith?

Few will have difficulty accepting as fact that religion is built on a foundation of faith. Some who tend to be antagonistic to religion insist that this means that faith is accepting something for which there is no evidence. Christians and especially Christians skilled in the philosophic enterprise, would disagree with this definition and, while willingly admitting that science is a well recognized and accepted "way of knowing" based on experimentation and observation of the natural world, would insist that there are other ways of knowing that are of importance in our personal and social lives, ways which rely on opinion, belief, and factors other than evidence and testing. A significant obstruction in this dialog occurs when a definition of science is presented which arbitrarily and specifically excludes any extra-natural or super-natural possibility.

2. Is the argument that presupposition is a *sine qua non* of all thinking a valid one?

Again, the answer comes down to the definitions involved. It appears reasonable to conclude that since presupposition is the pre-requisite of all science, as has been demonstrated, faith and presupposition may be synonyms, at least in the scientific enterprise. There is incompleteness in faith and assumption, in both the theological and scientific arenas, and therefore the metamorphosis of faith into knowledge requires a 'leap'. This 'leap' does not necessarily exclude empirical observation.

3. What are the principal common features and dissimilarities of the faith dynamic as the foundation for both religion and the scientific theory of evolution?

There is much agreement that science has its own faith-based belief system and that all science proceeds on the assumption that nature is ordered in a rational and intelligible way. Physicists, as they probe the minutiae of the atom, assume in advance that they will find order and so far their presupposition-faith has been justified. Science assumes the universe is governed by dependable, immutable, absolute, universal, mathematical laws of an unspecified origin. In this research it is taken as a given that the prerequisite for the scientific enterprise is conscious or unconscious acceptance of the "faith-based-presuppo-sitional-assumption" that there is rational order in nature. If the natural world were random and lacked order, scientific study would be impossible. However, the reason why the world might be law-governed is ultimately a question not for science but for philosophy. Science at this stage engages *ab initio* in the "faith-based-presuppositional-assumption" that the world is law-governed. Science cannot progress without basic philosophical commitments about the nature of the world and of humanity. Science depends on a consis-tent order and uniformity in nature.

4. On the basis of the above findings, is it possible to describe science as a secular religion?

The conclusion is that it is not appropriate to label evolution as a secular religion, although there are many areas in which evolutionary theory and religion overlap. The problem is that such a comparison cannot be made with any degree of accuracy until an acceptable definition of religion has been formulated. Although many characteristics of religion are similar to characteristics of science and evolu-tionary theory, no precise definition of religion is available. If such should be formulated, then a more precise contrast and comparison of religion and science may be possible. It should be pointed out, however, that the claim by Bible-believing Christians that evolution is a secular religion often appears to be defensive rather than objective. The difficulty in formulating an adequate and satisfactory definition of religion is not unique, because, as this study has demon-strated, to formulate an adequate definition of science is not as simple and straightforward as it might appear on the surface.

Study and Review Question for Chapter Ten

Only One: From the four (4) concluding questions, choose one and provide your best answer in one paragraph.

GLOSSARY OF TECHNICAL TERMS

A priori -- in philosophy denotes something supposed without empirical evidence.

Ab initio -- from the beginning.

Aeonian – everlasting or lasting an immeasurable period of time.

Ad infinitum -- designate a property that repeats in all cases in mathematical proof.

Amicus curiae –friend of the court.

Anothen – can mean "again" or "from above," in the Gospel of John the preferred meaning is "from above."

Anthropic -- relating to humans or the era of human life.

Dysphoria -- a state of feeling unwell or unhappy.

Dysteleology --no final cause from purposeful design.

Entweder-oder – one way or the other..no alternative.

Ephemeral – short-lived, transitory; from the Greek "lasting only one day."

Exegeted—past participle of exegete meaning "to lead out" or a critical explanation or interpretation of a text.

Ex cathedra – speaking with the authority derived from one's office or position.

Ex nihilo – out of nothing.

Fideists – reliance on faith alone rather than scientific reasoning or philosophy in questions of religion.

Ictic **creation** – refers to a physiologic state or event such as a seizure. The word originates from the Latin ictus, meaning a blow or a stroke.

Immanentist -- belief that God indwells and operates directly within the universe or nature.

Kerygma – the Greek word for preaching in the New Testament.

Memes -- ideas, behavior, or style that spreads within a culture.

Myth – a traditional attempt to explain the origins of natural phenomena.

Neptunism – is a discredited and obsolete scientific theory of geology.

Presuppositionalism – a school of apologetics that believes that Christian faith is the oly basis for rational thought.

Processive creation -- the belief that God created new forms of life gradually over a period of millions of years.

Progressionist – a person who advocates social, political, or economic progress.

Proleptical -- the anticipation of possible objections in order to answer them in advance.

Qua science -- in the capacity or character of science

Qualia – the subjective or qualitative properties of experiences.

Reductionism - the theory that every complex phenomenon can be explained by analyzing the simplest, most basic mechanisms.

Scientia --knowledge based on demonstrable and reproducible data

Sine qua non – an indispensable and essential action, condition, or ingredient.

Teleonomical - the principle that the body's structures and functions serve an overall purpose, as in assuring the survival of the organism.

Telos - end, purpose or goal.

Uniformitarianism – is the assumption that the same natural laws and processes that operate now have always operated in the universe.

Vide supra -- *a term used to refer a reader to an earlier place in a text.*

ABOUT THE AUTHOR

E. Basil Jackson, MD, JD, DLitt, PhD is a Distinguished Professor of Psychiatry, Medicine and Law. Born in Ireland, and received his early education there. He studied at the Queen's University of Belfast Medical School and shortly after graduation received a fellowship in psychiatry at the Menninger School of Psychiatry in Topeka, Kansas. After completion of training in Adult Psychiatry, he entered the Child Psychiatry program at the University of Rochester in Rochester, New York. Shortly after completing training as a pediatric psychiatrist, he became Director of Graduate Psychiatric Education at Marquette University School of Medicine in Milwaukee, Wisconsin. The American Board of Psychiatry and Neurology certified Dr. Jackson in Psychiatry, Child Psychiatry and Forensic Psychiatry.

Dr. Jackson also holds certification as a Psychoanalyst and in Addictionology and Compulsive Disorders, practicing these disciplines all of his professional life. He also holds doctorates in theology, law and philosophy and is a member of the Bar of the State of Wisconsin. Presently Dr. Jackson continues to consult in the field of law and psychiatry, but his principal interest lies in the integration of faith and society. He continues to serve various institutions as a graduate professor.

AFTERWORD

JACKSON, EDGAR BASIL, Philosophiae Doctor (Dogmatiek)
NORTH-WEST UNIVERSITY, Potchefstroom, South Africa.

E. Basil Jackson was born in Omagh, Northern Ireland, as the son of Francis and Helena Jackson. Apart from his qualification in Theology, he also qualified in Medicine, Surgery, Psychiatry, Addictionology, Paediatric Psychiatry and Law. His present vocation is a practice of General and Forensic Psychiatry and Law. He is the author of thirty scientific articles and has delivered over seventy papers. He and his wife Leila have a daughter Lorraine who also holds an MD.

In the doctoral thesis, *The Faith Dynamic in Creationism and Evolutionary Theory*, Dr. Jackson examines evolutionary theory and creationism objectively without engaging in an apology for or a criticism of either. He compares the presuppositions and assumptions of both systems and examines the role of faith in religion and in the scientific theory of evolution. The study explores the dichotomy of faith in religion and reason, the ways in which these operate in theories of intelligent design and theistic evolution, and in the question of whether scientific evolutionary theory can be considered to be a secular religion.

The thesis argues that acceptance of the scientific theory of evolution is as dependent upon a faith commitment as is adherence to religion, though the type and quality of the two respective faith systems are very different and therefore worthy of comparison and contrast. According to one of the doctoral examiners, Dr Jackson proved that he is a master of research, that he can interpret and that he can apply the sound methods required of study of this nature. – Prof. S. T. Rochester, NWU

BIBLIOGRAPHY

Abel, Ernest L. 1973. *Ancient Views On The Origin Of Life*. Madison, NJ: Fairleigh Dickinson University Press.

Addison, Joseph. 1983. "The Spacious Firmament" Hymn 103 In *Hymns Ancient & Modern*. New Standard Edition. Norwich: Canterbury Press.

Alexander, Denis. N.D. Creation And Evolution. Http://Www.Bethinking.Org/Science-Christianity/Advanced/Creation-And-Evolution.Htm, accessed 26.8.12.

Allegro, John M. 1970. *The Sacred Mushroom And The Cross*. Garden City, NY: Doubleday.

Anderson, Leith. 2004. A Steady Christian Influence. *Christianity Today* 48(8), 1 August.

Aquinas, Thomas. 1998. *In* Philosophy Of Religion: Selected Readings. William L. Rowe & William J. Wainwright, *Eds*. New York And Oxford: Oxford University Press.

Asimov, Isaac. 1981. *In The Beginning: Science Faces God In The Book Of Genesis*. New York: Crown Publishing.

Asimov, Isaac. I982. Foreword: The Way Of Reason. *In* Paul Levinson, Ed. *Pursuit Of Truth: Essays On The Philosophy Of Karl Popper On The Occasion Of His 80th Birthday*. Atlantic Highlands, Nj: Humanities Press.

Atran, S. 1998. Folk Biology And The Anthropology Of Science. *Behavioural And Brain Sciences* 21(5): 547-609.

Augustine, St. 1961. *Confessions*. Translated By R. S. Pine-Coffin. New York: Penguin.

Augustine, St. 1982. *The Literal Meaning Of Genesis*. Translated By J.H. Taylor. New York: Paulist Press.

Avise, John C. 1998. *The Generic Gods: Evolution And Belief In Human Affairs*. Cambridge, Ma: Harvard University Press.

Ayala, Francisco, 1974. Biological Evolution: Natural Selection Or Random Walk? *American Scientist* 62:700. November-December.

Ayala, Francisco J. 1978. The Mechanisms Of Evolution. *Scientific American* 239(3):56-69. September.

Bahnsen, G.L. 1974. On Worshipping The Creature Rather Than The Creator. *Journal Of Christian Reconstruction* 1: 89.

Bailey, David H. 2011. Is The Bible A Scientific Textbook? Online: Http://
Www.Sciencemeetsreligion.Org/Blog/2011/02/Is-The-Bible-A-
Scientific-Textbook/. Accessed 30 July 2012.

Bales, J. D. And R. T. Clark. 1966. *Why Scientists Accept Evolution?* Grand
Rapids, Mi: Baker Books.

Barbour, Ian G. 1997. *Religion And Science: Historical And Contemporary
Issues*. First Revised Ed. San Francisco: Harper San Francisco.

Barbour, Ian. 1990. *Religion In An Age Of Science*. San Francisco: Harper
And Row.

Barbour, Ian G. 1990. Religion In An Age Of Science. Volume 1 Of Gifford
Lectures 1989-1990. Chapter 1: Ways Of Relating Science And
Religion. Norwich: Scm Press. Online: www.Religion-Online.Org/
Showchapter.Asp?Title=2237&C=2064, Accessed 8.30.12.

Barkow, Jh; Cosmides, L & Tooby, J (Eds). 1995. *The Adapted Mind:
Evolutionary Psychology And File Generation Of Culture*. New
York, Ny: Oup. 666pp.

Barrow, John D., & Frank J. Tipler. 1988. *The Anthropic Cosmological
Principle*. Oxford: Oxford University Press.

Barth, Karl. 1958. *Church Dogmatics*, Vol. 3. Edinburgh: T&T Clark.

Barzun, Jacques. 1959. *Darwin, Marx, Wagner*. 2nd Edition. New York:
Doubleday And Co.

Batson, C. Daniel, Schoenrade, Patricia, And Ventis, W. Larry. 1993.
Religion And The Individual: A Social-Psychological Perspective.
Oxford: Oxford University Press.

Baumgardner, John. 1998. Interview Reported By James Bell. Http://Www2.
Asa3.Org/Archive/Evolution/199802/0063.Html, Accessed 30 July
2012).

Baxter, Batsell Barrett. 1971. *I Believe Because*. Grand Rapids, Mi: Baker
Books.

Beck, Stanley. 1963. Science And Christian Understandings. *Dialog* 2:316-
317, August.

Behe, Michael. 1996. *Darwin's Black Box: The Biochemical Challenge To
Evolution*. New York: The Free Press.

Behe, Michael. 1997. Molecular Machines: Experimental Support
For The Design Inference.   Http://Www.Apologetics.Org/
Molecularmachines/Tabid/99/Default.Aspx Accessed 10 January
2012.

Behe, Michael. 2001. The Modern Intelligent Design Hypothesis. *Philosophia
Christi* (Series 2) 3/1:165-6.

Behe, M. J. 2007. *The Edge Of Evolution*. New York: Free Press.

Bethell, Tom. 2005. *The Politically Incorrect Guide To Science*. Washington, Dc: Regnery Publishing Company.

Berger, Peter. 1967. The Sacred Canopy: Elements Of A Sociological Theory Of Religion. New York: Anchor Books.

Bickel, Bruce And Jantz, Stan. 2008. *Evidence For Faith 101*. Eugene, Or: Harvest Publishers.

Birch, L.C. And *Ehlich,* P.R. 1967. Evolutionary History And Population Biology. *Nature 214: 349 - 352 (22 April).*

Bird, Wendell R. 1991. *The Origin Of Species Revisited: The Theories Of Evolution And Of Abrupt Appearance.* Nashville, Tn: Regency.

Bjorklund, David F., Carlos Hernandez Blasi, Amy K. Gardiner, 2008. When Development Matters: From Evolutionary Psychology To Evolutionary Developmental Psychology. *Anuario De Psicologia* 39/2, 177-192.

Blasing, Craig A., And Darrell L. Bock. 1993. Progressive Dispensationalism. Grand Rapids: Baker Academic.

Borg, Marcus. 2003. The Heart Of Christianity: Rediscovering A Life Of Faith. San Francisco: Harper.

Bottero, J. 2004. *Religion In Ancient Mesopotamia*. Chicago: University Of Chicago Press.

Boyer, Pascal. 2001. Religion Explained: The Human Instincts That Fashion Gods, Spirits And Ancestors. London: Vintage.

Boyer, Pascal. 2004. Why Is Religion Natural? *Skeptical Enquirer* 28.2, March/April. Http://Www.Csicop.Org/Si/Show/Why_Is_Religion_ Natural, Accessed 15 Sept 2012.

Brady, R. 1982. Dogma And Doubt. *Biological Journal Of The Linnean Society* 17:79, 96.

Britton, Karl. 1935. The Truth Of Religious Propositions. *Analysis* 3, No. 1/2: 21-27, October. Http://Www.Jstor.Org/Discover/10.2307/3326614 ?Uid=3737536&Uid=2&Uid=4&Sid=21101149782881. Accessed 4.8.12.

Brockman, John. 1995. *The Third Culture: Beyond The Scientific Revolution.* New York: Simon & Schuster.

Buffaloe, Neal. 1969. God Or Evolution. *Mission,* April.

Buffaloe, Neal, And Patrick Murray. 1981. *Creationism And Evolution*. Little Rock, Ar: The Bookmark.

Bumiller, Elisabeth. 2005. Bush Remarks Roil Debate On Teaching Of Evolution. *New York Times*, 3 August. Barnhart, Joe. 1996. Karl Popper, Philosopher Of Critical Realism. *The Humanist*, 56 (4).

Burgess, Stuart . 2004. *The Origin Of Man*. Leominster: Day One Publications.

Burton, Alan C. 1957. The Human Side Of The Physiologist: Prejudice And Poetry. *Physiologist* 1(1): 1-5.

Calne, Donald B. 1999. *Within Reason: Rationality And Human Behavior.* New York: Pantheon.

Camp, Robert. 1972. Theistic Evolution. *In* Robert Camp, Ed. *A Critical Look At Evolution.* Atlanta, GA: Science And Communication Research And Development Corporation.

Carlson, Richard (Ed.). 2000. *Science And Christianity: Four Views.* Downers Grove, Il: Intervarsity Press.

Carree, Diana. 2010. The Good, The Bad and The Ugly. *Reasons To Believe Newsletter.* Glendora, Ca, July/August. Http://Www. Reasons.Org/Articles/The-Good-The-Bad-And-The-Ugly-Of-One-Liners, Accessed 25.8.2012.

Carroll, William E. 2000. Creation, Evolution, And Thomas Aquinas. *Revue Des Questions Scientifiques* 171 (4): 319-347.

Carter, Brandon. 1974. Large Number Coincidences And The Anthropic Principle In Cosmology. *In* M.S. Longair, Ed., *Confrontation Of Cosmological Theory With Observational Data,* Pp. 291-298. Dordrecht: Reidel.

Cech, Thomas R. 1995. The Origin Of Life And The Value Of Life. *In* Holmes Rolston Iii, Ed., *Biology, Ethics, And The Origins Of Life.* Boston: Jones & Bartlett.

Chambers, Robert. 1994 [1844]. *Vestiges Of The Natural History Of Creation.* Reprint Edition, J. Secord (Ed.). Chicago: University Of Chicago Press.

Chang, Kenneth. 2005. Explaining Life's Complexity, Darwinists And Doubters Clash. *New York Times,* August 22.

Clark, John D. 1976. Some Philosophical Implications Of The Theory Of Evolution. *Origins* 3(1):38–45.

Clark, Robert E.D. 1943. Evolution And Entropy. *Journal Of The Transactions Of The Victoria Institute* 75: 49-72.

Cline, Austin. 2012. Is Evolution A Religion? Is Evolution A Religious Belief System Based On Faith? Http://Atheism.About.Com/Od/ Evolutionreligionreligious/P/Evolutionrelig.Htm, Retrieved 7.2.12.

Cobb, Micah. 2011. Alvin Plantinga's "The Reformed Objection To Natural Theology" (Summary). Http://Micahcobb.Com/Blog/?P=1863, Accessed 6.8.12.

Collins, Francis S. 2003. Faith And The Human Genome. *Perspectives On Science And Christian Faith* 55:142-153.

Collins, Francis S. 2006. *The Language Of God: A Scientist Presents Evidence For Belief.* New York: Free Press.

Collins, C. John. 2006. *Genesis 1-4: A Linguistic, Literary, And Theological Commentary*. Phillipsburg, Nj: P&R Publishing.

Connelly, Paul. 1996. Definition Of Religion And Related Terms. Http://Www.Darc.Org/Connelly/Religion1.Html, Accessed 21 May 2012.

Cookson, Clive. 2005. Evangelicals Converted On The Environment. *The Financial Times*, December 23.

Cornford, F.M. 1965. Pattern Of Ionian Cosmogony. In Munitz, Milton K. (Ed.) *Theories Of The Universe*. New York: The Free Press. Http://Www.Amazon.Com/Theories-Of-The-Universe-Ebook/Dp/B003dygovy#Reader_B003dygovy Accessed 2 April 2012

Cosmides, L. And Tooby, J. 1995. Function To Structure: The Role Of Evolutionary Biology And Computational Theories In Cognitive Neurosciences. In M. Gazzaniga (Ed.), *The Cognitive Neurosciences*. Cambridge, Ma: Mit Press.

Cosmides, L. & J. Tooby. 2005. Neurocognitive Adaptations Designed For Social Exchange. *In* W. Sinnot-Armstrong (Ed.), *Moral Psychology, Vol. 2*. Cambridge, Ma: Mit Press.

Council For Secular Humanism. 1980. A Secular Humanist Declaration. Http://Www.Secularhumanism.Org/Index.Php?Page=Declaration&Section=Main . Accessed 2 April 2012.

Creationwiki Contributors. 2009. Exact And Inexact Science. *Creationwiki, The Encyclopedia Of Creation Science*. Http://Creationwiki.Org/Exact_And_Inexact_Science. Accessed 2 April 2012.

Crick, Francis. 1981. *Life Itself: Its Origin And Nature*. New York: Simon & Schuster.

Darlington, C.D. 1959. The Origin Of Darwinism. *Scientific American* 200:60-65. May.

Darwin, Charles. 1872. *On The Origin Of Species*. 6th ed. London: Collier Macmillan.

Darwin, Charles. 1881. Personal Letter To William Graham, 3 July, 1881. Darwin Correspondence Project. Http://Www.Darwinproject.Ac.Uk/Entry-13230. Accessed 2 August, 2012.

Darwin, Charles. 1895. *On The Origin Of Species*. Facsimile 1st Ed. Cambridge, Ma: Harvard University Press, 1964.

Darwin, Charles. 1958. *The Autobiography Of Charles Darwin*. Edited With Appendix And Notes By His Grand-Daughter Nora Barlow. London: Collins. Online: Http://Darwin-Online.Org.Uk/Content/Frameset?Itemid=F1497&Viewtype=Text&Pageseq=1, Accessed 26 July 2012.

Darwin, Charles. 1959. Letter To C. Lyell, October 11, 1859. *In* Darwin F. (Ed.) *The Life And Letters Of Charles Darwin, Vol. Ii*. New York: Basic Books.

Darwin, C. 1964. *On The Origin Of Species*. Cambridge, Ma: Harvard University Press. 488pp.

Darwin, Charles. 1981. *The Descent Of Man*. Princeton, Nj: Princeton University Press.

Darwin, Charles. 1996. *The Origin Of Species*. Oxford: Oxford University Press.

Darwin, Charles. 2004. Quoted In Nancy Pearcey, *Total Truth: Liberating Christianity From Its Cultural Captivity*. Wheaton, Il: Crossway Books.

Darwin Correspondence Project. Darwin And Design. Retrieved 2009-02-17. Http://Www.Darwinproject.Ac.Uk/Darwin-And-Design-Article

Darwin, Francis, Ed. 1887. *The Life And Letters Of Charles Darwin, Including An Autobiographical Chapter*. London: John Murray.

Davies, Paul. 1983. *God And The New Physics*. New York: Simon And Schuster.

Davies, Paul. 1988. *The Cosmic Blueprint*. New York: Simon & Schuster.

Davis, Percival And Dean Kenyon. 1993. *Of Pandas And People: The Central Question Of Biological Origins*. 2nd Edition. Texas: Foundation For Thought And Ethics.

Dawkins, Richard. 1976. The Selfish Gene. Oxford: Oxford University Press.

Dawkins, Richard. 1996 [1986]. *The Blind Watchmaker*. New York: Norton.

Dawkins, Richard. 2006. *The God Delusion*. New York: Houghton Mifflin.

De Chardin, Pierre Tielhard. 2008. *The Phenomenon Of Man*. New York: Harper.

Dembski, William A. & Jonathan Wells. 2008. *The Design Of Life: Discovering Signs Of Intelligence In Biological Systems*. Dallas, TX: The Foundation For Thought And Ethics.

Dembski, William. 1998. *The Design Inference*. Cambridge: Cambridge University Press.

Dembski, William A. 1999. *Intelligent Design*. Downers Grove, Illinois: Intervarsity Press.

Dennett, Daniel C. 1987. *The Intentional Stance*, Cambridge, MA

Dennett, Daniel C. 1995. *Darwin's Dangerous Idea: Evolution And The Meaning Of Life*. New York, NY: Simon & Schuster.

Dennett, Daniel C. 2005. Show Me The Science. *New York Times*, 28 August.

Denton, Michael. 1986. *Evolution: A Theory In Crisis*. Bethesda, MD: Adler & Adler.

Dewey, John. 1962. *A Common Faith*. New Haven, CT: Yale University Press.

Dewitt, David. 2004. Why I Rejected 'Theistic Evolution'. Creation Ministries International, January 12. Http://Creation.Com/Why-I-Rejected-Theistic-Evolution. Accessed 12 December 2011.

De Young, Kevin. 2012. What's Wrong With Theistic Evolution? *The Christian Post*, April 24, 2012. Http://Www.Christianpost.Com/News/Whats-Wrong-With-Theistic-Evolution-73714/, Accessed 21 Nov 2012.

Dicke, R.H. 1957. Gravitation Without A Principle Of Equivalence. *Reviews Of Modern Physics* 29:363–376.

Dimitrov, Tihomir. 2008. *50 Nobel Laureates And Other Great Scientists Who Believe In God*. E.Book, Http://Nobelists.Net .

Discovery Institute, 2007. Ranks Of Scientists Doubting Darwin's Theory On The Rise. Www.Discovery.Org/A/2732 Accessed 20 July 2012.

Dobzhansky, Theodosius. 1955. *Evolution, Genetics And Man*. New York: John Wiley & Sons.

Dobzhansky, T. 1958. Evolution At Work. *Science* 127(3306):1091-8. May 9.

Dobzhansky, Theodosius. 1973. Nothing In Biology Makes Sense Except In The Light Of Evolution. *The American Biology Teacher* 35: 125-129, March.

Dolphin, Lambert. 2006. The Limits Of Science. Http://Ldolphin.Org/Scilim. Shtml . Accessed 2 April 2012.

Domning, Daryl P. 2001. Evolution, Evil And Original Sin. *America* Magazine, 12 Nov. Http://Www.Americamagazine.Org/Content/Article. Cfm?Article_Id=1205, Accessed 23 Nov 2012.

Down, Martin. 2007. *Deluded By Darwinism*. Eastbourne: Kingsway.

Drake, Henry L. 1958. *The People's Plato*. New York: Philosophical Library.

Drury, Nevill. 2004. *The New Age: Searching For The Spiritual Self*. London: Thames and Hudson.

Dulle, Jason. N.D. Theistic Evolution: The Illegitimate Marriage Of Theism And Evolution. Http://Www.Onenesspentecostal.Com/Theisticevolution.Htm, Accessed 21 Nov 2012.

Durkheim, Emile. 2001 [1912]. *The Elementary Forms Of Religious Life*. Oxford: Oup.

Eaton, Heather. 2008. The Revolution Of Evolution. *Journal Of Religion And Society*. Supplement Series 3:27-46.

Ebert, Michael H. (Ed.) 2008. Current Diagnosis And Treatment In Psychiatry. 2nd Edition. London:Mcgraw-Hill.

Eccles, J.C. 1980/1991. *Evolution Of The Brain: Creation Of The Self.* New York: Routledge.

Eccles, Jc. 1991. *Evolution Of The Brain: Creation Of The Self.* New York, Ny: Routledge. 282pp.

Eddington, Arthur S. 1930. *On The Instability* Of Einstein's Spherical World. *Monthly Notices Of The Royal Astronomical Society* 90:672, May.

Eigen, Manfred. 1971. Self-Organization Of Matter And The Evolution Of Biological Macromolecules. *Die Naturwissenschaften* 58: 465-523.

Einstein, Albert. 1940. Religion And Science. Http://Www.Onbeing.Org/ Program/Einstein039s-God-Einstein039s-Ethics/Extra/Einstein-Science-And-Religion-1940/1986. Accessed 2 April 2012.

Eiseley, Loren C. [1946] 1957 Reprint. *The Immense Journey.* New York: Vintage Books.

Elliott, Paul. 2003. Erasmus Darwin, Herbert Spencer And The Origins Of The Evolutionary Worldview In British Provincial Scientific Culture. *Isis* 94: 1-2.

Erbich, Paul, 1985. On The Probability Of The Emergence Of A Protein With A Particular Function. *Acta Biotheoretica* 34:53-80.

Fikes, Thomas G. 2001. Evolutionary Psychology As Computational Theory In The Cognitive Sciences. *Journal Of Psychology And Theology* 29/4: 340ff.

Flew, Antony. 2004. As Quoted In The Article "Famous Atheist Now Believes In God." Associated Press, December 9. Http://Www. Sciencefindsgod.Com/Famous-Atheist-Now-Believes-In-God.Htm. Accessed 10 Jan 2012.

Flew, Anthony. 2007. *There Is A God: How The World's Most Notorious Atheist Changed His Mind.* New York: Harper One.

Foster, B.R. 1995. *From Distant Days: Myths, Tales, And Poetry Of Ancient Mesopotamia.* Bethesda, Md: Cdl Press.

Fraser, A. 1958. Monte Carlo Analyses Of Genetic Models. *Nature* 181 (4603): 208-209.

Frazer, James George. 1922. *The Golden Bough: A Study In Magic And Religion.* Republished 2008 By Forgotten Books. Quoted Online At Http://Www.Religioustolerance.Org/Rel_Defn3.Htm, Retrieved 7.2.12.

Freud, Sigmund, And Breuer, Joseph. 1895. Studies In Hysteria. Standard Edition, Vol. 2. *Trans.* James Strachey.

Freud, Sigmund. 1900. *The Interpretation Of Dreams.* Standard Edition Vol. 4: 1-338.

Freud, Sigmund. 1923. *The Ego And The Id.* Standard Edition, Vol. 19.

Freud, Sigmund. 1935. *A General Introduction To Psychoanalysis.* New York: Liveright.

Freud, Sigmund. 1950 [1895]. *Project For A Scientific Psychology. Standard Edition, Vol. 1: 281-387.* Trans. James Strachey.

Freud, Sigmund. 1961 [1927]. *The Future Of An Illusion.* Translated From German By James Strachey. London: The Hogarth Press.

Fromm, Eric. 1941. *Escape From Freedom.* New York: Rinehart.

Geertz, Clifford. 1973. *The Interpretations Of Cultures.* New York: Basic Books.

Gefter, Amanda. 2009. How To Spot A Hidden Religious Agenda. *New Scientist* Saturday, 28th February.

Geisler, Norman L. And Turek, Frank. 2004. *I Don't Have Enough Faith To Be An Atheist.* Wheaton, Illinois: Crossway.

Giberson, Karl. 2008. Adventist Origins Of Young Earth Creationism. Http:// Biologos.Org/Uploads/Projects/Giberson-Scholarly-Essay-1.Pdf. Accessed 26 July 2012.

Gitt, Werner. 1995. Dangers Of Theistic Evolution. Http://Creation.Com/10-Dangers-Of-Theistic-Evolution, Accessed 23 Nov 2012.

Gitt, Werner. 2006. *Did God Use Evolution? Observations From A Scientist Of Faith.* Green Forest, Ar: New Leaf Publishing Group. Http:// Www.Answersingenesis.Org/Articles/Dgue/Basic-Assumptions-Of-Theistic-Evolution And Http://Www.Answersingenesis.Org/Articles/ Dgue/Basic-Assumptions-Of-Evolution . Accessed 12 Dec 2011.

Gliedman, John. 1982. Miracle Mutations. *Science Digest* 90: 90-96, February.

Goethe, J. W. 1827. *Gott Und Welt.* Gedichte 22. Vollständige Ausgabe Letzter Hand, Bd. 1-4: Gedichte. Stuttgart Und Tübingen: Cotta.

Gould, Stephen Jay. 1977. *Ever Since Darwin.* New York: W.W. Norton.

Gould, Stephen J. 1980. Shades Of Lamarck. In *The Panda's Thumb.* New York: W.W. Norton.

Gould, S.J. 1982. Darwinism And The Expansion Of Evolutionary Theory. *Science Magazine* 216: 380-387, 23rd August.

Gould, Stephen Jay. 1991. Exaptation: A Crucial Tool For Evolutionary Psychology. *Journal Of Social Issues* 47(3): 43-65.

Gower, Barry. 1997. *Scientific Method: An Historical And Philosophical Introduction.* London: Routledge.

Gregerson, Niels. 2001. The Cross Of Christ In An Evolutionary World. *Dialog: A Journal Of Theology* 40, 192-207.

Gregersen, Niels Henrick. 2002. Beyond The Balance: Theology In A Self-Organizing World. *In* Niels Henrick Gregersen And Ulf Gormon

(Eds), *Design And Disorder.* London And New York: T&T Clark.

Grene, Marjorie. *1959.* The Faith Of *Darwinism. Encounter 74*: 48, November.

Griffith, Ted. 2011. Christianity And Evolution: Impossible Doublethink? Www.Creationconversations.Com/Profiles(Blogs)Christianity-And-Evolution-Impossible. Accessed 9.11.11

Hall, Mark A. And Milton S. Lesser. 1966. *Review Texts In Biology.* New York: Amsco School Publications.

Hall, Marshall And Sandra. 1974. *The Truth: God Or Evolution?* Grand Rapids, Mi: Baker Books.

Hall, Thomas William; Richard B. Pilgrim, & Ronald R. Cavanagh. 1985. *Religion: An Introduction.* New York: Harper & Row.

Ham, Ken. 2008. *The New Answer Book.* Green Forest, Ar: Master Books.

Hamer, Dean H. 2004. *The God Gene: How God Is Hardwired Into Our Genes.* New York, Doubleday.

Hamilton, Edith. 1942. *Mythology.* Boston: Little, Brown And Co.

Hamlyn, D. W. 1978. *The Theory Of Knowledge.* London: Macmillan.

Hanegraaff, Hank. 2009. *Crisis In Christianity.* Nashville: Thomas Nelson.

Hansen, V.L. N.D. Mathematics Through Millenia. Encyclopedia Of Life Support Systems (Eolss). Www.Eolss.Net/Sample-Chapters/Co2/E6-01-01-01.Pdf, Accessed 8 25.11).

Hanson, Joseph R. N.D. Faith Vs Science: Irreducible Complexity. Http://Truth-Saves.Com/Intelligent-Design-Vs-Evolution, Accessed 8.18.12.

Harris, C. Leon. 1975. A Axiomatic Interpretation Of The Neo-Darwinian Theory Of Evolution. *Perspectives In Biology And Medicine* 18:179-184.

Harris, S. 2006. *Letter To A Christian Nation.* New York, NY: Bantam Press. 112pp.

Harrison, E. 1974. Universe, Origin And Evolution Of. Encyclopaedia Britannica, 14th Ed. Vol. 18: 1007-1008.

Hasker, William. 1983. *Metaphysics: Constructing A Christian World View.* Downers Grove, Illinois: Intervarsity Press.

Hastings, Ross. 2011. What Science And Theology Have In Common. *Faith Today,* November / December, 20-21.

Hearn, Walter. 1961. *Journal Of The American Scientific Affiliation,* June.

Heft, Fr. James I., 2005. Evolution And Creationism: The Relationship Between Science And Catholicism. Annual Faith And Culture Lecture, University Of Dayton, September 30th.

Helm, Paul. 1997. *Faith And Understanding*. Grand Rapids, MI: Wm. B. Eerdmans.

Henry Carl F. H. 1990. *Toward A Recovery Of Christian Belief*. Westchester, Illinois: Crossway Books.

Hertzog, H.S., Pensavalle, M.T. & Lemlech, J.K., 2000. Collegial Relationships: What Does It Mean To Be A Colleague? Paper Presented At The Annual Meeting Of The American Educational Research Association, New Orleans, La., April 24-28.

Hexham, Irving. 1993. *Concise Dictionary Of Religion*. Downers Grove: Intervarsity Press, 186-187. Quoted Online: Http://Www. Religioustolerance.Org/Rel_Defn2.Htm (Accessed 4 July 2012).

Holloway, Carson. 2006. Darwinism And Religion. *Science And Theology News* July/August.

Horgan, John. 1996. *The End Of Science: Facing The Limits Of Knowledge In The Twilight Of The Scientific Age*. New York: Addison-Wesley.

Horgan, John. 2011. Can Science Solve—Really Solve—The Problem Of Beauty? *Scientific American*. November 13.

Hoskins, Michael. 2008. William Herschel. *In New Dictionary Of Scientific Biography*, Vol. 3. New York: Charles Scribner's Sons.

Hösle, Vittoria, and Illies, Christian (Eds). 2005. *Darwinism And Philosophy*. Indiana: University Of Notre Dame Press.

House, Wayne H. (Ed.) 2008. *Intelligent Design 101: Leading Experts Explain The Key Issues*. Grand Rapids, Mi: Kregel Publications.

Hsu, Kenneth J. 1986. Sedimentary Petrology And Biologic Evolution. *Journal Of Petrology* 56: 730.

Hull, David L. 1973. *Darwin And His Critics*. Cambridge, Ma: Harvard University Press.

Hunter, Cornelius G. 2001. *Darwin's God: Evolution And The Problem Of Evil*. Grand Rapids, Mi: Brazos Press

Hurlbut, William, And Kalanithi, Paul. 2001. Evolutionary Theory And The Emergence Of Moral Nature. *Journal Of Psychology And Theology* 29 (2001): 330-39. Online: Http://Findarticles.Com/P/Articles/ Mi_Hb6566/Is_4_29/Ai_N28884060/Pg_2/?Tag=Content;Col1, Accessed 7.5.12.

Huxley, Julian. 1960. Essays Of A Humanist. *In* Sol Tax, Ed., *Issues Of Evolution*. Chicago: University Of Chicago Press.

Huxley, Thomas H. 1903. *Life And Letters Of Thomas Henry Huxley, Vol. 1*. London: Macmillan.

Huxley, Thomas. 1903. Quoted In Leonard Huxley, *Life And Letters Of Thomas Henry Huxley*, Vol. Ii. 1903. Online: Http://Www.Gutenberg. Org/Ebooks/5799 Accessed 2 April 2012.

Israel, Jonathan I. 2001. *Radical Enlightenment: Philosophy And The Making Of Modernity 1650–1750*. Oxford: Oxford University Press.

Jäckel, C., Kast, P. And Hilver, D. 2008. Protein Design By Directed Evolution. *Annual Review Of Biophysics* 37:153-173.

Jacobsen, T. 1976. *The Treasures Of Darkness: A History Of Mesopotamian Religion*. New Haven: Yale University Press.

James, William. 1902. *The Varieties Of Religious Experience*, Chapter 3. Http://Csp.Org/Experience/James-Varieties/James-Varieties3.Html, Retrieved 7.2.12.

Jantsch, E. 1979. *Die Selbstorganisation Des Universums*. München: Carl Hanser.

Jauncey, James H. 1961. *Science Returns To God*. Grand Rapids, Mi: Zondervan.

Joad, C.E.M. 1955. *The Recovery Of Belief*. London: Faber And Faber.

Johnson, Phillip. 1993. *Darwin On Trial*. Downers Grove: Intervarstity Press.

Johnson, Phillip E. 2000. *The Wedge Of Truth: Splitting The Foundations Of Naturalism*. Downers Grove, Illinois: Intervarsity Press.

Jones, Do-While. 2001. Some Real Scientists Reject Evolution. Http://Scienceagainstevolution.Org/V5i10f.Htm Accessed 20 July 2012.

Jones, Shirley. 1994. *The Mind Of God And Other Musings*. San Rafael, Ca: New World Library.

Kant, Immanuel. 1788. *Critique Of Practical Reason*.

Keith, Sir Arthur. Quoted In W.A. Criswell, 1972, *Did Man Just Happen?* Grand Rapids, Mi: Zondervan.

Kerkut G.A., 1960. *Implications Of Evolution*. New York: Pergamon.

Koestler, Arthur. 1978. *Janus: A Summing Up*. New York: Vintage Books.

Kourany, J., Ed. 1987. *Scientific Knowledge: Basic Issues In The Philosophy Of Science*. Belmont, Ca: Wadsworth Publishing Company.

Kreeft, Peter. 1994. *Handbook Of Christian Apologetics*. Downers Grove, Il: Intervarsity Press.

Kreis, Steven. 2005. The History Guide: Lectures On Modern European Intellectual History. Lecture 3: The Medieval World View (2). Www.Historyguide.Org/Intellect/Lecture3a.Html, Accessed 8.4.10.

Kuhn, Thomas. 1977. Objectivity, Value Judgment, And Theory Choice. *In The Essential Tension: Selected Studies In Scientific Tradition And Change*. Chicago: University Of Chicago Press. Pp. 320-339.

Kutschera, U. 2003. A Comparative Analysis Of The Darwin–Wallace Papers And The Development Of The Concept Of Natural Selection. *Theory In Biosciences* 122 (4): 343–359.

Kuyper, Abraham. 1943. *Calvinism: Six Stone Foundation Lectures*. Grand Rapids, MI: Eerdmans.

Kuyper, H.H. 1903. *Evolutie Of Revolutie*. Amsterdam: Hoveker & Wormser.

Koenig, Harold. 1997. *Is Religion Good For Your Health*? New York: Haworth Pastoral Press.

Koenig, H.G., 1998. Religious Attitudes And Practices Of Hospitalized Medically Ill Older Adults. *International Journal Of Geriatric Psychiatry*. 13/4: 213-224.

Koenig, H.G. And Larson, D.B. 1998. Use Of Hospital Services, Church Attendance And Religious Affiliation. *Southern Medical Journal* 91: 925-932.

Koenig, H.G. *Et Al*. 1998a. The Relationship Between Religious Activities And Blood Pressure In Older Adults. *International Journal Of Psychiatry In Medicine* 28/2: 189-213.

Koenig, H.G. *Et Al*. 1998b. Religious Coping And Health Status In Medically Ill Hospitalized Older Adults. *Journal Of Mental And Nervous Disease* 186:513-521.

Koenig, H.G. *Et Al*. 1998c. Religiosity And Remission From Depression In Medically Ill Older Patients. *American Journal Of Psychiatry* 155: 536-542.

Koenig, H.G. *Et Al*. 1998d. The Relationship Between Religious Activities And Cigarette Smoking In Older Adults. *J Gerontol. A Biol. Sci. Med. Sci. 53:* M426–34.

Koenig, H.G., Hays, J.C., Larson, B.D., *Et Al*. 1999. Does Religious Attendance Prolong Survival? A Six-Year Follow-Up Study Of 3,968 Older Adults. *J Gerontol. A. Biol. Med. Sci*. 54/7: M370-M377.

Larson, Edward J. 2002. The Theory Of Evolution: A History Of Controversy. The Teaching Company. Http://Www.Scribd.Com/Doc/38410656/ Theory-Of-Evolution Accessed 16 May 2012.

Larson, Edward J. 2006. *Evolution: The Remarkable History Of A Scientific Theory*. New York: Random House.

Larson, Edward J. 2009. "I Had No Intention To Write Atheistically": Darwin, Od, And The 2500-Year History Of The Debate. *Religion Dispatches* 24 Nov 2009. Accessed 16 May 2012. Http://Www. Religiondispatches.Org/Archive/Science/1813/%E2%80%9ci_Had_ No_Intention_To_Write_Atheistically%E2%80%9d%3a_Darwin,_ God,_And_The_2500-Year_History_Of_The_Debate

Lavine, T.Z. 1989. *From Socrates To Adler*. New York: Bantam.

Leeming, David A. 2010. *Creation Myths Of The World*. 2nd Ed. Santa Barbara, Ca: Abc-Clio.

Lennox, J.G. 2000. *Aristotle's Philosophy Of Biology: Studies In The Origins Of Life Science*. Cambridge: Cambridge University Press.

Leming, Michael R. 2003. Religion And The Mediation Of Death Fear. *In* Clifton D. Bryant, Ed., *Handbook Of Death And Dying, Vol. 1.* Thousand Oaks, Ca: Sage Publications, Pp. 117-125.

Lemoine, Paul. 1937. Introduction: De L'evolution? *Encyclopedie Francaise*, Volume 5.

Lessl, T. 1985. Science And The Sacred Cosmos: The Ideological Rhetoric Of Carl Sagan. *Quarterly Journal Of Speech* 71:178.

Levine, Joseph S. And Kenneth Miller. 1994. *Biology: Discovering Life*, 2nd Ed. Lexington, Ma: D.C. Heath And Company.

Lipson, H.S. 1980. A Physicist Looks At Evolution. *Physics Bulletin* 31:138 (May).

Lisle, Jason. 2006. God And Natural Law. In *Answers* Magazine, Vol. 1, No. 2, Oct.- Dec. Pp. 74-78. Http://Www.Answersingenesis.Org/Articles/Am/V1/N2/God-Natural-Law Accessed 2 April 2012.

Livingstone, David N. 1987. *Darwin's Forgotten Defenders.* Grand Rapids, Mi: Eerdmans.

Livingstone, James C. 1971. *Modern Christian Thought From The Enlightenment To Vatican Ii.* New York: Macmillan.

Lucas, J.R. 1979. Wilberforce And Huxley: A Legendary Encounter. *The Historical Journal* 22 (2): 313–30, June.

Luskin, Casey. 2008. The Positive Case For Design. Http://Www.Discovery.Org/Scripts/Viewdb/Filesdb-Download.Php?Id=986. Accessed 10 January 2012.

Luskin, Casey. 2012. Did Michael Behe State Exaptation Has Been "Shown" To Produce Irreducible Complexity? Www.Evolutionnews.Org/2012/08/Did_Michael_Beh063271.Html, Accessed 9.10.12.

Lyell, Charles. 1830. *Principles Of Geology*, Vol. 1. London: John Murray. Http://Darwin-Online.Org.Uk/Content/Frameset?Viewtype=Text&Itemid=A505.1&Pageseq=1 Accessed 8 Dec 2011.

Lyell K.M. (Ed.) 1881. *The Life And Letters Of Sir Charles Lyell.* 2 Vols. London: John Murray.

Lyons, Eric. 2007. Yesterday's "New Reality Of Evolution" Debunked Again. (Http://Www.Apologeticspress.Org/Apcontent.Aspx?Category=9&Article=2236). Accessed 2 April 2012.

Mahoney, Michael J., 1988. Self-Deception In Science. Paper Presented At The Annual Meeting Of The American Association For The Advancement Of Science (Philadelphia: May 28, 1986), Also Published In *Origins Research.* 11, No. 1 (Colorado Springs, Colorado: Students For Origins Research, Spring 1988), Pp. 1-2, 6-7, 10.

Malinowski, Bronislaw. 1961. *Argonauts Of The Western Pacific.* New York: Dutton.

Malthus, T.R. 1798. *An Essay On The Principle Of Population*. Online: Http://
Www.Econlib.Org/Library/Malthus/Malpopcover.Html

Marks, Paul. 2007. Evolutionary Algorithms Now Surpass Human Designers.
New Scientist, July 28. (Http://Www.Newscientist.Com/Article/
Mg19526146.000-Evolutionary-Algorithms-Now-Surpass-Human-
Designers.Html)

Marr, D. 1982. *Vision: A Computational Investigation Into Human
Representation And Processing Visual Information*. San Francisco:
Freeman.

Marsden, George M. 1984. *Understanding Fundamentalist* Views Of
Science. *In* Ashley *Montagu (Ed.) Science And Creationism*. New
York: *Oxford University Press*, Pp. 95-116.

Marsden, Neil. 2006. The Father Of Lies. *Creation* 28 (1), December 2005-
February 2006.

Martin, D. John. 2010. Survival Of The Metaphysically Fittest. S*alvo
Magazine Archives*. 6 July. Http://Www.Salvomag.Com/New/
Articles/Archives/Philosophy/Martin.Php, Accessed 22.8.12.

Marx, Karl. 1844. *Critique Of Hegel's Philosophy Of Right,* Introduction.
(Http://Www.Marxists.Org/Archive/Marx/Works/1843/Critique-Hpr/
Intro.Htm, Accessed 21.8.12).

Mastin, Luke. 2008: The Basics Of Philosophy. Www.Philosophybasics.
Com/Branch_Naturalism.Html, Accessed 22.8.12.

Matthews, Kenneth A. 1996. *Genesis 1-11:26: An Exegetical And
Theological Exposition Of Holy Scripture*. New York: Broadman &
Holman

Matthews, L.H. 1971. Introduction To *The Origin Of Species*, By Charles
Darwin. London: Dent.

Mayr, Ernst. 1963. *Animal Species And Evolution*. Cambridge, Ma: Harvard
University Press.

Mayr, Ernst. 1977. Darwin And Natural Selection. *American Scientist* 65,
May/June.

Mayr, Ernst. 1991. *One Long Argument: Charles Darwin And The Genesis
Of Modern Evolutionary Thought*. Cambridge, Ma: Harvard
University Press.

Mayr, Ernst. 2000. Darwin's Influence On Modern Thought. *Scientific
American* 283/1: 67-71, July.

Mayr, Ernst. 2001. *What Evolution Is*. New York: Basic Books.

Mccarthy, John F. 1991. *The Science Of Historical Theology*. Rockford, Il:
Tan Books And Publishers, Inc.

Mcgiffert, A.C. 1961. *Protestant Thought Before Kant*. New York: Harper.

Mcgrath, A.E. 2004. *Dawkins' God: Genes, Memes And The Meaning Of Life*. Oxford: Blackwell.

Mcgrath, Alister. 2005. *Dawkins' God: Genes, Memes And The Meaning Of Life*. 2nd Edition. London: John Wiley & Sons.

Mcgrath, Alister. 2009. Augustine's Origin Of Species. *Christianity Today*, 8 May 2009. Http://Www.Christianitytoday.Com/Ct/2009/May/22.39. Html?Paging=Off, Accessed 21 Nov 2012.

Mcintyre, J. 1999. 'Evolution's Fatal Flaw.' *Perspectives On Science And Christian Faith*, 51 (3), 162-164.

Mckevitt, P., 1961. Psychoanalysis And Faith. *Irish Theological Quarterly* 28/4: 318, October.

Mencken, H.L.1946. Treatise Of The Gods, Revised Ed. New York: Alfred A. Knopf.

Merriam-Webster Online Dictionary. Http://Www.Merriam-Webster.Com/ Dictionary/Logic. Accessed 30 July 2012.

Mesoudi, A., 2011. Culture And The Darwinian Renaissance In The Social Sciences And Humanities. *Journal Of Evolutionary Psychology* 9/2: 109.

Meyer, Stephen C., *Et Al*. 2003. The Cambrian Explosion: Biology's Big Bang. *In* John A. Campbell And Stephen C. Meyer, Eds, *Darwinism, Design And Public Education*. Michigan State University Press.

Meyer, Stephen C. 2004a. The Cambrian Information Explosion. *In* William A. Dembski And Michael W. Ruse, Eds, *Debating Design*. Cambridge: Cambridge University Press.

Meyer, Stephen C. 2004b. The Origin Of Biological Information And The Higher Taxonomic Categories. *Proceedings Of The Biological Society Of Washington* 117(2): 213-239.

Meyer, Stephen. 2007. Intelligent Design: The Origin Of Biological Information And The Higher Taxonomic Categories. *Proceedings Of The Biological Society Of Washington* 117/2: 213-239, May 18.

Miller, Kenneth R. 1999. *Finding Darwin's God*. New York: Harper Collins.

Miller, Kenneth R. 2009. Quoted By Center For Inquiry & The Clergy Letter Project. Http://Www.Teachthemscience.Org/Belief. Accessed 20 Nov 2012.

Millhauser, Milton. 1959. *Just Before Darwin: Robert Chambers And Vestiges*. Middletown, Ct: Wesleyan University Press.

Milliken, Robert. 1925, Quoted In *The Nashville Banner*, August 7th.

Mitchell, Milo. 2012. What Is The Current Status Of The Assumed Bible/ Science Conflict? Http://Www.Selahministries.Net/Subpage12.Html Accessed 2 April 2012.

Mithen, Steven. 1999. Symbolism And The Supernatural. In Robin Dunbar, Chris Knight, And Camilla Power, Eds. *The Evolution Of Culture.* Edinburgh: Edinburgh University Press. Cited By Max Andrew Taylor (2005) *The Evolutionary Basis And Function Of Religion.* University Of More, Louis Trenchard. 1925. *The Dogma Of Evolution.* Princeton, Nj: Princeton University Press.

Moody, Paul. 1970. *Introduction To Evolution.* 2nd Ed. New York: Harper & Row.

Moore, James R. 1979. *The Post-Darwinian Controversies: A Study Of The Protestant Struggle To Come To Terms With Darwin In Great Britain And America, 1870-1900.* London: Cambridge University Press.

Morris, Henry M. 1963. *The Twilight Of Evolution.* Grand Rapids, Mi: Baker Books.

Morris, Henry M. 1966. *Studies In The Bible And Science.* Grand Rapids, Mi: Baker Books.

Morris, Henry M. 1989. *The Long War Against God.* Grand Rapids, Mi: Baker Books.

Morris, Henry M. 1997. *That Their Words May Be Used Against Them: Quotes From Evolutionists Useful For Creationists.* Green Forest, Ar: Master Books Inc.

Mortenson, T., 2009. In 'The New Answers, Book 1,' Ed. K. Ham., Masters Books, Green Forest, Arkansas,

Mueller, P.S., Plevak, D.J. And Rummans, T.A. 2001. Religious Involvement, Spirituality, And Medicine: Implications For Clinical Practice. *Mayo Clin. Proc.* 76(12):1225-35. Http://Www.Ncbi.Nlm.Nih.Gov/Pubmed/11761504, Retrieved 7.2.12.

Mullahy, Patrick. 1948. *Oedipus Myth And Complex: A Review Of Psychoanalytic Theory.* New York: Hermitage Press.

Muller, H. J. 1959. Experimental Variation. *In* Encyclopaedia Britannica 22: 988. Online: Http://Gluedideas.Com/Content-Collection/Encyclopedia-Britannica-Volume-22-Part-2-Tromba-Marina-Vascular-System/Experimental-Variation_P2.Html Accessed 2 April 2012.

Munitz, Milton K. 1965. *Theories Of The Universe.* New York: The Free Press. Tennessee Honors Thesis Projects. Http://Trace.Tennessee.Edu/Cgi/Viewcontent.Cgi?Article=1921&Context=Utk_Chanhonoproj, Accessed 8.28.12.

Murphy, Nancey. 2008. The New Atheism And The Scientific-Naturalist Tradition. Kripke Center Lecture. *Journal Of Religion And Society* 10.

Ncse. 2008. Project Steve. National Center For Science Education. Http://Ncse.Com/Taking-Action/Project-Steve Accessed 20 July 2012.

Ncse. 2008a. Ayala Profiled In *Scientific American*. Http://Ncse.Com/News/2008/10/Ayala-Profiled-Scientific-American-002660, Posted October 22nd. Accessed 20 Nov 2012.

Neff, L. 1987. Christianity Today Talks To George Gilder. *Christianity Today*, March 6.

Nelson, Paul And Jonathan Wells. Homology In Biology. *In* John A. Campbell And Stephen C. Meyer, Eds, *Darwinism, Design And Public Education*. Michigan State University Press.

Niewoehner, W.A. 1997. A Philosophy That Makes Sense Of Life. *The Washington Times*. 19 Jan.

Noebel, David A. 2001. *The Battle For Truth*. Harvest House Publishers.

Numbers, R.L. 1998. *Darwinism Comes To America*. Cambridge, Ma: Harvard University Press.

Numbers, Ronald. 2006. *The Creationists: From Scientific Creationism To Intelligent Design*. Expanded Edition. Cambridge Ma: Harvard University Press.

O'connor, John. 2006. Quotations By Pierre Simon Laplace. Http://Www-History.Mcs.St-Andrews.Ac.Uk/Quotations/Laplace.Html. Accessed 2 April 2012.

O'leary, Denyse. 2004. *By Design Or By Chance*. Minneapolis: Augsburg Fortress.

Oman, John W. The Sphere Of Religion. *In* Joseph Needham (Ed.) 1955 (1926). *Science, Religion And Reality*. New York: George Braziller, Pp. 265-306.

Ona, Robert. 2007. Conversion – Crisis And Process Conversion In A Congregation. Dissertation. Dayton,Tn: Oxford Graduate School.

Osborn, Henry Fairfield. 1918. *The Origin And Evolution Of Life*. New York: Charles Scribner's Sons.

Osborn, Henry Fairfield. 1929. *From The Greeks To Darwin*. New York: Charles Scribner's Sons.

Ospovat, Alexander. 2008. Werner, Abraham Gottlob. *In Complete Dictionary Of Scientific Biography*. Online: Http://Www.Encyclopedia.Com/Doc/1g2-2830904607.Html . Accessed 9 December 2011.

Overton, William. 1982. Mclean V. Arkansas Board Of Education, 529 F.Supp. 1255 (E.D. Ark. 1982).

Paley, William. 1802. *Natural Theology, Or, Evidences Of The Existence And Attributes Of The Deity, Collected From The Appearances Of Nature*. London: Rivington. 12th Edition (London, 1809) Online At Http://Darwin-Online.Org.Uk/Content/Frameset?Itemid=A142&Viewtype=Text&Pageseq=1

Pals, Daniel L. 1997. *Seven Theories Of Religion*. Oxford: Oxford University Press.

Pember, George H. 1876. *Earth's Earliest Ages And Their Connection With Modern Spiritualism, Theosophy, And Buddhism.* Reprint Ed. Grand Rapids, Mi: Kregel, 1975.

Penzias, Arno. 1992. *In* Henry Margenau & R.A. Varghese, Eds., *Cosmos, Bios, And Theos.* La Salle, Il: Open Court.

Penzlin, H. 1987. Das Theologie-Problem In Der Biologie. *Biologische Rundschau* 25:7-26.

Perlas, Nicky. 1982. Neo-Darwinism Challenged At Aaas Annual Meeting. *Towards 2:29,* Spring.

Peters, Ted & Martinez Hewlett. 2006. *Can You Believe In God And Evolution?* Nashville Tn: Abingdon Press.

Philbin, William J. 1953. Faith And Christianity. *Irish Theological Quarterly* 20 (4): 337-349, October.

Philpott, Kent., 2012. "Born Again,' Internet Christian Journal, 2;2).

Pierce, J. Kingston. 2000. Scopes Trial. Originally Published In *American History,* August 2000. Published Online June 12, 2006. Www. Historynet.Com/Scopes-Trial.Htm, Accessed 26 July 2012.

Pieters, Albertus. 1947. *Notes On Genesis.* Grand Rapids, Mi: Eerdmans.

Pigluicci, Massimo. 2001. Design Yes, Intelligent No: A Critique Of Intelligent Design Theory And Neocreationism. *Skeptical Inquirer* 25/5, September/October. Http://Www.Csicop.Org/Si/ Show/Design_Yes_Intelligent_No_A_Critique_Of_Intelligent_ Design_Theory_And_Neocr/, Accessed 21 Nov 2012.

Plantinga, Alvin. 1997. Methodological Naturalism? *Perspectives On Science And Christian Faith* 49/3: 143-54. September. A Version Of This Article Is Given At Www.Arn.Org/Docs/Odesign/Od181/Methnat181. Htm, Accessed 22.8.12.

Plotkin, Hc. 1998. *Evolution In Mind: An Introduction To Evolutionary Psychology.* Cambridge, Ma: Harvard University Press.

Polkinghorne, John. 1986. *One World: The Interaction Of Science And Theology.* Princeton, Nj: Princeton University Press.

Poole, Michael, And Wenham, G.J. 2001. Creation Or Evolution - A False Antithesis. Oxford: Latimer House.

Poppe, Kenneth. 2006. *Reclaiming Science From Darwinism.* Eugene, Or: Harvest House.

Popper, Karl. 1959. *The Logic Of Scientific Discovery.* New York: Routledge.

Popper, Karl. 1974, Scientific Reduction And The Essential Incompleteness Of All Science. *In* Studies In The Philosophy Of Biology. Berkeley, Ca: University Of California Press. Pp. 259-284.

Popper, Karl R. 1985. *In* David Miller, Ed., *Popper Selections.* Princeton, Nj: Princeton University Press.

Popper, Karl. 1992. *Unending Quest: An Intellectual Biography.* Oxford: Routledge.

Provine, Will. 1988. Geneticists And Race. *American Zoologist* 26:857-887.

Ramm, Bernard. 1954. *The Christian View Of Science And Scripture.* Grand Rapids, Mi: Eerdmans.

Rance, Hugh. 1999. Hutton's Unconformities. In *Historical Geology: The Present Is The Key To The Past.* Queensborough Community College Press. Http://Geowords.Com/Geohisthr.Htm. Accessed 9 Dec 2011.

Randall, John Herman. 1962. *The Career Of Philosophy.* New York: Columbia University Press.

Ratzch Del. 2000. *Science And Its Limits.* Downers Grove: Intervarsity Press.

Reynolds, Vernon. 1986. Religious Rules And Reproductive Strategies. *Essays In Human Sociobiology* 2:105-117.

Ricci, Paul. 1986. *Fundamentals Of Critical Thinking.* Lexington, Ma: Ginn Press.

Richards, Robert J. 2008. *The Tragic Sense Of Life: Ernst Haeckel And The Struggle Over Evolutionary Thought.* Chicago: University Of Chicago Press.

Rifkin, Jeremy. 1983. *Algeny.* New York, Viking Press.

Roach John. 2005. Does "Intelligent Design" Threaten The Definition Of Science? *National Geographic News*, April 27th.

Rolston, Holmes Iii. 1998. Evolutionary History And Divine Presence. *Theology Today* (Princeton) 55: 415-434.

Rosazak, T. 1975. *Unfinished Animal: The Aquarian Frontier And The Evolution Of Consciousness.* Chicago: Harper And Row.

Rose, H. & Rose, S. (Eds). 2000. *Alas, Poor Darwin: Arguments Against Evolutionary Psychology.* New York, Ny: Harmony Books. 346pp.

Ross, Hugh. 1991. *The Fingerprint Of God.* 2nd Edition. Orange, Ca: Promise Publishing.

Ross, Hugh. 1993. *The Creator And The Cosmos.* Colorado Springs: Navpress.

Ross, Hugh. 2006. *Creation As Science.* Colorado Springs: Navpress.

Rothman, Tony. 1987. A "What You See Is What You Beget" Theory. *Discover Magazine,* May.

Rudwick, M.S.J. (Ed.) 1997. *Georges Cuvier, Fossil Bones And Geological Catastrophes.* Chicago, Il: University Of Chicago Press.

Rusbult, Craig. 2006. Divine Action In Natural Process: Is Natural Process

Guided By God? Http://Www.Asa3.Org/Asa/Education/Origins/Te-Guided.Htm, Accessed 21 Nov 2012.

Ruse, Michael, 2000. Saving Darwin From The Darwinians. *National Post*, May 13: B3.

Ruse, Michael. 2003. Is Evolution A Secular Religion? *Science* 299 (#5612): 1523-1524. 7 March. Http://Www.Sciencemag.Org/Content/299/5612/1523.Full Accessed 2 April 2012.

Ruse, Michael. 2003. *Darwin And Design: Does Evolution Have A Purpose?* Cambridge, Ma: Harvard University Press.

Rush, J.H. 1962. *The Dawn Of Life*. New York: Signet.

Sagan, Carl. 1994. *Pale Blue Dot: A Vision Of The Human Future In Space*. New York: Random House.

Sarkar, Sahotra. 2007. *Doubting Darwin: Creationist Design In Evolution*. Cambridge, Ma: Harvard University Press.

Schadewald, Robert J. 1984. The Evolution Of "Bible-Science": Young Earthers, Geocentrists, And Flat Earthers. *In* Laurie R. Godfrey (Ed.), *Scientists Confront Creationism*. New York: Norton. Http://Www.Philvaz.Com/Apologetics/P43.Htm. Accessed 26 July 2012.

Schafersman, Steven D. 1997. Naturalism Is Today An Essential Part Of Science. A Paper Presented At The Conference On Naturalism, Theism And The Scientific Enterprise, Dayton, Oh, Feb. 20-23, 1997. Online: Http://Www.Stephenjaygould.Org/Ctrl/Schafersman_Nat.Html, Accessed 8.10.11.

Schaub, Edward L. 1923. Bosanquet's Interpretation Of Religious Experience. *The Philosophical Review* 32, No. 6 (Nov., 1923): 652-667.

Schleiermacher, Friedrich. 1799. *On Religion: Speeches To Its Cultured Despisers*. Http://Archive.Org/Stream/Onreligionspeech00schluoft (Accessed 21.8.12).

Schmidt, Karen A. 1993. Evolution In A Test Tube. *Science News*, Col. 144, August 7.

Schoenheit, John W. 2006. What Is "Faith"? Http://Www.Truthortradition.Com/Modules.Php?Name=News&File=Print&Sid=692, Accessed 5.12.10.

Schönborn, Christoph. 2005. Finding Design In Nature. *New York Times*, July 7.

Schönborn, Christoph. 2007. Reasonable Science, Reasonable Faith. *First Things*, April. Online: Http://Www.Firstthings.Com/Article/2007/05/Reasonable-Science-Reasonable-Faith-44 . Accessed 10 Jan 2012.

Schroeder, Gerald L. 1977. *The Science Of God*. New York: Free Press.

Schwartz, Gary E. 2006. *The G.O.D. Experiments: How Science Is Discovering God In Everything, Including Us*. New York: Atria Books.

Secord, J. 1997. Introduction To Charles Lyell, *Principles Of Geology*, Ix-Xliii. London: Penguin.

Seiglie, Mario. 2006. The Intelligent Design Revolution. *The Good News Magazine,* United Church Of God, January-February. Http://Www. Ucg.Org/Science/Intelligent-Design-Revolution. Accessed 10 January 2012.

Sigmund, 2012. Elaine Ecklund Finds Scientists Are Reluctant To Admit Being Non-Religious. Http://Whyevolutionistrue.Wordpress. Com/2012/07/06/Guest-Post/, Accessed 21 Nov 2012.

Silvert, W. (N.D.) Hard Science Vs. Soft Science. Http://Bill.Silvert.Org/ Notions/Ecology/Hardsoft.Htm. Accessed 2 April 2012.

Simmons, Geoffrey. 2004. *What Darwin Didn't Know*. Eugene, Oregon: Harvest House Publishers.

Simon, Richard M. 2010. Damning Criticism: Historical Perspectives On The Evolution/Intelligent Design Conflict. *Journal Of Religion And Society* 12:1-19. Http://Moses.Creighton.Edu/Jrs/2010/2010-11.Pdf. Accessed 10 Jan 2012.

Simpson, George Gaylord. 1967. *The Meaning Of Evolution*, Revised Edition. New Haven: Yale University Press.

Sissons, T. Herman. 2010. How Certain Are Proven Facts? Http:// Thebigbangtonow.Wordpress.Com/2010/04/07/How-Certain-Are-Proven-Facts . Accessed 15 May 2012.

Sosis, R. And C. Alcorta. 2003. Signaling, Solidarity, And The Sacred: The Evolution Of Religious Behavior. *Evolutionary Anthropology* 12:264–274.

Spencer, Herbert. 1864. *Principles Of Biology*, Vol. 1. London: William And Norgate.

Spiegel, Alix. 2010. Is Believing In God Evolutionarily Advantageous? Http:// Www.Npr.Org/Templates/Story/Story.Php?Storyid=129528196, Accessed 16 Sept 2012.

Stenger, M.J. 2007. *God, The Failed Hypothesis: How Science Shows That God Does Not Exist*. New York, Ny: Prometheus Books. 287pp.

Stenger, Victor J. 2004. Is The Universe Fined-Tuned For Us? *In Matt Young And Taner Edis, Eds.,* Why *Intelligent Design Fails*: A *Scientific Critique* Of The *New Creationism. New Brunswick Nj: Rutgers University Press: 172-84*. Online: Http://Www.Colorado.Edu/ Philosophy/Vstenger/Cosmo/Finetune.Pdf

Stone, Jerome A., 2009. *Religious Naturalism Today: The Rebirth Of A Forgotten Alternative*. Albany, Ny: State University Of New

York Press. Online Excerpt: What Is Religious Naturalism? Http://Faculty.Uml.Edu/Rinnis/2000_Stone_2_1.Pdf, Accessed 8.10.11.

Sullivan, J.W.N. 1933. *Limitations Of Science*. New York: The Viking Press.

Swenson, Donald. 1999. *Society, Spirituality, And The Sacred: A Social Scientific Introduction*. Peterborough, Ca: Broadview Press.

Terzian, Yervant, Ed. 1997. *Carl Sagan's Universe*. Cambridge: Cup.

Thaxton, Charles. 1998. A New Design Argument. *Cosmic Pursuit,* March 1st.

Theocharis, T. & M. Psimopoulos. 1987. Where Science Has Gone Wrong. *Nature* 329: 595-598. 21 Oct.

Thiry, Paul Henri (Baron D'holbach). 1797. *System Of Nature, Or, The Laws Of The Moral And Physical World*, Vol. 1. Online: Http://Www.Gutenberg.Org/Catalog/World/Readfile?Fk_ Files=1472519&Pageno=21 . Accessed 2 April 2012.

Thomas, J. D. 1965. *Facts And Faith*. Abilene, Tx: Biblical Research Press.

Thompson, Bert. 2001a. Creation—Will It Stand The "Test Of Science"? Http://Www.Apologeticspress.Org/Apcontent. Aspx?Category=9&Article=679 . Accessed 6 Dec 2011.

Thompson, Bert. 2001b. What's Wrong With Theistic Evolution? Http://Www. Apologeticspress.Org/Apcontent.Aspx?Category=9&Article=306&T opic=64 . Accessed 6 Dec 2011.

Thomson, Keith Stewart. 1997. Marginalia: Natural Theology. *American Scientist* 85:219-221. May/June.

Thomson, Keith Stewart. 2001. Vestiges Of James Hutton. *American Scientist* 89(3) May-June. Online (Accessed 16 July 2012): Http:// Www.Americanscientist.Org/Issues/Pub/2001/5/Vestiges-Of-James-Hutton .

Tipett, Krista. 2010. *Einstein's God*. New York: Penguin Books.

Topoff, Howard. 1997. A Charles Darwin (187th) Birthday Quiz. *American Scientist* 85:104-107. March/April.

Toptenz.Net. 2012. Top 10 Most Famous Scientific Theories (That Turned Out To Be Wrong). Http://Www.Toptenz.Net/Top-10-Most-Famous-Scientific-Theories-That-Turned-Out-To-Be-Wrong.Php. Accessed 26 July 2012.

Triggs, Roger. 1993. *Rationality And Science*. Oxford: Blackwell.

Ulett, Mark A. 2010. Form And Function, By Edward Stuart Russell. Embryo Project Encyclopedia Issn: 1940-5030. Online: Http://Embryo.Asu. Edu/View/Embryo:127835. Accessed 2 April 2012.

Urpeth, J. 2009. 'Naturalism And Religion': Nietzsche And Bergson On Religious Life. British Society For Phenomenology Conference,

3-5 Apr 2009, St Hilda's College, Oxford, Uk. Online: Www.Gala. Gre.Ac.Uk/1379/2/Urpeth_Phenomenology_Of_Religious_Life.Pdf Accessed 9.3.11.

Ussery, David. 2000. A Review Of *Darwin's Black Box*. Http://Www.Cbs. Dtu.Dk/Staff/Dave/Behe.Html . Accessed 10 January 2012.

Van Till, Howard. 1999. The Fully Gifted Creation. *In* J. Moreland & John H. Reynolds (Eds) *Three Views On Creation And Evolution*. Grand Rapids, Mi: Zondervan.

Van Till, Howard, Davis A. Young, Clarence Menninga. 1988. *Science Held Hostage*. Downers Grove, Illinois: Intervarsity Press.

Van Till, Howard. 1999. The Fully Gifted Creation. *In* J. Moreland & John H. Reynolds (Eds) *Three Views On Creation And Evolution,* Pp. 161–218. Grand Rapids, Mi: Zondervan.

Verduin, Leonard. 1956. *Towards A Theistic Creationism*. Pamphlet. Baker Book House, 1969.

Voltaire, François-Marie Arouet. 1901. *The Works Of Voltaire, A Contemporary Version,* Vol. X The Dramatic Works. Trans. William F. Fleming. New York: E.R. Dumont. Online: Http://Oll.Libertyfund. Org/Title/2240/211123 , Accessed 21 July 2012.

Von Ditfurth, Hoimar. 1984. *Wir Sind Nicht Nur Von Dieser Welt*. München: Deutscher Taschenbuch-Verlag.

Von Roeschlaub, Warren Kurt. 1998. God And Evolution. Www.Talkorigins. Org/Faqs/Faq-God.Html, Accessed 21 Nov 2012.

Waddington, C. H. 1962. *The Nature Of Life*. New York: Athenum.

Waggoner, Ben. 1996. Georges Cuvier (1769–1832). University Of California, Berkeley. Http://Www.Ucmp.Berkeley.Edu/History/Cuvier. Html Accessed 19 July 2011.

Wald, George. 1963. *Biological Science: An Inquiry Into Life*. New York: Harcourt, Brace & World, Inc.

Wald, George, 1974. Fitness In The Universe: Choices And Necessities, In J. Oro *Et Al*., Eds., *Cosmochemical Evolutions And The Origin Of Life*. Dordrecht, Netherlands: D. Reidel.

Wallace, Anthony F.C. 1966. *Religion: An Anthropological View*. New York: Random House.

Warburton, Nigel. 2004. *The Basics Of Philosophy*. London: Routledge.

Warfield, Benjamin Breckinridge. 1915. Calvin's Doctrine Of The Creation. *Princeton Theological Review* 13/2: 190-255, April.

Warfield, B. B. 2000. *Evolution, Science And Scripture: Selected Writings*. Edited By Mark A. Noll And David N. Livingstone. Grand Rapids, Mi: Baker Books.

Watson, D.M.S. 1929. *Molecular Biology Of The Gene*. New York: W.A. Benjamin.

Watson, Lyall. 1982. The Water People. *Science Digest* 90 (May).

Weinberg, Steven. 1999. A Designer Universe? Address At The Conference On Cosmic Design. American Association For The Advancement Of Science. Washingto, Dc (April). Http://Www.Physlink.Com/ Education/Essay_Weinberg.Cfm. Accessed 16 July 2012

Wells, Jonathan. 2000. *Icons Of Evolution*. Washington, Dc: Regnery Publications.

Wells, Jonathan. 2004. Using Intelligent Design Theory To Guide Scientific Research. *Progress In Complexity, Information And Design* 3(1), November.

Whatley, Richard. 2011. Science As A Way Of Knowing. Http://Www.Ucsusa. Org/Scientific_Integrity/What_You_Can_Do/Science-As-A-Way-Of-Knowing.Html . Accessed 25 Oct 2011.

White, Alexander & Robert S. White. 2004. *Science, Faith And Ethics*. Peabody, Ma: Hendrickson Publishers.

White, Ellen Gould. 1958. *Patriarchs And Prophets*. Hagerstown, Md: Review And Herald Publishing Company.

Whitehead, Alfred North. 1926. Religion And Dogma. Lecture Delivered February 1926 At The King's Chapel, Boston, Usa. Http://Www. Mountainman.Com.Au/Whiteh_2.Htm, Accessed 21 Aug. 2012.

Whitehead, A.H. 1926. *Science In The Modern World*. New York: Macmillan.

Whitehead, Alfred North. 1929. *The Function Of Reason*. Princeton, Nj: Princeton University Press.

Wickenden, Arthur C. 1948. *Youth Looks At Religion*. New York: Harper.

Wikipedia Contributors. 2012. Irreducible Complexity. Http://En.Wikipedia. Org/Wiki/Irreducible_Complexity. Accessed 25/8/12.

Wilder-Smith, A.E. 1975. *Man's Origin And Destiny*. Minneapolis, Mn: Bethany House Publishers.

Wilgoren, Jodi. 2005. Politicized Scholars Put Evolution On The Defensive. *New York Times*, 21 August, 6. Http://Www.Nytimes. Com/2005/08/21/National/21evolve.Html?_R=2&Pagewanted=1&E i=5088&En=24bc7c9b16cac8a8&Ex=1282276800&Partner=Rssnyt &Emc=Rss . Accessed 27 July 2012.

Wilkins, John S. & Wesley R. Elsberry. 2001. The Advantages Of Theft Over Toil: The Design Inference And Arguing From Ignorance. *Biology And Philosophy* 16: 711-724, November. Online: Http://Www. Talkdesign.Org/Cs/Theft_Over_Toil . Accessed 10 Jan 2012.

Wilson, E. Bright. 1952. *An Introduction To Scientific Research*. New York: Mcgraw-Hill.

Wilson, E.O. 1978. *On Human Nature*. Cambridge, Ma: Harvard University Press.

Wilson, Edward O. 1982. Toward A Humanistic Biology. *The Humanist* 42:38-41, 56-58, September/October.

Wolf, Gary. 2006. The Church Of The Non-Believers. *Wired Magazine* 11:14. New York: Conde Nast Publishers, November.

Woodward, Kenneth L. 1999. 2000 Years Of Jesus. *Newsweek*, March 29, 1999:54.

Woodward, Thomas. 2006. *Darwin Strikes Back*. Grand Rapids, Mi: Baker.

Wyhe, John Van. 2007. Mind The Gap: Did Darwin Avoid Publishing His Theory For Many Years? Notes And Records Of The Royal Society 61(2):177-205. Online (Accessed 16 July 2012): Http://Rsnr. Royalsocietypublishing.Org/Content/61/2/177.Full

Wysong, R.L. 1976. *The Creation-Evolution Controversy*. Midland, Mi: Inquiry Press.

Yerxa, Donald. 2002. *Species Of Origins: America's Search For A Creation Story*. Rowman & Littlefield Publishers, Inc.

York, Michael. 1995. A Report On The Citizen Ambassador Program's Religion And Philosophy Delegation To The People's Republic Of China. *Journal Of Contemporary Religion* 10.2 (1995):197. Www. Michaelyork.Co.Uk/Domus/Cv/Confpapers/Cp-63, Retrieved 7.2.12.

Young, Willard. 1985. *Fallacies Of Creationism*. Calgary, Ab: Detselig Enterprises.

Notes and References

1. ^ William Blakestone. *Book 3 Chapter 10: Of Injuries to Real Property, And First of Dispossession, or Ouster, of The Freehold* footnote 47

2. ^ a b James T. Bretzke, *Consecrated phrases: a Latin theological dictionary : Latin expressions commonly found in theological writings* (Liturgical Press, 1998), p. 10. ISBN 0-8146-5880-6, ISBN 978-0-8146-5880-2

3. ^ Peter Jones (2006). *Reading Ovid: Stories from the Metamorphoses.* Cambridge University Press. p. 223. ISBN 0-521-84901-2.

4. ^ See Google books.

5. ^ Ovidi Nasonis Epistvlae Heroidvm, XIII. Laodamia Protesilao

6. ^ cacoëthes. Charlton T. Lewis and Charles Short. *A Latin Dictionary* on Perseus Project.

7. ^ κακοήθης. Liddell, Henry George; Scott, Robert; *A Greek–English Lexicon* at Perseus Project

8. ^ "Abbreviations"

9. ^ "Abbreviations", University of Sussex

10. ^ Jon R. Stone, *More Latin for the Illiterati,* Routledge, 1999, p. 53.

11. ^ Giles Jacob, *A Law Grammar,* W. Clarke & Sons, 1817, p. 3.

12. ^ Ablative of present participle *vivens + pater*

13. ^ Actus non facit reum, nisi mens sit rea: An Investigation into the Treatment of Mens Rea in the Quest to Hold Individuals Accountable for Genocide Mens Rea: The Mental Element quoting and citing William A. Schabas, "The Jelisic Case and the Mens Rea of the Crime of Genocide," Leiden Journal of International Law 14 (2001): 129.

14. ^ Clan Fergus(s)on Society Retrieved on 14 December 2007

15. ^ *Sancti Aurelii Augustini Opera*, vol. IV, p. 412

16. ^ "University of Minnesota Style Manual: Correct Usage". .umn. edu. 2010-11-22. Retrieved 2011-01-19.

17. ^ Gray, John (2006), *"Lawyer's Latin (a vade-mecum)"*, Hale, London, ISBN 9780709082774.

18. ^ "Pliny the Elder: the Natural History, Liber VIII". Penelope.uchi-cago.edu. Retrieved 2011-01-19.

19. ^ *Exempli gratia* (e.g.) and *id est* (i.e.) are commonly confused and misused in colloquial English. The former, *exempli gratia*, means "for example", and is used before giving examples of something ("I have lots of favorite colors, e.g., blue, green, and hot pink"). The latter, *id est*, means "that is", and is used before clarifying the meaning of something, when elaborating, specifying, or explaining rather than when giving examples ("I have lots of favorite colors; i.e., I can't decide on just one"). In British style, the stops may be omitted: "I have lots of favourite colours, *eg* blue, green and hot pink". "I have lots of favourite colours; *ie* I can't decide on just one"

20. ^ American style guides tend to recommend that "e.g." and "i.e." should generally be followed by a comma, just as "for example" and "that is" would be; UK style tends to omit the comma. See Dictionary.com and their discussion of commas for more information. Search "comma after i.e." for other opinions.

21. ^ Rapini, Ronald P. (2005). *Practical dermatopathology*. Elsevier Mosby. ISBN 0-323-01198-5.

22. ^ Webb-Johnson AE (May 1950). "Experientia docet". *Rev Gastroenterol* **17** (5): 337–43. PMID 15424403.

23. ^ *The Diwan of Abu'l-Ala* at Project Gutenberg

24. ^ Rutilius Namatianus: *De reditu suo*, Liber primus at The Latin Library

25. ^ Jon R. Stone (2005). *The Routledge Dictionary of Latin Quotations*. Routledge NY. p. 253. Retrieved 2012-11-13.

26. ^ Gravis Dulcis Immutabilis at classicpoetryaloud.com

27. ^ P. Ovidius Naso: *Epistulae Ex Ponto*, Liber Quartus, X. Albinovano at The Latin Library

28. ^ *Res Rusticae – De agri cultura*

29. ^ http://dictionary.reference.com/help/faq/language/g58.html

30. ^ http://grammar.quickanddirtytips.com/ie-eg-oh-my.aspx

31. ^ "Ite Missa Est" from the *Catholic Encyclopedia*

32. ^ Home page of St. Julian's School

33. ^ Harbottle, Thomas Benfield (1906). *Dictionary of Quotations (Classical)*. The Macmillan Co.

34. ^ The Latin Library: SVETONI TRANQVILII VITA DIVI CLAVDI

35. ^ Larry D. Benson, ed. *The Riverside Chaucer*. 3rd ed. Boston: Houghton Mifflin, 1987. p. 939, n. 3164.

36. ^ Chamberlin, Yves. "Omnia Extares, seriously?". Cooper Point Journal. Retrieved 29 July 2012.

37. ^ "Myths Unveiled: The Social History of The Evergreen State College" by Ty Rosenow (2009). Unpublished manuscript, The Evergreen State College, Olympia, WA.

38. ^ "Masonic mottoes"

39. ^ St Mark's Square

40. ^ Trademark registration

41. ^ Kinsey, Alfred Charles (1998) [1953]. *Sexual Behavior in the Human Female*. Indiana University Press. p. 638. ISBN 978-0-253-33411-4. (Kinsey Reports)

42. ^ Blakesley, Christopher L. (2009). "18. Jurisdiction Ratione Personae or the personal reach of the courts jurisdiction". *The Legal Regime of the International Criminal Court*. Martinus Nijhoff. pp. 421–454. ISBN 9789004180635.

43. ^ John Nery. "The Jesuits' Fault". Philippine Daily Inquirer.

44. ^ Quintus Horatius Flaccus (14 BC). "Q. Horati Flacci Epistvlarvm Liber Secvndvs" (in Latin). The Latin Library. Retrieved 10 September 2008.

45. ^ Column 1532, Lords Hansard, 21 January 1998

46. ^ Michael Bush, "Calvin and the Reformanda Sayings," in Herman J. Selderhuis, ed., *Calvinus sacrarum literarum interpres: Papers of the International Congress on Calvin Research* (Göttingen: Vandenhoeck & Ruprecht, 2008) p. 286. ISBN 978-3-525-56914-6

47. ^ Hildebrand, J. H. and Scott, R. L. (1950),*The Solubility of Nonelectrolytes*, 3rd ed., American Chemical Society Monograph No. 17, Reinhold Publishing Corporation.

48. ^ "Spartam nactus es; hanc exorna", note from *Reflections on the Revolution in France* (1790) by Edmund Burke

49. ^ "University motto". Cayetano-pae.org. 1989-10-14. Retrieved 2012-01-03.

50. ^ "Augustini Sermo LXXVI". Hiphi.ubbcluj.ro. Retrieved 2012-01-03.

51. ^ *The Tragedy of Doctor Faustus* by Christopher Marlowe (at Wikisource)

52. ^ Czech Brewery Rakovník — The Brewery

53. ^ Trans-Lex.org

54. ^ Image at York University, Department of Languages, Literatures & Linguistics.

55. ^ "Latin Pronunciation Demystified" by Michael A. Covington. Program in Linguistics, University of Georgia. December 31, 2005]

References:

Adeleye, Gabriel G. (1999). *World Dictionary of Foreign Expressions.* Ed. Thomas J. Sienkewicz and James T. McDonough, Jr. Wauconda, IL: Bolchazy-Carducci Publishers, Inc. ISBN 0865164223.

Hardon, John, Fr. *Modern Catholic Dictionary.*

Stone, Jon R. (1996). *Latin for the Illiterati.* London & New York: Routledge. ISBN 0415917751.

Lightning Source UK Ltd.
Milton Keynes UK
UKOW03f2256131013

218992UK00001B/13/P